'*New Theory and Practice of Transactional Analysis in Organizations* is an important, contemporary collection of chapters that – contrary to its title – is placing TA contribution at the heart of OD practice. Coming out for publication in the midst of one of the most turbulent periods of recent times, it will offer some stability in its sense-making of organizational and development practice which we all need.'
Dr. Eliat Aram, *CEO, The Tavistock Institute of Human Relations, London, UK*

'As *New Theory and Practice of Transactional Analysis in Organizations* is a book focused on innovation of organizational TA, we also asked a newer TA organizational generation from different countries to write a sentence or two why this book is important for TA and for the organizational field. An impressive synergy of thought leaders in the field of TA in organizations that inspire us to innovate our approach to organizations, leaders and teams.'
Danijela Djuric, *Growth Code Consultant*

'In the 60's, Berne ingeniously connected the individual and the collective dimension inside a single theoretical approach. If human beings barely changed since then, organizations have transformed very deeply. This wonderful book pushes "Berne's organisational theory (BOT)" towards the 21st century. BRAVO!'
Olivier Bettach, *Executive Coach and Method Actor, Paris, France*

'The book opens your eyes on the resources of agile organizations which are able to use the ability to "be" (and not to "do") in uncertainty, remaining impassive, facing loss of meaning, without wanting at all costs to reach results and certainties.'
Rossella Iannucci, *Head of Internal Coaching Academy Intesa Sanpaolo Group*

'It's been said many times that organisations are heading into crisis over and over again. The research into how Transactional Analysis can help leaders make practical choices is growing: this book is at the cutting edge and is a must read for anyone that's serious about effective leadership through volatile times.'
Andrew Tailby, *MA, Chief Executive Officer, TRESC Ltd*

'The authors are highly experienced Organisational TA Professionals. What they don't know about working on the edge with teams and organisations is probably not worth knowing. When reading this book, you will be immersed by its wealth and blend of knowledge, wisdom, theory, and practical application. A must have for all coaches, managers and consultants ready to take risks in order to promote the wellbeing, growth and development of organisations and teams. No Risk, No Result!'
Anjana Rajani, *Trainer/Coach, Power2Progress*

NEW THEORY AND PRACTICE OF TRANSACTIONAL ANALYSIS IN ORGANIZATIONS

This innovative book presents state-of-the-art thinking on using transactional analysis (TA) to change the structure, relationships and culture in organizations. Actual and sustainable change starts where people dare to work on the edge.

The book is arranged according to the three levels of organizations described by Eric Berne – the structural, interpersonal and psychodynamic levels – and the chapters expand on his concepts at each level. With contributions by an international range of authors, incorporating a selection of practical case studies, the book illuminates key themes including group and team dynamics, psychological safety, emotion and, most foundationally, boundaries.

Exploring the tensions of boundaries that can determine both the stability of a system as well as its innovative potential, this book provides a strong structural framework for TA coaches, consultants and analysts, as well as other professionals working with and within organizations.

Sari van Poelje, TSTA-O, MSc team coaching, is an international team coach and expert on agility and innovation. Sari has been the director of Intact Academy for 35 years, offering TA, ICF and EMCC accredited training to coaches and consultants all over the world. She works as a consultant in Agile Business Innovation with multinational organizations, family businesses and start-ups to help them innovate their business more quickly than their products, so that they can accelerate their time to market. Sari has 35 years' experience of coaching and consulting with managers and directors and has been a director in multinational organizations for 23 years. She herself is a licensed teaching and supervising transactional analyst, PCM trainer, NOBCO-EMCC accredited master coach and master systemic team coach. She has published numerous articles and books on leadership, coaching and organizational change including *TA in Organisations* (1996) and *Learning for Leadership* (2002).

Anne de Graaf, MA, is TSTA in the field of management and organizational development and CTA in the field of psychotherapy. For over 30 years, Anne was consultant, trainer and coach to a large number of companies and organizations, using TA, Group Relations and System Theory. He is co-author (together with Klaas Kunst) of the successful TA book about leadership *Einstein and the Art of Sailing* and co-editor (together with Bill Cornell, Trudi Newton and Moniek Thunnissen) of the comprehensive introduction to TA called *Into TA*. Anne has published several articles on organizational TA topics in *Transactional Analysis Journal* and other magazines. For 10 years he was general director of the Dutch TA academie. Currently he is the owner of RondHeel, consultancy and training. He is a lecturer at the MSc Organisational TA program at the Berne Institute in the UK.

INNOVATIONS IN TRANSACTIONAL ANALYSIS: THEORY AND PRACTICE
Series Editor: William F. Cornell

This book series is founded on the principle of the importance of open discussion, debate, critique, experimentation, and the integration of other models in fostering innovation in all the arenas of transactional analytic theory and practice: psychotherapy, counseling, education, organizational development, health care, and coaching. It will be a home for the work of established authors and new voices.

TRANSACTIONAL ANALYSIS OF SCHIZOPHRENIA
The Naked Self
Zefiro Mellacqua

CONTEXTUAL TRANSACTIONAL ANALYSIS
The Inseparability of Self and World
James M. Sedgwick

GROUPS IN TRANSACTIONAL ANALYSIS, OBJECT RELATIONS, AND FAMILY SYSTEMS
Studying Ourselves in Collective Life
N. Michel Landaiche, III

NEW THEORY AND PRACTICE OF TRANSACTIONAL ANALYSIS IN ORGANIZATIONS
On the Edge
Sari van Poelje and Anne de Graaf

www.routledge.com/Innovations-in-Transactional-Analysis-Theory-and-Practice/book-series/INNTA

NEW THEORY AND PRACTICE OF TRANSACTIONAL ANALYSIS IN ORGANIZATIONS

On the Edge

Edited by Sari van Poelje and Anne de Graaf

LONDON AND NEW YORK

First published 2022
by Routledge
2 Park Square, Milton Park, Abingdon, Oxon OX14 4RN

and by Routledge
605 Third Avenue, New York, NY 10158

Routledge is an imprint of the Taylor & Francis Group, an informa business

© 2022 selection and editorial matter, Sari van Poelje and Anne de Graaf; individual chapters, the contributors

The right of Sari van Poelje and Anne de Graaf to be identified as the authors of the editorial material, and of the authors for their individual chapters, has been asserted in accordance with sections 77 and 78 of the Copyright, Designs and Patents Act 1988.

All rights reserved. No part of this book may be reprinted or reproduced or utilised in any form or by any electronic, mechanical, or other means, now known or hereafter invented, including photocopying and recording, or in any information storage or retrieval system, without permission in writing from the publishers.

Trademark notice: Product or corporate names may be trademarks or registered trademarks, and are used only for identification and explanation without intent to infringe.

British Library Cataloguing-in-Publication Data
A catalogue record for this book is available from the British Library

Library of Congress Cataloging-in-Publication Data
Names: Poelje, Sari van, editor. | Graaf, Anne de, 1951– editor.
Title: New theory and practice of transactional analysis in organizations : on the edge / edited by S.J. van Poelje and Anne de Graaf.
Description: Abingdon, Oxon ; New York, NY : Routledge, 2021. | Series: Innovations in transactional analysis: theory and practice | Includes bibliographical references and index.
Identifiers: LCCN 2021008394 (print) | LCCN 2021008395 (ebook) | ISBN 9781032002941 (hardback) | ISBN 9781032002965 (paperback) | ISBN 9781003173564 (ebook)
Subjects: LCSH: Organizational behavior. | Transactional analysis. | Organizational change.
Classification: LCC HD58.7 .N4826 2021 (print) | LCC HD58.7 (ebook) | DDC 302.3/5—dc23
LC record available at https://lccn.loc.gov/2021008394
LC ebook record available at https://lccn.loc.gov/2021008395

ISBN: 978-1-032-00294-1 (hbk)
ISBN: 978-1-032-00296-5 (pbk)
ISBN: 978-1-003-17356-4 (ebk)

DOI: 10.4324/9781003173564

Typeset in Times New Roman
by Apex CoVantage, LLC

CONTENTS

	List of contributors	viii
1	Editors' introduction	1
2	Three levels of leadership	6
3	Adapting leadership power to its purpose	16
4	Leading self-organising teams: a paradox or a necessity?	30
5	Force fields in organisations: a new perspective on intervening in groups, systems and organisations	51
6	Managing boundary dynamics	87
7	Leading through people – managing vulnerability in working relationships	107
8	Managing fear and anxiety	118
9	Learning practices at work: a case for cognitive apprenticeship	130
10	Organizational cultures and change interventions	156
11	Berne's organizational theory applied to the prevention of psychosocial risks: a European phenomenon	174
12	Transactional analysis: a passport for the next decades	189
	Index	197

CONTRIBUTORS

Ugo De Ambrogio, TSTA-O, degree in social and political science at the University of Milan. He is a sociologist and director of the IRS (Institute for Social Research) where he directs research, consultancy, planning, evaluation and coaching and training activities with public administrations and non-profit organizations. He is the director, teacher and coach of the "Scuola IRS per il Sociale" (IRS School for Social) and director, teacher and co-founder of Eureka Academy OrganizzAT: School of Transactional Analysis in the organizational field. He has been a professor of planning and social evaluation at the University of Milan "Bicocca", at the "Ca Foscari" University of Venice and at the Polytechnic University of Milan. He is the author of over 100 scientific publications and four Italian books about TA in the organizational field.

Patrice Fosset is a PTSTA in the field of organizational psychology. After 15 years' experience in sales for a large industrial group, Patrice trained to become a practitioner in systemic and integrative psychology. He founded a consultancy firm specialized in accompanying change as well as a coaching school. For more than 25 years, he has used the concepts of transactional analysis as a foundation to support leaders and their teams to develop their skills and improve the efficiency of their organizations. He was particularly interested in the health of employees in companies, the prevention of psychosocial risks and the problems linked to moral harassment in professional circles. He contributes to the development of TA in France as a member of SEMLAT, an association which organizes a summer week devoted to training in transactional analysis. Now, he teaches transactional analysis and supervises professionals within organizations. He is an author and a speaker. His research focuses on the practice of energetics and transactional analysis.

Rosa R. Krausz, PhD, is TSTA – O & Ed. of ITAA and UNAT-Brasil. Rosa worked 40 years as a consultant, trainer and executive coach applying TA. She is the founder and first president of UNAT-Brasil, of ABRACEM (Brazilian Association of Executive Coaching), secretary of ITAA, member of ITAA

CONTRIBUTORS

Executive Committee and the *Transactional Analysis Journal (TAJ)* Editorial Board. Rosa was also editor of *REBAT – Brazilian Journal of Transactional Analysis* for 20 years. She authored three books on TA in organizations and more than 50 articles – some of which were published in *TAJ* and the *Script* and several of which were translated into German, French, Italian and Portuguese. Rosa is the recipient of the Eric Berne Award 2012 for two of her articles published in *TAJ*: "Organizational Scripts" (1993) and "Power and Leadership in Organizations" (1986).

Mandy Lacy, PhD, is a TSTA in the field of organisational psychology. Mandy works with leaders, teams and organisations involved with change and digital transformation. She is also a coach and a benefits realisation management specialist. Her PhD research investigated the conceptualisations of group memory enhancing learning and knowledge practices in the workplace. Mandy has published on TA topics, and has several articles and a book from her research in press. Mandy has taught at the University of Sydney Business School and currently leads a postgraduate leadership programme at The Mind Lab in New Zealand. She is the director of Mandy Lacy Consulting, Beyond Benefits and MQ Meeting Intelligence.

Corinne Laurier is a consultant in managerial and organizational development and TSTA in the field of organizations. She has been supporting companies or associations from various sectors in their organizational and managerial issues for 37 years, first as HR director and then as a consultant for 20 years. She is committed to combining personal growth and organizational development through the necessary changes in systems and leadership issues. She is co-author of a book on professional interviewing and author of *Manage with Transactional Analysis: Dare Your Managerial Style!* and various articles. Passionate about learning and pedagogical issues, she also passes on her experience and the wealth of transactional analysis in the field of organizations to consultants and coaches. She has also been very involved in TA associations for more than 10 years, occupying various positions or missions.

Marleine Mazouz is a consultant and coach. After many years within training organizations, she created a training company, specialized in professional efficiency and management, and served as a director and associate with a group of accounting firms. In 1993, she created Mediation Training Counsel ("Mediation Formation Conseil") to meet the needs of her clients: manage manager-employee relationship issues. She strengthens this area by integrating the prevention of psychosocial risks. In 2013, she created a preparation school for certification in transactional analysis in Paris. Today, with P.T.S.T.A. Organisation, she attaches great importance to the ethical and deontological dimension. Her guideline: Respect, Care, No judgment, No interference. Her field experiences allow her to measure, understand and help her customers clear up their discounting by relying on Eric Berne's organizational theory.

Jacques Moreau has held management positions in a context of international development. He is a TSTA in the field of management and organizational development. Thirty-five years ago, he founded the Ressources & Changement Group, a consulting and training firm. He works as a consultant as a resource person for individuals and groups undergoing change and as a facilitator of transformation processes. He also devotes himself to the transmission of his experience and research in transactional analysis in its "tensions orientation model", particularly adapted to intervention within groups. As a certified system engineer, he is interested in the relationships between individuals and groups. He has written scientific articles and collaborated in collective works in this field. He has an integrative perspective of psychological, sociological and anthropological aspects. He promotes the symbolic dimension and the involvement of the body.

Kathrin Rutz, MA, is TSTA in the organisational field. She is a co-director of the Eric Berne Institute in Zurich and conducts TA-training programmes. As a former primary school teacher and principal and as an organisational psychologist, she is also a lecturer and consultant at the Zurich University of Teacher Education. There she conducts courses and programmes for leaders and acts as coach and organisational consultant to schools and other (higher) educational institutions. Her focus is on personnel and leadership development, coaching, career counselling, team development and organisational consultancy. She brings together the individual, relational and systemic perspectives. As a freelance consultant, she works with individuals, teams and organisations to facilitate change, enhance skills and improve workplace performance. Her clients include profit and non-profit organisations from the public and private sectors.

Graeme Summers is a freelance executive coach and trainer based in the UK. He is also a lead coach at London Business School where he has worked since 2005. Graeme works internationally with leaders from a wide variety of organizations and sectors. He is a CTA in the field of psychotherapy, and prior to his coaching career, he was a psychotherapist for 19 years. He was also Director of Training for the Counselling and Psychotherapy Training Institute in Edinburgh. Graeme combines his passion for people development, psychology and learning to make academic insights accessible, relevant and practical. He is co-author, with Keith Tudor, of their book *Co-creative Transactional Analysis: Papers, Responses, Dialogues, and Developments* (2014). Graeme is co-recipient, alongside Keith, of the 2020 Eric Berne Memorial Award for their work on co-creativity.

1

EDITORS' INTRODUCTION

Sari van Poelje and Anne de Graaf

In 2018 we decided to co-create a new handbook on the theory and application of transactional analysis (TA) in organisations, with nine of our colleagues from all over the world. We were curious about how TA professionals in the field of management & organizational development (M&OD) perceive the rapid changes in the world and our profession today. It seems to us we live in days of constant crises. All these developments – from trade wars to climate threats to virus outbreaks – do not go beyond the doors of organisations. All of us are authors, teachers and supervisors in TA, and experienced managers, coaches, trainers and consultants in our own right.

Rapid change

At the structural level organisations have changed, under the influence of volatile markets and socio-environmental developments. The need to create structures that enable cooperation across functions and disciplines has increased. The challenge at this level is to maintain boundaries and identity while at the same time allowing enough permeability that new information, partnerships and thinking can impact the organization. At the relational level the need to create communication and cooperation across distance and difference has become greater. Increased pressure from the environment and developments that are not in the realm of one organization alone to influence has increased the need for systemic thinking in relationships. At the existential level the need to switch from I-thinking to We-thinking in organizational cultures has increased.

This is dramatically illustrated by the response to the COVID-19 crisis, which shows us that the world cannot function on the basis of individual responsibility anymore. We are forced to accept collective responsibility for our actions. The confusion this causes is clearly illustrated by the call for 'social distancing' in days when people need each other more than ever. The choice of 'social distancing' instead of 'physical distancing' shows that thinking about boundaries between individual and group – certainly among policymakers – is under pressure. For us two things are clear: Firstly, in organisations we never walk alone. Secondly, organisations need top learners, because top learners are successful managers (van Poelje, 2004).

On the edge

We believe that TA can contribute at all of these levels. TA can offer innovative, on-the-edge thinking for this new world. TA can stimulate daring, on-the-edge acting for this new reality. Central to this thinking and acting is the notion of boundary. Eric Berne (1963) defined a boundary as a constitutional, psychological or spatial distinction: "A group may be defined as any social aggregation that has an external boundary and at least one internal boundary (p. 54)".

Three elements of this boundary definition are important. First: the idea that boundaries are (mostly) imaginary lines, demarcations that exist primarily in the mind of the perceiver. Every organisation is always and above all an organisation in the mind. Second: boundaries are essential in defining groups and organisations because they are their main structural element. One can even say that the clearer the boundaries – contracts – the higher the functioning. Third: boundaries refer not only to separate areas but also to their interrelation and possibly to the dynamics as well (e.g. Friedlander, 1987). Transactions exist because there are boundaries.

For a TA coach or consultant boundaries are an organising principle guiding their interventions, both as a structural frame and as the main relational and psychological principle. The permeability of boundaries can determine both the stability of a system and its innovative potential. On a medieval map the boundary would show up as the distinction between what is known and what is not known. Any TA coach or consultant has to walk this line between known and not known, between being in a system and at the same time being an outsider.

Any group or organisation that wants to change – grow or innovate – needs to cross the boundary between being 'conservative and stable' and being 'innovative and unstable', between 'knowing what you have' and 'not knowing what you get'. Doing so is often experienced as risky. We think that looking at change from a dialectical perspective is necessary here, because we believe there always is a dialectical tension between order and disorder, between integration and differentiation, between stability and instability, between balance and disbalance. When order is a fact, the longing for disorder emerges. When integration is a fact, differentiation becomes a need. When stability has had its time, instability beckons. We have to learn to deal with these dynamic contradictions, with the interplay between complementary or opposing tendencies (Baxter & Montgomery, 1996). Tension is part of life, at home and at work. Dealing with all these tensions is the challenge. We call this being on the edge.

Effectivity

Petriglieri and Wood (2003) wrote:

> Behavioral professionals are constantly warned by their teachers, supervisors, and colleagues about the risk of losing their 'objective' and 'unbiased' perspective – of 'going native', of having 'their buttons pushed' and being 'hooked' into their clients' games, of 'falling out of role' and so on. If this is a risk when working with an individual client, it is even more of a risk when working with a group, the gravity of whose psychological pull is considerably stronger and much more multidimensional. We are suggesting here, however, that there is something to be said for allowing oneself to be drawn into the emotional field of a group – if it is done responsibly.

One will never understand an organisation or group by just being an observer. Being in or part of it, 'getting your shoes dirty', allows for a deeper understanding of what is really going on.

So whoever wants to work on the edge first needs to be mindful of the boundaries. No boundary, no edge. Eric Berne was, in our opinion, very much in favour of working on the edge. To really make a difference a TA professional needs to be willing to take a risk. His very first article about applying TA in an organisational context, called "Institutional Games" (Berne et al. 1962), ends with a question: "How efficient can I be without getting fired?" Whoever looks up 'edge' or 'on the edge' in a dictionary will notice that being or working on the edge is referring to something bad or disastrous. We are not advocating to engage oneself in bad or disastrous situations. We do think however that any TA professional, working in or with groups and/or organisations, must be prepared to at least take a risk. No risk, no result!

The book

In this book we have collected articles by leading thinkers and practitioners in the TA organisational field. Their mission was to write a chapter from their 'on-the-edge perspective' on TA in the organisational world today, based on original conceptualisation with practical edge.

- In Chapter 2 on the three levels of leadership, **Dutch** TA professional **Sari van Poelje** talks of the management of paradoxes: the paradox between market reactivity and corporate identity, between centralised control and delegation and between independence and interdependence of teams.
- In Chapter 3 **Corinne Laurier** from **France** argues that organisational, personal and historical power factors need to be adapted to role and goals; in today's world power *over* needs to be replaced by power *for* dynamics.

In Chapter 4 **Kathrin Rutz** from **Switzerland** uses her wide experience in expert organisations to explore the four essential conditions to work with self-organising teams: (1) clear structures, (2) strong leadership, (3) negotiated contracts and a (4) culture of dialogue.

In Chapter 5, our **French** colleague, **Jacques Moreau**, offers a new perspective on working with large living systems in the boundary zone. The boundary zone is the area between outside and inside, the transitional space that allows us to work with the tension between love, conflict and destruction.

In Chapter 6 on boundary dynamics, our **French** colleague, **Patrice Fosset**, gives practical guidelines on how to move from diagnosis to problem resolution in organisations by changing the force and permeability of boundaries.

In Chapter 7 **Graeme Summers** from the **UK** shows the power of vulnerability in leading downwards, upwards, across and outwards, and that courage, creativity and cooperation will bring is to a new edge in working in today's organisations.

In Chapter 8 on managing fear and anxiety **Anne de Graaf** from the **Netherlands** argues that organisations are in a sense systems of emotions, often constructed to manage the fear of their managers. On the one hand this anxiety can lead to innovation, but if unchecked it is merely a container for life scripts.

In Chapter 9 **Mandy Lacy** from **New Zealand** focuses on her PhD research on cognitive apprenticeship and collaborative reflection in the workplace as a way to stimulate innovation.

In Chapter 10 on organisational cultures and change, **Italian Ugo De Ambrogio** describes five models of organisational culture: Culture of Cohesion (paternalistic), Culture of Order (efficient), Culture of Challenge (spontaneity), Culture of Rules and Procedures (hyper-bureaucratic) and Culture of Obedience (closed).

In Chapter 11, the case study by **Marleine Mazouz** from **France** shows us how to work with psychosocial risk prevention. In France this is dictated by law, and managers are personally responsible. She shows us how to work with primary, secondary and tertiary risk prevention strategies using TA.

In Chapter 12, the closing chapter of this book, **Rosa R. Krausz** from **Brasil** outlines the changes she expects in the organisational environment and the contribution TA can make to understanding and adapting to these changes.

Finally

Working together is a challenge, but there is no alternative if you want to grow and innovate. Efficiency is key but so is cooperation. Our task is to keep relationship and contracted goals in balance. This is not easy. It's edgy work. After having read all the articles, you will see how true this is.

Writing this book together has been a testimony to the need to take risks and to cooperate. We – Anne and Sari – are colleagues, but despite our similar roles and development, we spent twenty years in friction. One day we met decided to explore our tension as a systemic consequence within our community and both our life scripts. We have been on a beautiful journey together, building our cooperation on the edge. This is what transactional analysis in the end is all about – to build the capacity to meet and work together in appreciation of each other's similarities and differences. We would like to finish with a quote from our colleague Jim Allen, taken from his keynote at the Eric Berne centennial TA conference in 2010 in Montreal: "People meet based on their similarities. They grow based on their differences". We couldn't agree more. Have a good read!

References

Baxter, L., & Montgomery, B. (1996). *Relating: Dialogues and Dialectics*. New York: The Guilford Press.

Berne, E. (1963). *The Structure and Dynamics of Organizations and Groups*. New York: Grove Press.

Berne, E., Birnbaum, R., Poindexter, R., & Rosenfeld, B. (1962). Institutional Games. *Transactional Analysis Bulletin*, 1(2), 12–13.

de Graaf, A. (2013). The Group in the Individual, Lessons Learned from Working with and in Organizations and Groups. *Transactional Analysis Journal*, 43, 311–320.

Friedlander, F. (1987). 'The ecology of work groups' in *Handbook of organizational behavior*. J. Lorsch (ed.), 301–314. Englewood Cliffs, NJ: Prentice Hall.

Petriglieri, G., & Wood, J. D. (2003). The Invisible Revealed: Collusion as an Entry to the Group Unconscious. *Transactional Analysis Journal*, 33(4), 332–343.

Van Poelje, S. (2004) Learning for Leadership. *Transactional Analysis Journal*, 34(3), 223–228.

2
THREE LEVELS OF LEADERSHIP

Sari van Poelje

In this chapter I focus on expanding Berne's original ideas about the different structures in an organization and relate it to leadership. Leadership is a position, a relationship and a symbol. My purpose is to increase awareness of the fact that effective leadership is focused on congruency at all three levels of organizational structure.

What is leadership?

Studies of leadership since the 1940s have focused on two main dimensions of leadership: task-oriented and relationship-oriented leadership (Boje, 2000). This later evolved into other perspectives, including research into these dimensions, focused on leadership traits, situational leadership and transactional and transformational leadership (Mann, 1959; Hersey & Blanchard, 1998; Vroom & Jago, 1988).

As a result of this research, leadership has often been defined as (1) having the position of a leader and/or (2) the ability to lead a group of people in a common task. Consequently, a lot of publications focus on the structural role and tasks of leadership or on the relational ability of leaders.

New challenges for leadership

Though this research gave us a good idea of what leaders should do and how they should do it, it didn't take into account the rapid changes we face today.

We live in an accelerated turbulent world. Increasing complexity, drastically shortened production cycles and lack of resources are forcing us to come up with new answers.

Within leadership there are new and different challenges that require new answers: The complexity and speed of change is such that the demands on leaders are rapidly outdistancing the capabilities of any single person (Wageman et al., 2008). How can we shift from an individual leadership to a team leadership focus?

The boundaries of control are shifting. Where before leadership was focused on distributing resources within the organization, nowadays a lot of the resources for production are outsourced in a network and are outside of direct control of the leaders. How can we shift from a focus on direct supervision to a focus on leading virtual networks?

The basis of power is shifting. Where before the most experienced leader rose to the top, nowadays there is a shift towards autonomous workers, where innovative ideas count for more than experience. How can we shift from a focus on sustainable production to a focus on anticipation and innovation?

These challenges indicate a need to shift to a more interdependent and purposeful form of leadership to deal with today's turbulence. Leaders today should be focusing more on creating leadership teams, virtual networks and innovation. The question is: what concepts and tools can we offer to enable this shift?

The structure of organizations and leadership

What is an organization?

Transactional analysis (TA) offers a comprehensive set of concepts and tools at the organizational level, which offers a systemic view beyond the well-known concepts at the individual level.

A group may be defined as any social aggregation that has an external boundary and at least one internal boundary (Berne, 1963, p. 54).

The major external boundary distinguishes between members and non-members, that is, between the group and its environment. The major internal boundary distinguishes between two classes of people, the leadership and the membership. Minor internal boundaries distinguish one class of membership from another class. An organization may be considered a more complicated type of group.

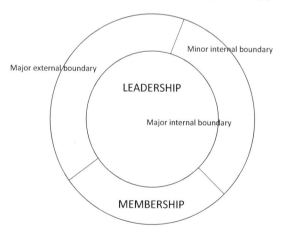

Figure 2.1 Organizational boundaries

Public and private structure

One of the major contributions of Berne (1963) is the recognition that an organization has both a public and a private structure that operate simultaneously.

The public structure is observable in the leadership and membership boundaries and roles (organizational structure) and through the relationships and dynamics between the individuals who fulfil these roles (intrapersonal structure). This public structure determines the structure of roles and relationships within the organization.

An organization also has a private structure, consisting of interlocking scripts and imagoes. This private structure is determined by the personal wishes, archaic needs and experience of the leadership and the membership. It is visible in the culture of communication in an organization (transactions). For instance, any organization has a formal structure of roles and hierarchy, which defines the power distribution in an organization. At the same time, an informal structure of relationships is at work, which determines the dynamics of influence at work. And underneath all of that, a constellation of transference is at work, profoundly influencing our reactions to leadership, belonging and culture.

Transactional analysis focus on leadership

In Berne's (1964) *The Structure and Dynamics of Organizations and Groups*, leadership is described as a role on three levels of organization:

1 Responsible leadership: legitimate power in organizational structure, accountable if things go wrong
2 Effective leadership: actual decision-making power in individual structure, dominant during organization activity
3 Psychological leadership: symbolic, god-like in private structure, important in times of crisis

Berne also provides three concepts to describe the historical development of leadership in a group (see also Fox, 1975):

1 Euhemerus: the mythical leader of the group in the imago, seen as omnipotent
2 Primal leader: establishes organization and gives meaning to canon through heroic deeds
3 Personal leader: current leader and sub-leaders in the organization

In later TA articles, the focus is mostly on relationship-oriented leadership. For example, Krausz (1986) writes about the various uses of power in leadership to influence others toward results. Campos (1971) writes about leadership as the potency to allow clients, in particular employees, to make a choice in the direction of their contract.

Some transactional analysts write more about task-oriented leadership. For instance, Clarkson (1991), following Berne's description of the development of group imago, writes about the different tasks of leadership in different developmental stages. Gurowitz (1975) links the establishment of safe external group boundaries to the ability of the leader to establish strong internal boundaries.

Some have written more about the development of leadership in different settings, for example in articles on autocratic systems and on learning for leadership (van Poelje, 1995, 2004).

The levels of leadership

In this part of the chapter, I focus on the main tasks of leadership in each level of the organization.

Level 1. Leadership in the organizational structure

In the organizational structure, leadership is defined as a role in the organizational hierarchy. It is distinguished from organizational membership, through the major internal boundary.

This is the domain of what Berne (1963) called the responsible leaders. They lead on the basis of their formal position and the sanction and reward power that are associated with that position. This is supported by the organizational constitution, which describes the purpose, boundaries, tasks and procedures in a group.

At this level, the task of leadership is to manage the organizational boundaries and processes to fulfil the purpose of the organization. I believe at this level the main focus of leadership should be dealing with three major organizational dilemmas concerning boundaries.

Paradox 1: You can maximize the reactivity to market – open major external boundary – or the corporate identity – closed major external boundary – but not maximally at the same time.

Paradox 2: You can maximize delegation – open major internal boundary – or control – closed major internal boundary – but not maximally at the same time.

Paradox 3: You can maximize the independence – open minor internal boundaries – or interdependence – closed minor internal boundaries – but not maximally at the same time.

Figure 2.2 Organizational boundaries and paradoxes

Leadership of organizational structure is like being a DJ

At this level, leadership is like being a DJ with a boundary mixing panel with three switches. You open or close boundaries depending on the purpose of the organization and the dynamics in the environment.

For example, if the organization's purpose is to produce at maximum efficiency at the same quality level time after time in a stable environment, the major internal and external boundaries and minor boundaries should be more closed. As a consequence, the organization will be characterized by a strong corporate identity, with centralized control and independent business units.

Think of a corporation like McDonald's – an international company with affiliates all over the world – that has to produce hamburgers in the same way with the same quality everywhere. They have a relatively stable market and low-level work, so they don't need a lot of innovative input from the market, and they need a clear hierarchical structure to deal with the routine tasks. All the processes are standardized, so there is little need for delegation of leadership to employees.

Another example is an organization whose purpose is to innovate and remain flexible in a fast-moving market, like Apple. In that case, it is important to be reactive to the market and keep a more open external boundary and encourage interdisciplinary cooperation amongst departments through more open minor internal boundaries. To keep the organization stable with this kind of openness it is important that the leadership remains directive and stable, underpinned with clear processes.

Every opening or closing of one boundary affects the opening or closing of the other boundaries. Every organization has to maintain a dynamic balance between open and closed boundaries to serve their purpose at different times.

Level 2. Leadership of the individual structure

In the individual structure, leadership is defined as the ability to influence others to achieve breakthrough performance. In Berne's terms this concerns effective leadership, based on the authority of the person in their role (persona).

It is supported by the personal authority of the leader and the laws and regulations governing group dynamics. At this level, the focus of leadership is to manage relationships and enhance group cohesion to counteract dysfunctional group dynamics.

Cohesion is the need of members to preserve the existence of the group (Berne, 1966). It is the cohesive force, which can counteract the disruptive forces of pressure, agitation and intrigue. When there is not a balance between the disruptive dynamics and the internal cohesion, the group becomes a combat or process group instead of a work group.

At this level, leadership is focused on increasing cohesion in a group. Research shows that the more cohesive a group, the higher the performance (Wageman et al., 2008).

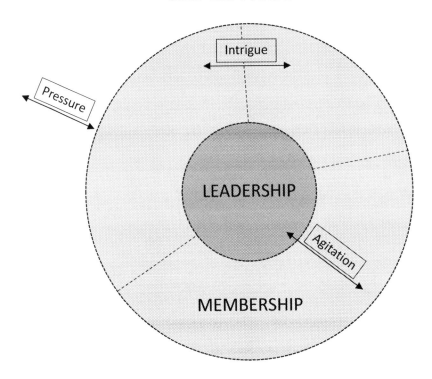

Figure 2.3 Managing cohesion

On the whole, there are three strategies to increase cohesion:

1. Increase the interpersonal attraction (Lewin, 1952, p. 162; Festinger et al., 1950)
    - Increase perceived similarity between members
    - Increase the interdependence of shared goals
    - Increase the social interaction in the group
2. Enhance the social identity (Tajfel, 1979)
    - Create a positive in-group and a negative out-group
    - Minimize intragroup differences and maximize intragroup differences
    - Manipulate social beliefs about mobility, the possibility of change and legitimacy of the group to encourage people to stay
3. Strategize social exchange (Thiebault et al. 1959)
    - Increase the reward while lowering the cost of membership while manipulating the number of options outside the group, the investment of the members in the group and the expectations of the group

For example, when using this last strategy there are several important implications for increasing cohesion. To increase cohesion, it is important for leadership to keep tabs on the rewards versus the cost of membership. Leadership can pursue a strategy based on giving higher than average salaries for instance, and/or lowering the cost of membership by introducing flexible work hours, transport options, day care and so forth.

Apart from reward and cost, leadership can influence cohesion through the three mediating factors. For instance, if you are the only employer in that region offering this type of job, there are limited options. If the members have invested a lot of work for a long time in the organization, their investment is large, and they will be more reluctant to leave. Lastly, if the organization exceeds the previous expectations of members, then people will be more likely to stay.

For example, CLAAS Hungária is the only large employer offering this type of agricultural engineering job in the east of Hungary. People enter the company at a very young age, often passing on the job from father to son, and they stay for lifetime employment. They offer a very good benefits package, compared with Hungarian employers, because their benefits are modeled on the German head office packages. They actively increase the benefits of membership by offering for example sports facilities and transportation to and from work.

Level 3. Leadership in the psychodynamic structure

At the psychodynamic level, the relationship between leaders and members is determined by the group imago and based on the implicit script-based expectations of both leaders and members.

Each of us has learned about leadership and membership in our first experience of group, which is usually our family of origin. This is the domain in which we create our first script beliefs, about leadership and membership. These color our group imagoes until they are decontaminated and clarified.

The leadership focus at this level is on managing the culture and on clarifying the group imago to minimize the archaic influence on actual performance. This is done through a continuous process of decontamination of the leadership-membership relationship.

Berne (1963) defined three elements of organizational culture: the etiquette, techniques and character of a culture as introjected and experienced by the individual (see also: Drego, 1983).

In our archaic scripts the leader is seen as omnipotent. In the process of decontamination, the leader has to become more of a delegating mentor, to gradually create a culture of realistic expectations, competency and participative leadership.

Lessons learned

Leadership is a position in the organizational structure, a relationship in the relational structure and an imago in the psychodynamic structure of organizations.

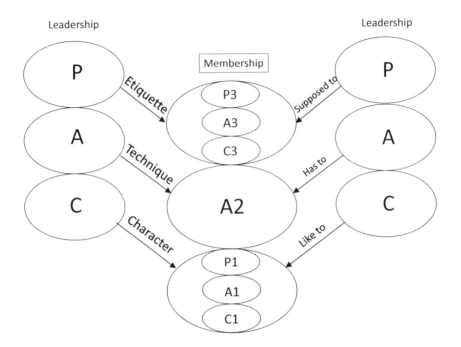

Figure 2.4 Organizational script matrix

All the levels of leadership are active at the same time and require a different focus.

In the organizational structure, leadership is focused on managing the permeability of the boundaries and can be likened to be being a boundary DJ with a three-slide mixing panel.

In the relational structure, leadership is focused at increasing cohesion, to counteract any disruptive pressure, agitation or intrigue. Leadership at this level is focused on improving the relationships within the organization by balancing the rewards and costs of membership.

In the psychodynamic structure, leadership is focused on clarifying the group imago and decontaminating archaic transferential processes on leadership. Leadership at this level is preoccupied with creating and maintaining clear communication and a healthy culture of performance.

Leadership is most powerful when all three levels of leadership are managed in a congruent way.

References and further reading

Bennett, D. (1980). Successful Team Building Through TA. *Amacom*.
Berne, E. (1963). *The Structure and Dynamics of Organizations and Groups. A Transactional Analysis Handbook*. New York: Grove Press.

Berne, E. (1966). *Principles of Group Treatment*. New York: Oxford University Press.
Boje, D. (2000). *The Isles Leadership: The Voyage of the Behaviorists*. Michigan, USA: The Leadership Box (Northern Michigan State University).
Campos, L. P. (1971) Transactional Analysis Group Leadership Operations. *Transactional Analysis Journal*, October, 1(4), 21–24.
Clarkson, P. (1991). Group Imago and the Stages of Group Development. *Transactional Analysis Journal*, January, 21(10), 36–50.
Drego, P. (1983). *Transactional Analysis Journal*, 13(4).
Festinger, L., Schachter, S., & Back, K. (1950). *Social pressures in informal groups; a study of human factors in housing*. Harper.
Fox, E. M. (1975). Eric Berne's Theory of Organizations. *Transactional Analysis Journal*, October, 5(4), 345–353.
Gurowitz, E. M. (1975). Group Boundaries and Leadership Potency. *Transactional Analysis Journal*, April, 5(2), 183–185.
Hersey, P. & Blanchard, K. H. (1977). *Management of Organizational Behavior: Utilizing Human Resources* (3rd ed.) New Jersey/Prentice Hall, ISBN 978-0132617697
Hersey, P., Blanchard, K., & Johnson, D. (2008). *Management of Organizational Behavior: Leading Human Resources* (9th ed.). Upper Saddle River, NJ: Pearson Education.
Iverson, R. D., & Buttigieg, D. M. (1999). Affective, Normative and Continuance Commitment: Can the Right Kind of Commitment Be Managed? *Journal of Management Studies*, May, 36(3).
Kapur, R., & Miller, K. (1987). A Comparison Between Therapeutic Factors in TA and Psychodynamic Therapy Groups. *TAJ*, 17(1), 294–300.
Krausz, R. R. (1986). Power and Leadership in Organizations. *Transactional Analysis Journal*, April, 16(2), 85–94.
Lee, A. (2014). The Development of a Process Group. *Transactional Analysis Journal*, January, 44(1), 41–52. first published on 14 March 2014.
Lewin, K. (1952). *Field Theory in Social Science*. New York: Harper & Row.
Mann, R. D. (1959). A Review of the Relationship Between Personality and Performance in Small Groups. *Psychological Bulletin*, 56(4), 241–270.
Peck, H. B. (1978). Integrating Transactional Analysis and Group Process Approaches in Treatment. *TAJ*, October, 8(4), 328–332.
Tajfel, H. & Turner, J. C. (1979). "An integrative theory of intergroup conflict". In W. G. Austin & S. Worchel (eds.). *The social psychology of intergroup relations*. Monterey, CA: Brooks/Cole. pp. 33–47.
Thibaut, J. W., & Kelley, H. H. (1959). *The Social Psychology of Groups*. New York: John Wiley & Sons.
Van Poelje, S. (1995). Development of Autocratic Systems. *Transactional Analysis Journal*, July, 25(3), 265–270.
Van Poelje, S. (2004). Learning for Leadership. Sari van Poelje. *Transactional Analysis Journal*, July, 34(3), 223–228.
Vroom, V. H., & Jago, A. G. (1988). *The New Leadership: Managing Participation in Organizations*. Englewood Cliffs, NJ: Prentice-Hall.
Wageman, R., Nunes, D. A., Buruss, J. A., & Hackman, J. R. (2008). *Senior Leadership Teams: What It Takes to Make Them Great*. HBR Press.

3
ADAPTING LEADERSHIP POWER TO ITS PURPOSE

Corinne Laurier

Introduction

Power is not a given. There can be too much or too little power depending on the purpose you want to pursue as a leader. In this article we will explore how to adapt your use of power depending on the level and role of leadership in the system.

Organisational transformation usually creates insecurity, a sense of loss of structure, relationship or identity. Attempts to inject a sense of security, through leadership containment and control, can be risky, as this could give way to an autocratic form of power (Jacobs, 1987) or to disengagement of members (van Poelje, 1995).

The use of the correct type of power is therefore a key theme in accompanying change. Power has been the subject of a whole raft of publications in transactional analysis (TA; C. Boyd, A. Jacobs, R. Krausz, J. Kreyenberg, R. Massey, S. van Poelje, C. Steiner), some of which I refer to here. Most of these publications are focussed on understanding how an autocratic system arises as opposed to a democratic one, on how leader-follower relationships develop, as well as describing the various types of power and their impact on the organisation and analysing power plays.

In this chapter, we take a different route: how to make your leadership power fit to purpose.

"Adapted" power

Power can be defined from the perspective of influence, as defined by Rosa Krausz (1986, p. 85). She sees power as "the ability to influence the actions of others, individuals or groups." In the case of leaders, this influence is used to enable teams to meet their operational and strategic goals and to implement change effectively, in other words to maintain a healthy team.

Perceptions of power are often extreme nowadays, seemingly a choice between autocracy and democracy, between "having power" or "being powerless". Yet everyone holds some form of power in their own way and according to their role (Crozier & Friedberg, 1977).

In companies, being a manager or a member naturally involves exerting power. The key is to use that power in a manner that is suited to the company culture, one's role and one's objectives.

Each employee adapts their action to the organisation in which they work.

My assumption is that "adapted power" is more beneficial to the leader and environment and ensures long-term efficiency than autocratic power or an absence of power. I base this assumption chiefly on theories of motivation, which show that we get better results when we have motivated teams, and on Sari van Poelje's (1995) study of autocratic systems and their limits. I also draw on my own experience in various organisations, where different types of leadership require different ways of using power.

With adapted power, the leader shows that each employee, at their own level in the context of the organisation, can have access to sufficient sources of power to reach their goals. These sources of power are based on personal characteristics and on a whole set of organisational, personal, cultural and historical characteristics, which I explain next.

These sources can be analysed and applied using the three levels of leadership defined by van Poelje (2021), and power factors, as defined by Eric Berne's (1963, 1966) authority diagram. The aim is to obtain a "framework for the systemic analysis" of "adapted power".

The three levels of leadership

Drawing on the work of Berne (1963), van Poelje (2021) describes three levels of leadership and the main tasks of the leader at each level. She concludes, "Leadership is most powerful when all three levels of leadership are managed in a congruent way".

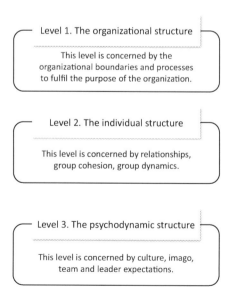

Figure 3.1 The three levels of leadership

The three power factors

In my work with organisations, I use Berne's idea that leadership is influenced by four factors (organisational, personal, cultural and historical) in relation to the levels of leadership described previously, to teach leaders how to use adapted power.

Organisational power

Organisational power stems from the power granted by the system, determined by the sharing of responsibilities and the areas of activity officially delegated to a "responsible leader". A responsible leader is the person holding the position of leader in the company's organisation structure and legally responsible for his or her decisions (Berne, 1963).

A number of elements relevant to adapted power can be identified here:

- Decision-making power: What is the breakdown of responsibilities between the various levels of management? How autonomous is the leader in decision making?
- Accountability: To whom is the leader accountable? What does he or she report on?
- Resources: What financial, material and human resources does the leader have? How much room to manoeuvre does he or she have in respect to these resources?
- Information: Is the leader provided with the necessary information to ensure the performance of his or her team? Is the information about his or her decision-making power and responsibilities officially recognized?
- Application of laws and regulations: Does the leader have autonomy in the enforcement of laws and regulations? Can the leader make a one-off autonomous decision not to apply a rule that would impinge on performance?

Other factors impacting organisational power:

- Having authority over a particular person (as director, founder, shareholder)
- Titles and diplomas (depending on the company activity or culture)
- Being a member of a specific organisation: for example, a representative of labour inspection services is recognised as having power granted by the Ministry concerned, whomever that person may be

Another identifiable aspect here is that of roles. As I said earlier, these power factors differ depending on the role played.

Let's begin by defining a role: "A role is a coherent system of attitudes, feelings, behaviours, perspectives on reality, and accompanying relationships" determined by one's position in an organisation or society (Schmid, 2008, p. 20). In sociology, the role theory approach gives us another, similar, definition: "*The role is an organized model of behaviours relating to a certain position of the individual in an interactional whole*" (Rocheblave-Spenlé, 1969, p. 306). These definitions link the personal and cultural with the organisational aspects of role definition.

In our professional lives, we play several roles simultaneously: manager, co-worker, colleague, boss's cousin, former employee. Each of these roles forms a coherent whole.

We can identify three main types of professional roles in organisations: those of leaders, those of team members, and those of apparatus (Berne, 1963).

The role relates to an organisational purpose: the role "serves" the operating targets and involves "externally assigned" concerns (Crespelle, 1985). It is therefore delineated by a number of obligations, for example to respect laws and regulations, and also by certain responsibilities, for example the performance of one's team, the atmosphere among staff, customer satisfaction, anticipating change, making decisions and ensuring rules are respected.

Different roles involve different obligations and responsibilities. Someone who has a dual role like engineer and manager has two systems of obligations and responsibilities to deal with. The risk would be to confuse the two roles and, hence, their associated obligations and responsibilities. Their reactions, for instance to the absence of a team member at a crucial stage in the project, will differ according to whether they are in their role as engineer or as leader.

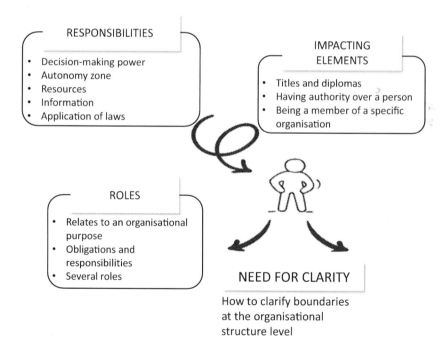

Figure 3.2 Organisational power factors

When a single person holds several roles, these responsibilities and obligations need to be clearly stated and kept separate to ensure they are able to lead at the structural level. That might involve making explicit what is implicit and sharing this information. The clearer the boundaries of the leader's role, the better their ability to activate organisational power factors and to intervene effectively at this first level.

These organisational power factors enable the leader to act at the structural level of the organisation. They are observable and identifiable elements of official power. If these are impaired, the leader may be prevented from taking action formally. However, a leader who has access only to this level of power would be at risk of exercising a coercive form of leadership, based on position only: "I am the boss, you must obey me". In other words, when the leader does not have power factors at their disposal to motivate employees, they may be obliged to demand that orders be carried out, which will mean putting their "organisational power factors" to work to ensure they are obeyed.

Let's see how this works in practice: Julie as CEO

Julie has created an e-reputation monitoring firm. When we meet, her company has been around for 10 years and has 15 employees. The company is at a key stage in its development. Julie says, "Something has become stuck: my colleagues no longer follow my lead, they're afraid of me and I don't know why. They need to improve their skills. I'm prospecting new markets and have ideas for growth. We will need to recruit, and the team needs to be more cohesive and dynamic. I find them sluggish, uninvolved; they don't take any responsibilities and don't understand what's at stake."

Observations

Together, we take the time needed to assess the factors just discussed.

Julie's role is that of CEO. She has sole responsibility for the company. Each of the 15 employees deals with her directly. She makes all of the decisions.

Organisational power factors

Julie never delegates; she shoulders all of the responsibility.

She has total decision-making power, from purchasing to the recruitment and dismissal of staff, to the growth or termination of the company. She has no-one with whom to discuss these decisions.

She says she feels "scattered, I change levels all of the time, I feel alone".

She is accountable only to legal bodies, such as chartered accountants and the Ministry of Work. She finds no meaning in these levels of leadership; she experiences them more as legal obligations than as blocking points.

Julie has little means at her disposal: due to the size of the company, its expenses are only just balanced by its profits. The company has reached critical size and needs to grow if it wants to generate real profits. She can do that only by winning new business, which requires a different skill set to that which she currently uses in the company.

Julie complains about there being "too much useless information". She has her own resources, in terms of information on markets, her obligations and so forth. However, with respect to daily operations and customer processing, she simply receives unsorted information from her 15 colleagues.

She has autonomy in terms of applying laws and regulations. The difficulty at this level lies in the lack of an established internal framework. Julie reacts on a case-by-case basis, with no real consistency in her approach, leading some people to say she has favourites within the team.

Together, we notice that the lack of organisational power factors is preventing her from acting at the structural level in a consistent, structured manner. While her power is indeed official, it is also unique.

When she is annoyed, Julie sometimes threatens to punish her employees, saying she doesn't "know how to react" at such times. In these cases, she is exerting a form of coercive power.

Julie agrees that her role should primarily involve steering the company and making decisions with regard to its growth. She holds multiple roles and sometimes makes inappropriate decisions due to being caught up in role confusion.

She understands that the fear she feels among her colleagues stems from her power to punish, and which is reinforced by the threats she makes. This is not what she wants. She is uncomfortable with this kind of power.

Personal power factors

These lie in the individual person: personality, how they developed psychologically and integrated new relational experiences, needs for stimulation, structure and recognition (Berne, 1961); existential and "externally assigned" concerns (Crespelle, 1985); the way in which we inhabit our role.

In terms of adapted power this is related to interpersonal skills, a set of attitudes and behaviours, stemming not just from our personality but also from our experience and knowledge. For instance, the ability to listen, pass on information, provide support, give meaning, be authentic, care for others, give others autonomy and provide structure. Leaders also exert influence through their relationships, their ability to build a relational network and their interpersonal skills, both in terms of groups and individuals.

Finally, the leader's power is also influenced by their sense of legitimacy, their self-confidence and their ability to distinguish existential concerns from externally assigned concerns.

Alain Crespelle (1985) identifies two types of concerns that drive our life. The first are "existential" personal concerns. These are about feeling accepted or rejected, recognised or neglected. The second type are "externally assigned" concerns, relating to our social roles. These are about success or failure, losing and winning compared with others. When a person unconsciously confuses these two concerns, they behave in a way that will prevent them from resolving their problem. The more confusion there is, the more the person will be prevented from resolving the issue because the stakes become too high. For instance, the fear that no-one will like me if I make the wrong decision could result in me making no decision at all.

The way in which we inhabit a role also has an impact at this level and the various players interacting with the role each have their own expectations. These may differ depending on the type of organisation structure in place, the sector of activity, the co-worker in question and the level of management involved. They affect attitudes and relationships profoundly. We adapt our action to each of our roles by changing the way we speak, our vocabulary, the way we dress and even the way we say hello.

By ensuring attitudes are consistent with the expectations of their role, the leader can develop the relational level power, the ability to bring a certain amount of cohesion and momentum to their team.

Clarifying what is expected of their role, first in their own mind, then with the main people with whom they have contact, will make it easier for managers to develop suitable attitudes and behaviour. This is particularly true for leaders whose roles are fragmented (Micholt, 2010, p. 67): "When a person gets lost in the multiplicity of his roles and loses perspective, we call that role fragmentation." When this happens, the leader will need to restore meaning and clarify his or her priorities in terms of responsibilities.

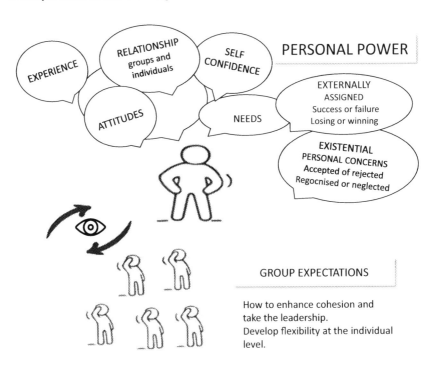

Figure 3.3 Personal power factors

This means becoming more flexible, that is, gaining the ability to "activate an adequate role and to momentarily deactivate the other roles in a given situation" (Micholt, 2010, p. 57).

The leader will also need to clarify his or her own expectations of co-workers' roles, to help them develop the appropriate behavioural skills.

The personal concerns impact the manager's individual and collective relationships with their staff and their environment. They enable them to establish a structure and suitable framework for the group, deal with strained interpersonal situations, cultivate team cohesion in the short and long term and give meaning to their actions.

van Poelje (2021) says, "At this level (2) the focus of leadership is to manage relationships and enhance group cohesion to counteract dysfunctional group dynamics". These personal power factors enable the leader to act at the interpersonal level. They are implicit and can be identified only through observation of the leader's impact on relationships and team cohesiveness and on their environment and will thus play in a part in the leader's "adapted power".

A leader who has access only to this level of power would be at risk of exercising an emotion-led symbiotic form of power: "Do that for me". A symbiotic relationship is defined as a dependent relationship in which one takes charge of the other, and in which the players are not using their Adult ego state at the same time Schiff, A. W., & Schiff, J. L. (1971). This symbiosis can apply at each hierarchic level, thus forming a symbiotic chain in which each level takes charge of the level below and willingly accepts to be taken charge of (Holdeman, 1989). The main problem posed by this symbiotic chain is the ensuing lack of autonomy within the organisation.

Let us now look at the practical with Julie

Julie is very energetic, always on the go and thinks fast. She has lots of ideas and gladly jumps from one subject to another. She arrives late at meetings, whether with colleagues or customers. She does not work in an orderly fashion and gives only sparse information to others. She holds few meetings with the full team and when she does, these are run without an agenda. She listens to her colleagues enough to know whether they have personal worries but not enough to know about their doubts and concerns.

She comes to realise that she does not give her staff any meaning or vision and that the organisation structure is not fixed. She also sees that she does not allow for any real autonomy, that she is very much in control. She becomes aware of her fear that the customers to whom she has committed will not be satisfied with the company's work. She feels the need to stay in control and is afraid to delegate. She is confusing externally assigned concerns with existential concerns: she is afraid her customers will no longer like her if she doesn't provide the expected service. She also wants to be recognised as a "super boss" by her team.

She has a sizeable network of relations, is developing a social network strategy and despairs that her staff are not doing likewise.

She notices that she has done little to enable group cohesion: the team is more a collection of individuals, with no team dynamic.

She doesn't know what her staff expects of her role and doesn't know what she expects of them in their role either.

Cultural and historical power factors

Berne (1963) identifies group culture and group history as two types of influence at the psychodynamic level. Historical influence is defined as the influence of predecessors that guides the organisation's activity. Predecessors are referred to as Primal Leaders: the group founder or any person who has significantly altered the group's rules, procedures, custom and practice, known as the Canon. And the "Euhemerus": any person whose qualities and values are idealised by the group after their death. We assume that historical factors are ultimately built into the organisation's broader culture.

Adapted power is related to the question how the leader's "personal culture" adjusts to that of the group and vice versa. I would highlight their belief system and values, key reference models (people and theory) and their career path.

In the course of our lives, we all form beliefs about ourselves, others and the world that influence our feelings and attitudes (Schiff, 1975). These beliefs enable us to differentiate what we describe as "justified power" from what we call "abuse of power, control, domination, and omnipotence" and so forth. (Micholt, 2009). These beliefs and values enable or prevent the leader from adapting to the group's culture.

Belief systems can be broken down in relation to cultural components (Berne, 1963):

- Technicalities: our perception of work and of the organisation. What we believe makes a "good" or a "bad" professional. What we believe to be the right ways of doing things, unacceptable mistakes, an "efficient" organisation. Knowledge and methods.
- Etiquette: connected to the culture values, norms and principles, that is, what is "right". For example, the "right" kind of authority, the "right" way of exerting power, cultural directives such as "you must be brave", "you should work without keeping score", "you must obey orders without question".
- Character: permissible deviations with respect to etiquette. There are generally areas of etiquette in which the expression of personality is tolerated without being considered incongruous. This is an "area of freedom to be oneself".

Key reference models may be family members, teachers or role models, as well as theoretical texts and key authors. For instance, John learnt about organisations from the Crozier model, while Marc's reference author is Mintzberg. These key sources of reference impact the way in which the leader more or less adjusts to their organisation and team.

ADAPTING LEADERSHIP POWER TO ITS PURPOSE

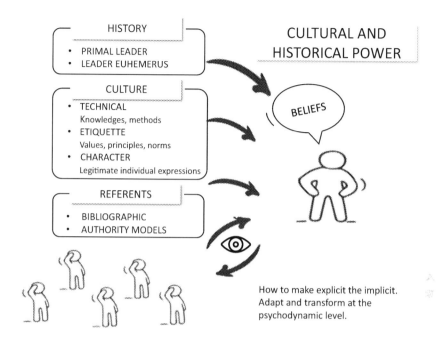

Figure 3.4 Cultural and historical power factors

Our beliefs about roles stem from our experiences and reference models. For instance, "a start-up founder must work 16 hours a day", "a manager should be close to his teams", "a leader is alone", and so forth. Identifying the leader's and the group's beliefs about roles supports leadership at the psychodynamic level, as this helps adjust one's mental representations (imago) and remove limiting beliefs.

The cultural power factors enable the leader to act at the psychodynamic level. Such factors are implicit and affect the leader's mental representation of the group as well as those made by the group about the leader.

A leader who has access only to this level of power would be at risk of exercising an outdated form of power, based on archaic transferential relationships, with the attendant risk of immobility and insufficient adaptation to change. This can be "I am the worthy representative of X (departed), who was respected by all, and we continue to transmit, analyse and decide as X would have done", meaning that changes in the environment are not taken into account.

Let us now look at the practical with Julie

The company's technical approach is focused on search and analysis. This gives rise to behaviours in relation to the need for isolation, calm and concentration. Different people in the team have different definitions of what makes a "good" e-reputation professional.

There is little information to go on in specifying what this label means. A few elements can be identified: most team members say things like "you can't be late for a client meeting", "we do our utmost but she doesn't see it", "we're not involved, a leader should involve the staff, particularly in a small company".

Meanwhile, Julie says, "this is my company, I can do what I want", "my staff should understand and follow me", "I'm nice to them, they shouldn't complain".

She regularly refers to her uncle, a freelancer. Julie worked freelance before setting up her company.

Here, we can see there is a gap between Julie's business culture and that of her team, which she discovers as part of our work together. She goes through phases of feeling surprise, indignation and then understanding.

While the company is free of "the weight of history", the corollary is that there is no history from which to build structure.

Julie's beliefs about her role start to emerge: "It's not easy being a woman CEO", "A CEO of a small company needs to control everything", "I don't know how to make difficult decisions".

Developing "adapted power"

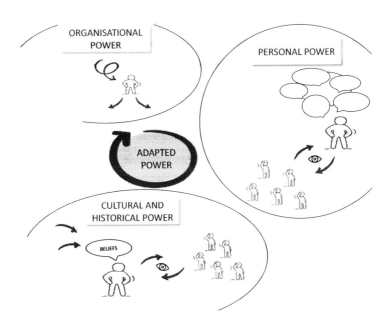

Figure 3.5 Adapted power

In conclusion, developing power that is adapted to the organisation, to one's role and one's goals, requires the accumulation of various power factors in relation to that role and targeting a specific level of leadership, in which the whole forms a dynamic system of interacting elements.

It involves the leader acquiring legitimacy, in respect of their position, their organisation and the people they work with at a given point in time. This "adapted power" allows them to support change and prepare for the future.

As such, it is not about wielding lasting power, but rather having the flexibility to grow over time, alongside people and across different spaces and situations.

In implementing change, an analysis of all of the previous factors, based on aspects of the specific role and context at hand, enables leaders to make the right adjustments.

Let us now look at the practical with Julie

Together, we examine the three sources of power, with a view to analysing Julie's specific case. Julie makes decisions, which she will implement over time.

Julie decides to focus chiefly on her role as CEO. This means delegating decisions about daily business issues. She writes up role descriptions and determines the responsibilities to be taken by each employee.

She gradually implements delegated powers to reassure both herself and her colleagues. Everyone takes the time needed to grasp the new guidelines. She and the team together establish group functioning rules.

She decides to work more collectively than individually. To that end, she determines different types of meetings she wants to set up and the specific content and information she wants to share. She approves this way of working with the whole team. Together, they also talk about what they expect of one another and for their customers.

By taking these steps, Julie is able to focus on her main role as CEO, and thus fully inhabit her organisational power in relation to this role.

Feeling more available, she is able to put her personal power to use in fostering group cohesion. At this level, the first step involved slowing down, to find a pace that better respected that of her team. Next, she provided vision. And, lastly, she sought the support of a colleague to help her organise meetings and workload.

Finally, now that the business culture has been shared, the group functions in a more fluid manner and any misunderstandings are of minor importance. Above all, the team has integrated discussions about ways of working into its etiquette.

This work, which took around one year, has enabled Julie to consolidate and develop her business. She can now use "adapted power" with respect to her employees, enabling her to move forward and grow the company with the entire team onboard.

Another example: John

John is Vice Chairman of a company with 86,000 employees. When he signs a contract with an external service provider, company procedure requires that the purchasing department first approves the budget and then drafts the contract, which will then need to be signed by three people before it can be validated. When payment time comes around, five people will need to give their approval.

It takes about a month between the contract request and contract signature. Payment is then made three months after the service provider issues the invoice.

John feels stuck as a result of these procedures (among other things), his organisational power is not adapted to suit his position and some of his unit's needs. He has to compensate for this shortfall through strategic circumvention and making use of his personal power in certain areas.

Conclusion

We can see that his "adapted power" is the result of a dynamic process involving several components.

Such power can be obtained by starting with the leader and placing them at the centre of this construction process, as demonstrated in this chapter. However, the issue can also be considered from the opposite angle: by looking at how a leader may be "prevented" from implementing their "adapted power" by the context, the situation or certain behaviours.

In an era of the "free" company, self-managing teams, networks of organisations, and so forth, we can also examine the question of power from the team's point of view: what means does the team have at its disposal to collectively exert its "adapted power"?

On a final note, we can also ask the question raised by Alter (2009): is not the challenge facing organisations less how to mobilise staff and more how to capitalise on their willingness to give?

References

Alter, N. (2009). *Donner et prendre, la coopération en entreprise*. Paris: La Découverte.

Berne, E. (1961). *Transactional Analysis in Psychotherapy: A Systematic Individual and Social Psychiatry*. New York: Grove Press.

Berne, E. (1963). *The Structure and Dynamics of Organizations and Groups*. Philadelphia: J. B. Lippincott.

Berne, E. (1966). *Principles of Group Treatment*. New York: Oxford University Press.

Crespelle, A. (1985). Trois pièges de la passivité: les enjeux confondus, les enjeux accrochés, les enjeux cachés. *Actualités en analyse transactionnelle*, 34(9), 92–96.

Crozier, M., & Friedberg, E. (1977). *L'Acteur et le système, Les contraintes de l'action collective*. Paris: Éditions du Seuil, Collection Points/Essais.

Holdeman, Q. L. (1989). The Symbiotic Chain. *Transactional Analysis Journal*, 19(3), 137–144. doi: 10.1177/036215378901900304.

Jacobs, A. (1987). Autocratic Power. *Transactional Analysis Journal*, 17(3), 59–71. doi: 10.1177/036215378701700303.

Krausz, R. (1986). Power and Leadership in Organizations. *Transactional Analysis Journal*, 16(2), 85–94. doi: 10.1177/036215378601600202.

Micholt, N. (2009). *Préface de Pouvoir et autorité, de l'organisation à la nation*. Paris: Editions d'AT.

Micholt, N. (2010). Organizational Roles. In *Keeping the TA-O Torch Alight*. Netherlands: Intact B.V., pp. 49–70.

Rocheblave-Spenlé, A. M. (1969). *La notion de rôle en psychologie sociale*. Paris: P.U.F.

Schiff, A. W., & Schiff, J. L. (1971). Passivity. *Transactional Analysis Journal*, 1(1), 71–78.

Schiff, J. E. A. (1975). *Cathexis Reader: Transactional Analysis Treatment of Psychosis*. New York: Harper & Row.

Schmid, B. (2008). The Role Concept of Transactional Analysis and Other Approaches to Personality, Encounter and Co-Creativity for All Professional Fields. *Transactional Analysis Journal*, 38(1), 17–30. doi: 10.1177/036215370803800104.

van Poelje, S. (1995). Development of Autocratic Systems. *Transactional Analysis Journal*, 25(3), 265–270. doi: 10.1177/036215379502500313.

van Poelje, S. (2021). New Theory and Practice of Transactional Analysis in Organizations – On the edge. Chapter 2 *Three levels of leadership*. Routledge.

4
LEADING SELF-ORGANISING TEAMS
A paradox or a necessity?

Kathrin Rutz

Self-organising teams have been the focus of debate for many years. But do they really increase effectiveness and efficiency? Using systemic TA concepts, this chapter shows they can, if organisations meet four essential conditions: (1) clear structures, (2) strong leadership, (3) negotiated contracts and a (4) culture of dialogue and co-creation.

Introduction

Self-organisation is a model for cooperation in today's working world, especially in expert organisations. Expert organisations are educational organisations such as schools, colleges and universities, but also health care organisations such as hospitals, care systems and centres or consulting companies and competence centres (cf. Janes, 2009; Thomann & Zellweger, 2016; Rybnicek et al., 2016).

Leading and managing experts is sometimes described as "herding cats" (Hengartner, 2012, presentation) – a (nearly) impossible task! Characteristically experts feel highly committed to their profession and demand a high degree of autonomy within an organisation. For this reason, it is essential to establish forms of collaboration and cooperation that enable a high level of participation and self-direction. The concept of self-organising or self-managing organisations (Laloux, 2015) is based on the premise that people have the knowledge and skills to deploy and structure their manpower in such a way that they achieve the defined goal in this manageable (sub)system. Working in expert interdisciplinary teams or project teams is common in expert organisations and often associated with distributed or shared leadership.

Teams imply cooperation

At the time Berne (1963) published his ideas about the structure and dynamics of organisations and groups, the term "team" was primarily used for sports teams. In the 1970s, the team concept evolved significantly.

In my use of the term in this chapter, I follow Hackman's (Hackman, 2002 in Kaltenecker, 2015a, p. 4) specific characteristics to define a team:

- "joint tasks to fulfil a compelling mission;
- clear boundaries in terms of information flow, alignment with other organisational units, resources, and decision-making policies;
- authority to self-manage within these boundaries; and
- stability over some reasonable period of time"

Working in teams implies cooperation and collaboration. In collaboration, people or teams work together in parallel on a part of the joint project, while in cooperation, individuals or teams work on different subtasks towards the result. Collaboration between specialists across disciplines is generally regarded as crucial to successful project implementation (Ashkenas, 2015).

Fruitful cooperation and collaboration imply that people within a company accept their dependence on the context such as organisational structure, task, functions and roles, and their mutual interdependence (Landaiche, 2012).

Self-organising teams seek autonomy

Before investigating the factors contributing to successful teamwork in more detail, let us have a closer look at self-organising teams. To put it simply, a

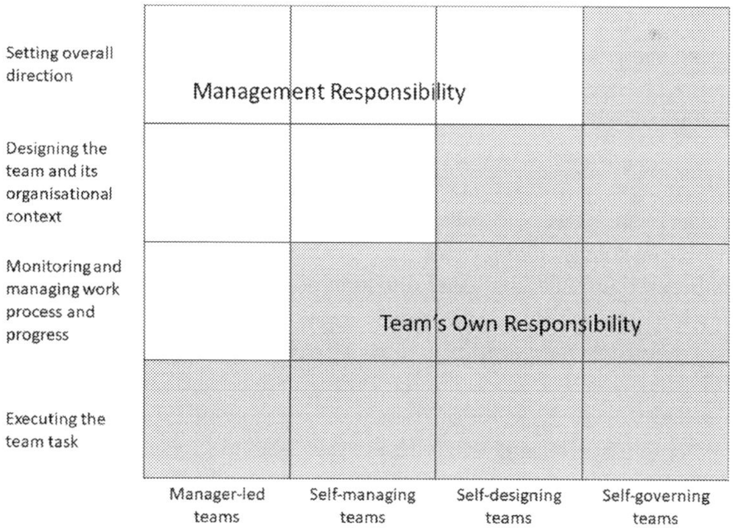

	Manager-led teams	Self-managing teams	Self-designing teams	Self-governing teams
Setting overall direction	Management Responsibility			
Designing the team and its organisational context				
Monitoring and managing work process and progress		Team's Own Responsibility		
Executing the team task				

Figure 4.1 Authority matrix (Hackman, 2002, p. 52)

self-organising team can be defined as a team that does not depend on or wait for a manager to assign work to it. Hackman (2002) offers an authority matrix to distinguish four levels of team self-organisation.

This illustrates that teams can be "self-organised" to varying degrees. What is relevant to the degree of self-organisation is the organisation or the structure in which the team is embedded, the task that the team should fulfil and finally the question of which kind of leadership the team needs in order to be successful. Let's explore these four aspects for successful self-organising teams further: clear structures, strong leadership, cooperation contracts and a culture of dialogue.

Clear structure support self-organisation

Psychiatric outpatient care

In Switzerland, medical outpatient services are available to people of all ages who, as a result of illness, accident, disability, age-related limitations or maternity, are dependent on short- or longer-term care and support. Local health care services, like the psychiatric care team, offer support at home in the case of mental health problems or psychosocial stress. The nurses providing this service cooperate with doctors, authorities and other institutions.

The team we'll use as an example consists of five part-time employees. The team has a formal hierarchical leader – who is, for different reasons, rarely available for the team. The team is struggling with the workload and as a result of this with their individual overload. It is difficult to recruit suitable personnel. The organisational and personnel structures are complicated, and the procedures and agreements are not clear. In order to establish a functioning and effective team, a team member was assigned the function of "coordinator".

In her thesis "Conditions for Self-Organizing in Human Systems" Eoyang (2001) explores questions about the reasons that some human systems are quick to organise themselves, while others take a long time, only to end up with unpleasant or unproductive patterns as a result. She points out "three system conditions that influence the speed, path, and direction of self-organising systems" (Human Systems Dynamic Institute, 2020):

"The emergence of patterns is governed by the interplay of three variables:

CONTAINER (C): Similarities that contain the system while patterns emerge;
DIFFERENCES (D): The significant distinctions that hold tension and have greatest influence on decision and action; and
EXCHANGES (E): Connections in the system that ensure the movement of information, energy, and other resources"

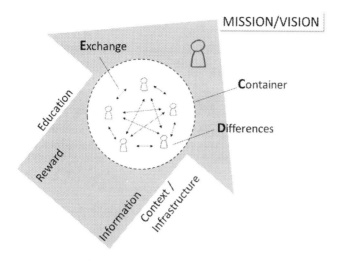

Figure 4.2 C/D/E-Model (cf. Kaltenecker, 2015b, p. 8)

The **container** sets the boundaries and defines the identity of a team. It builds on the organisational strategy, its mission, clear goals, guidelines and decision-making policies. The structural elements and the importance of boundaries is further explored later in this section.

The **differences** in knowledge, experience, age, cultural background and professions – if acknowledged and incorporated – contribute to the resources and strengths of a diverse team. This factor must be considered during the phase the team is constituted and roles and responsibilities are negotiated (Schmid & Messmer, 2005a, 2005b).

The **exchange** of information and knowledge between interdependent people or units facilitates the process of establishing successful self-organising teams and helps to spread the culture within a larger organisation. This aspect will be addressed again in the section about a "culture of dialogue".

Boundaries are a central element of the container

In his book *The Structure and Dynamics of Organizations and Groups*, Berne primarily defines the structure of a group by its boundaries (Berne, 1963, p. 56). The group structure specifies the roles and slots required to accomplish the purpose of the organisation or team. He defined an outer boundary and inner boundaries:

> The external boundary and the major inner boundary form the major boundaries of a group. . . . The external boundary, or boundary zone, separates the external environment from the group space, and the major

internal boundary divides the group space into a membership region and a leadership region.

(Berne, 1963, p. 56)

Berne defines the structure of a group in terms of its hierarchical relationships. There are simple groups in which a leader is distinguished from members, who are equal among themselves. Fox transferred Berne's ideas from its clinical setting to organisations (Fox, 1975, p. 345). According to Fox, simple diagrams represent "the minimal requirement for the existence of a group (Fox, 1975, p. 348)."

The structure of more diverse groups is called compound or complex. Here we also need to consider the Differences factor in the C/D/E-Model. Besides knowledge, experience, age, cultural background and professions I would suggest – in line with Schmid – adding functions and roles as further categories of difference (Schmid & Messmer, 2005b, 2008).

According to Fox, the compound diagram represents a hierarchical structure. The complex diagram is used to illustrate departmental or unit segments: "The organisational structure specifies the roles and slots required for accomplishing the purpose of the organization. It gives identity to the group and is an essential factor in determining how effective the activity will be" (Fox, 1975, p. 349).

Moreau (2005) points out that "there exist three dimensions supporting a team's existence, function, and development" (p. 356). These dimensions are *people*, as they create and develop a group or company. *Organisation* "refers to both the way the various missions and competencies are organized and also the machinery, instruments, buildings, and all other material and non-material . . . elements that make possible production of goods or delivery of services" (p. 356). He further describes that the two dimensions *people* and *organisation* are balanced by a third, which he refers to as "*value added*" or "*expected performance*".

He connects these three dimensions in a triangle with *people – organisation* as its base. This triangle also reminds one of the ordering elements of *strategy – structure – culture*, as defined and described in the St. Gallen Management Model by Rüegg-Stürm and Grand (2019). While the aspect of "value added" could be

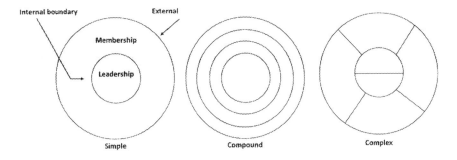

Figure 4.3 Structural diagrams (Fox, 1975, p. 359, based on Berne, 1963, pp. 58–59)

described as strategy, *organisation* matches *structure*. Very often an extended version of the strategy – structure – culture triangle is found, which adds people as a fourth element in order to focus on the people directly involved in the organisation, such as employees. In the St. Galler Management Model, people were originally described as stakeholders, which by definition would include all groups and individuals who are somehow affected by the value or damage created by a company.

In the earlier example, it was necessary and helpful for the psychiatric outpatient care team to map the different stakeholders. To take a closer look at the team itself, they used the structural diagram and explored the internal and external boundaries.

It became clear that it was a matter of identifying not only boundaries but also that they were of different characteristics. Minuchin (2015) explored and described boundaries within family systems. According to him, boundaries have the function to protect the differentiation (of roles) within the system (p. 71). The clarity of the boundaries within a family are described as a useful indicator for assessing the functioning of the family (p. 72). He further describes the clarity of boundaries on a continuum, whose two extremes of diffuse and excessively rigid boundaries respectively (p. 73).

Self-organising teams need permeable boundaries

By creating a team and belonging to a team, it's helpful to realise, how the "belonging to" or "not belonging to" and the process of creating a "belonging to" can be created. Berne (1963, pp. 116–117, 239) considered the permeably of a boundary as a relevant characteristic and described the peculiarity as "open" and "sealed". By open he meant that the boundary can be crossed freely in either direction, while a sealed boundary is described as "one which . . . is almost impossible to cross outwardly after the group is activated" (1963, p. 239).

Lee (2014, p. 43) picks up the subject and uses the concepts of attachment and boundaries to apply to all the elements of group-work process. She refers to the work of Salvador Minuchin (1975) and Vann Joines (1988) and defines the boundaries between person and person, person and others and person and environment as follows:

A   diffuse (lax and weak)
B   rigid (fixed and inflexible)
C   permeable (flexible and open)

Although Lee (2014) devoted her article to the principles and practice of transactional analysis process group work, many of her findings can be adapted to working groups and teams in organisations.

With respect to an organisation, we talk about boundaries between individuals (employees), between person and unit or team, and between person and environment. A closer look at permeable boundaries reveals that ideally, they "permit change, acknowledge differences, facilitate balanced empowerment and provide flexibility that fosters new experiences and relationships" (Lee, 2014, p. 43).

(Self-organising) Teams as specific groups in an organisation show, on inspection, that it is necessary to establish permeable boundaries. Owing to the fact that (self-organising) teams are set up for a certain period of time, with people who most probably belong to different teams in the same or in different organisations, flexible and mindful role management is crucial both for leaders and members. As Landaiche (2012, p. 195) puts it:

> I have come to see leadership as a secondary property or phenomenon, one that emerges from membership. The group member able to manage himself or herself has the potential to become a natural leader who is also able to follow.

Therefore, it is a leader's tasks – but also a member's task – to allow a team to grow and develop into a highly performing team and to ensure that it can stay agile. This leads us to the next aspect.

Strong leadership supports self-organisation

Curriculum development project

At a teacher training university, a project team is tasked with redeveloping the practical vocational training. The project owner is the head of the educational policy department. The heads of the different units in the department were recruited to form the project team. The assignment had been given by the head of the department, who also designated one of this team's members as project leader. The project owner – the department head – was convinced he had selected the right people, so the team was given the project schedule with goals and milestones. The project leader received few resources to coordinate the meetings and to document the process. Her role in the project team was unclear. The project was rarely a priority on the team member's agenda, and they got stuck in their work. The project leader asked for coaching to clarify her leadership role.

Lee (2014) specified five key aspects for analysing a group by adapting Berne's visualisation (Berne, 1966, p. 149) of group dynamics. The dashed lines in the figure represent permeable boundaries.

The ? Containment factor, is linked to the boundary zone which "separates the external environment from the group space" (Berne, 1963, p. 56).

Berne (1966, p. 151) also noted that the group cohesion is enforced by pressure from outside on the external boundary. In the containment phase of establishing a team or a group, Lee (2014) suggests three aspects to consider: membership,

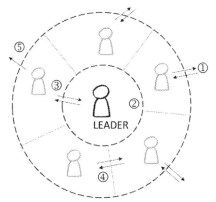

① Containment: The outer boundary of the group (extented boundary)
② Leadership: Establishing the leadership boundary (major internal boundary)
③ Responsiveness: Responsiveness of the group leader to individual group members
④ Interaction: The interactive group process (minor internal boundary)
⑤ Expansion: The expanded group process

Figure 4.4 Five aspects of group development (adapted from Lee, 2014, p. 44; Berne, 1966, p. 149)

group venue and time boundaries. It is important to raise questions around and to negotiate the administrative, psychological and content contracts. It is about getting to know each other in the mandated roles. Schmid and Messmer (2005a) are in favour of a system of complementary and related responsibility roles to allow members and leaders to contribute their part to the "value added", as Moreau (2005) puts it.

The ? Leadership boundary is defined by Berne as the major internal boundary, "representing those factors which meaningfully distinguish the membership form the leadership" (Berne, 1963, p. 57). It is the leader's task "to assume responsible leadership and ensure clarity about the group boundaries and group task" (Lee, 2014, p. 45). A responsible leader facilitates "the group to shape its own unique norms and create a healthy group culture (Berne, 1963)" (Lee, 2014, p. 45). It is about creating a secure base as defined by Kohlrieser et al. (2012, p. 8) in the form of "a person, place, goal or object that provides a sense of protection, safety and caring and offers a source of inspiration and energy for daring, exploration, risk taking and seeking challenge". With this in mind, the leader will encourage the group to get in touch with each other in an authentic way. He or she will allow and enhance curiosity, autonomy, coherent thinking and resonance (Rosa, 2019) towards context and content and will be available for members to come forward with their needs, wishes and ideas regarding the leader, the group and the group task.

Lee (2014, p. 46) describes the third aspect as ? Responsiveness and focuses on the boundary and the interaction between the leader and the group members. The people involved will ask themselves whether they are important to the leader and to other group members and they will wonder what their contribution might be. These thoughts "may relate to their position in their family of origin" (Lee, 2014, p. 46), and in such a group we often update our biographical experiences. It is about belonging, about power and influence and about intimacy (König & Schattendorfer, 2016, p. 34ff). Each member evaluates for themselves how congruent the leader is in relation to the principles formulated and the way they are lived in the team. It is about relating to each other and it is about the leader being responsive to relational needs (Erskine & Trautmann, 1996).

The next focus looks at ? Interaction among the group members and the group process. In the C/D/E-Model we talked about Exchange. From a neurobiological point of view, humans are designed for social resonance and cooperation. The core of all human motivation is finding and giving interpersonal recognition, appreciation and affection (Bauer, 2007, p. 21). It is the leader's task to initiate, stimulate and encourage contact and meaningful dialogue between individuals. The leader has an integrating role: it is through the mindful presence and empowerment of the group leader that the interaction in the group increases and working relations deepen. It is about developing and shaping the relationship skills of the team (Thiele & Korpiun, 2016).

With the fifth aspect Lee (2014) sets the focus on ? Expansion: How is the experience in the group spread to other parts of the organisation? Lee describes that at this stage

> the containment that was necessary for group formation and safe exploration can be dissolved. . . . As soon as all the group members personally value the relevance of this specific group experience, they are ready to dissolve the psychological outer boundary of the group and expand its relevance to other relationships and parts of their lives.
> (Lee, 2014, pp. 47–48)

In an organisational frame we must bear in mind that many employees in companies or institutions work in different constellations such as temporary working groups, project teams or expert teams simultaneously. In an ideal group process, in a group with permeable boundaries,

> the experience of authenticity and intimacy and the acceptance of self and new ways of relating to others are ready to be transferred beyond the external boundary of the group. This expansion of the boundary is necessary for the group leader too as she prepares to become a group member of the next group she enters.
> (Lee, 2014, p. 48)

As mentioned, Lee describes this process for transactional analysis group work processes. However, it also describes the process of agile, (self-organising) teams in organisations in a helpful way. For the team members this expansion is an important step as the group prepares for its end and members move outside the container. They can experience their availability for other parts of the organisation and contribute their competences in other areas of work. In this ending phase, it is essential to respect and honour what the individuals have contributed to the group and to give recognition to their "result". If each group member can articulate their learning outcomes from this co-created working process as well as their thinking about transferring it all into other working areas, then the organisation will benefit.

Differences as the second aspect of the C/D/E-Model cannot be assigned to a specific boundary quality. Rather, differences in the form of diversity and variety are an added value in a group, through increasing complexity. Significant distinctions generate tension and curiosity on the one hand, and on the other they can enhance clear differentiations where necessary and desirable, be it within a team or between units and groups.

To some readers of this chapter a link with Tuckman's (1965) stages of group development (i.e. forming, storming, norming, performing, adjourning) will be as obvious as the link with the adjustment of the group imago (Berne, 1963; Clarkson, 1991; Tudor, 2013) or the link with Levin's (1982) Cycles of Development.

It seems that Lee's diagram is very helpful in many ways when it comes to clarifying the structures, boundaries, tasks and roles of a group. Both models – Berne's structural model and the C/D/E-Model – consider the container with its boundaries; recognise and value any differences between the people involved regarding (professional) background, experience, competences, roles and functions; and focus on an exchange of information. While in Berne's model we talk about sharing knowledge and experience and establishing relationships, in the C/D/E-Model this exchange might have a touch of "trading". Yet it is about belonging to a temporary group, getting involved, reaching a goal together and sharing this experience.

In the structural diagram Berne (1966) and Lee (2014) describe the central role and the mediating task which are assigned to the leader. The aim is not to relieve the group of decisions, but to enable decision-making processes by exploring the possibilities while relating to each and keeping in contact.

Furthermore, Berne (1963, pp. 105–107) talks about three kinds of leadership: The *responsible leader* is described as the front man who also fills the role of the leader in the organisational or formal structure. This type of leadership is based on the organisation's constitution (p. 60) and is one factor that gives a group its organisational identity (p. 61). The actual members, assuming their roles in the organisational structure, form the individual structure of the group. The person with the most important role in this individual structure is the one who takes the actual decisions and is called the *effective leader*. The *psychological leader*, says Berne, "is the one who is most powerful in the private structures of the members and occupies the leadership slot in their group imagoes" (p. 105).

In her research, Krausz (1986) focuses on the power dynamics and correlates them with leadership styles in organisations. She concludes her findings as follows:

> Leadership styles may be expressed in terms of the use of different types of power. If a leader adequately uses available options, the probability of expanding his/her power will tend to increase. And being powerful often brings with it the tendency to share organisational power more effectively, as well as to stimulate the use of personal power in the group.
>
> (Krausz, 1986, p. 93)

It becomes quite apparent that leadership is a necessity in self-managing teams and that it is essential to fill and shape this role adequately. In the coaching with the project leader (see the case described earlier), it was important for her to recognise and locate the different aspects which interfered with her leadership. She gained clarity and was able to discuss her difficulties first with the project owner and at a later stage also with the project team members. By taking this step and claiming her responsibilities (Schmid & Messmer, 2005a), she gained what one would call leadership qualities.

So, when considering self-organising teams as one possible way to meet the challenges of today's and future working contexts, examining alternative leadership concepts seems indispensable. While a hierarchical understanding of leadership dominated over the last decades, an understanding of shared or distributed leadership is now emerging.

Lateral leadership – leading without hierarchical power

As mentioned, a trend towards less hierarchical and more flexible organisations is discernible in companies. More than two thirds of all managers who temporarily or permanently lead a team lead laterally, that is, they have no formal authority to issue instructions (Radatz, 2008). Lateral leadership places specific demands on both the leader and the organisation. Some of these conditions are discussed in the following section.

While hierarchical leadership tends to concentrate power, responsibility and decision-making sovereignty in one or in few persons only, lateral or shared leadership allows and forces many people – ideally all the team members – to take responsibility for the overall success and for their own development. This involves establishing a useful way of communication, critically examining the existing work processes, adjusting them if necessary, agreeing on decision-making procedures and achieving results together. There are a few factors to consider when focusing on the specificity of lateral leadership as a matter of directing non-subordinate members of the organisation towards a working goal.

Referring to research, Kühl suggests that lateral leadership is characterised by three mechanisms of influence: understanding/communication, trust and power.

Communication and dialogue (Kühl & Matthiesen, 2012; Kühl, 2017) are about understanding the other person's mental constructs in a way that opens new possibilities for action. Understanding therefore refers to discourse about facts and alternatives. This requires an openness for opposing arguments and presupposes that one's own constructs can be questioned and expanded through the examination of the counterpart's thinking frameworks. In transactional analysis (TA) language we also speak of an extension of the frame of reference. Willingness to engage in dialogue and an interest in the other person and their positions facilitate understanding. The basis for successful communication is, among other things, the ability to engage in dialogue (cf. Bohm, 2019), which requires attentive listening and meeting the other authentically in the here and now, revealing oneself and getting involved.

Trust, according to Kühl and Matthiesen (2012), is established when one party involved unilaterally makes an advance payment without the second party taking advantage of the possible short-term benefit, but in turn, in a further step, places their trust in the other party. Trust means that I do not need to understand the other's mindset in detail but must still be willing to deal with it. Building trust requires time and opportunities for encounters.

Power plays a role in lateral leadership by controlling internal, mostly informal communication (information power), expertise and the active use of contacts across and in relation to the organisation (cf. Kühl & Matthiesen, 2012; Scholl, 2012; Kühl, 2017).

These three components need to be kept in balance. If, for example, power or communication are taken more seriously than trust, or power games are played too aggressively, the basis of trust is put at risk. Transactional analysis holds a variety of concepts for thinking about ways to enable a culture of trust, power and communication:

While some readers might be familiar with these concepts, others might not know them. For those new to TA, the short definitions and/or descriptions that follow provide them with a first impression and offer the possibility of extending this knowledge by exploring the following references in addition to those already mentioned in this chapter. This list is not complete and provides only an overview of some concepts, their authors and some additional references.

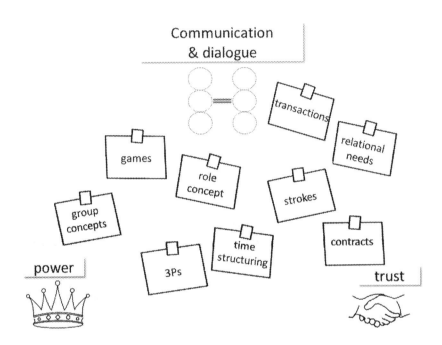

Figure 4.5 Building leadership

Group concepts		Group structure and group dynamics
Role concept	Berne, 1963 Schmid, 2008	In the role model of personality, a person is described as the portfolio of his or her roles played on the stages of her world. The stages of the world refer to the private, the professional and the organisational world of an individual.
Strokes	Berne, 1972	A stroke is a unit of recognition.
Time structuring	Berne, 1966 Stewart/Joines 1987, 2009	How people spend time when in pairs of groups.
Games	Berne, 1964 Choy, 1990 Summerton, 1993	Describe interactions with an ulterior motive that result in confusion and misunderstanding for everyone.
3 Ps	Crossman, 1966 Berne, 1972	Permission, protection and potency as resources and guidelines for ethical and resource-orientated criteria in mutual, but hierarchical relationships, as for exemple leader and employee of consultant and client.
Transaction	Berne, 1972 Stewart/Joines, 1987, 2009	A transaction is the smallest unit of interaction, consisting of stimulus and response.
Contract	Berne, 1972 English, 1975 Hay, 1992	A contract is a mutual agreement between two or more parties. The three-cornered contract (English) and multi-cornered contract (Hay) are helpful concepts for careful contracting in organisations.
Relational Needs	Erskine, 1996	Eight relational needs describe the needs that arise in human interaction. Awareness of these needs in ourselves and in others can help develop and foster relationships.

Figure 4.6 Overview of some concepts

Working together in teams, and even more so leading such a team, means adequately taking care of the previous aspects and establishing a container which allows constructive patterns to emerge.

Leadership can be recognised by the fact that someone asserts their influence and gives orientation and that people follow the impulses of this person. Many of us know situations in a professional context where the person who leads is not necessarily the person who has the hierarchical position to do so, but the one who can influence the team and is followed. Creating and establishing a supportive culture and working environment helps people to get involved in a given task and furthermore to get in contact and to relate well to the other group members.

In the previous explanations, the chapter has dealt with the prerequisites for self-organising teams. Moreover, leadership tasks and effects on the team dynamics have been described. The concept of lateral leadership has been applied to outline mechanisms that play a central role in cooperation. In the next two sections the importance of contracts and the culture of dialogue are explored.

Contracts

Expert exchange

This group's task is to supervise established safety standards and ensure that they are observed in the various departments of a large university hospital. The group members represent their departments as well as their professions (doctors, nurses, therapists, maintenance staff) in this matrix organisation. Each group member has been mandated by the head of their unit to ensure safety standards. The eleven members of the team are formally of equal status, irrespective of their rank and profession in the larger organisation. The group has been given resources (manpower, time) by the heads of the departments to be successful. It is the group's responsibility to devise a way of managing themselves. They report to the heads of department and to the person in charge of safety issues in this matter.

To enable cooperation that is based on mutual respect and goal orientation, it is necessary to create a safe place for exploring and developing ideas and defining "the nature of the work and the skills and tasks that each person will require" (Lapworth & Sills, 2011, p. 10). Self-organising teams or units are usually confronted with multilateral interests in their context, an issue which leads to three-cornered contracts (English, 1975) or multi-cornered contracts (Hay, 1992).

Berne (1966) distinguishes between the following three aspects of a contract: administrative, professional and psychological. In self-organising teams a central focus concerns the contract among the group members. Besides agreeing on items such as dates, available time and task responsibilities, what needs to be addressed is the question of who contributes which competences to achieve the objectives. At the psychological level, it is wise to find an answer to the questions, What could stop me from contributing my part to the work in this group? What could prevent us from reaching our goal?

Laugeri (2010) differentiates between the cooperation relationship among peers, for example, in a project team, and the collaboration relationships between subordinates and their superiors. Accordingly, she describes the necessity of what she calls a *cooperation contract*: "Through the cooperation contract the actors empower their team to become responsible for solving the difficulties that can be solved on their level" (Laugeri, 2010, p. 6).

The cooperation contract is negotiated by the team. Its purpose is to promote decision procedures by prioritising strategic information about activities to ensure goal-orientated reporting to the leader. The cooperation contract implies that everyone considers human relations a priority and is prepared to set aside personal considerations in order to carry out the common task. Well-defined cooperation contracts support structural cohesion and it is "through this unconditional solidarity within a team that they manifest their respect of their leader's values (structure unconditional support and co-operation)" (Laugeri, 2010, p. 7). Reaching clarity and a shared understanding of contracts among the group members and with their "great powers" (English, 1975, p. 383) is essential and requires a high level of communication and dialogue.

Working with well differentiated and clearly negotiated contracts also increases the awareness of ethical questions and issues as the people involved discuss dilemmas they are challenged with. De Graaf and Levy (2011) point out that at least three ethically loaded dilemmas arise in every organisation: the dilemma of time, of interest and of scope (Bryan et al., 2006 in De Graaf & Levy, 2011, p. 126). Self-organising teams are not only challenged by the question of What do we do in short-term and in long-term interventions?, but also with the issue of having any time at all. Mostly, the team members of one team also belong to another team and are invited to carefully manage their time. The dilemma of interest is also complex, as in such diverse teams, personal interests might clash with professional and organisational interests or even goals. Sorting out functions, roles, competences and responsibilities helps to generate a shared understanding and a common approach to contradictions or conflicts. Depending on the degree of self-organisation, the group will focus a limited, clear scope versus a wide, more complete and complex scope (De Graaf & Levy, 2011, p. 126). To overcome the paralysis that might occur when facing such divergent interests, it is essential to explore and pinpoint them so as to reach a clearer understanding of what and how the work can be done together.

The difficulty of this multidisciplinary working group was not about finding a way of working together. The difficulty lay in the fact that the people in charge were not clear about the task. The leaders agreed on a subject but had different ideas about the function and role of the delegates from their own units. It can be assumed that the dilemmas regarding time, interests and scope on the level of those in charge must have communicated themselves unconsciously and must thereby have been transferred to the mandated persons. Balling (2005) suggests using diagnosis of organisational culture in order to clarify contracts. This approach to the "stuck team" enhances the possibility of establishing contact and sets the focus on the organisation as a living system (Kreyenberg, 2005) rather than on the individuals. Therefore, the consultant's intervention was to invite the people in charge for a clarification and re-contracting with the group first.

Culture of dialogue

Pedagogical team

This pedagogical team is composed of the staff of the kindergarten level in a school community, including class teachers, subject teachers and curative teachers. They meet every two weeks for 1.5 hours to discuss joint teaching projects, parent nights and challenging situations with pupils. The school's principal then assigned the team the additional task of determining a method of evaluation in the framework of new curriculum. They received some training regarding the new competences and evaluation procedures. First proposals were due by the end of the first semester. These were to be coordinated with the next higher level of schooling, whose members were working on the same task. The time had always been short during meetings and now they had this additional task to fulfil. In order to get rid of this "burden", they quickly discussed one subject after the other and made decisions. Soon they started to realise that they questioned decisions already taken and got into discussions about fundamentals, which often ended in frustration.

Dialogue, as Bohm (2019) envisioned it, is an approach to group interaction, with an emphasis on listening and observation while suspending any culturally conditioned judgments and impulses. Suspending means taking note and observing emerging thoughts and feelings without having to act in accordance with them immediately (Isaacs, 2011, p. 123). Getting into a dialogue means getting in touch with oneself and the other(s). It is about fathoming and sharing individual mental images or imagos. It is about an encounter where I meet You (Buber, 1983).

The process of dialogue helps us to explore and analyse our thinking habits and patterns (Isaacs, 2011, p. 59). In communicating we create resonance (Rosa, 2019). Ideas arise and are developed further when listened to by me and others. Shared thoughts and feelings allow others to respond and to co-create the relationship and topics. To introduce and foster a culture of dialogue it takes – what Isaacs calls – a "container". According to him, the "container" is a receptacle "in which the intensity of human activity can be safely expressed" (Isaacs, 2011, p. 203).

When meeting in dialogue, people cannot be reduced to their function and roles. Schmid describes that in this encounter the "(1) individual behaviours, (2) attitudes, (3) personal myths (e.g., script stories), and (4) organizational, professional, and cultural myths are involved"(Schmid, 2008, p. 25). With this "background" they enter a dialogue and co-create realities. This also includes what de

Graaf (2013) calls to "spot the group(s) in the individual" (p. 318): each person involved in a dialogue is – at the same time – "at the nexus of many conversations" (p. 318). Furthermore, de Graaf encourages us not only to see the group in the individual but also to ask "what questions" when working with or in groups. "What questions" allow us to explore complexity and to see and recognise the context – or the "container".

In this chapter, the term "container" has now been used for the third time. Whereas the "container" in the C/D/E-Model refers to the similarities that hold the system while patterns emerge, containment also describes the outer boundaries. The "container" for dialogue refers to a setting, where people can express themselves, where they are listened to and where, to a certain extent, psychological security is provided. The philosophical underpinnings of TA support open and authentic communication and genuine dialogue. It is the leader's responsibility to ensure that the group or team have this container and the abilities to engage in dialogue.

A first intervention in working with the pedagogical team was to establish a culture of dialogue. This consisted primarily in the invitation to listen to each other. Although the bi-weekly 1.5 hours were short and the agenda for the meetings tight, the team agreed on establishing rituals which had a high focus on listening to each other: in the check-in they shared a few thoughts – concerns, joyful experiences e.g. – about how (work)life is for them. In the check-out each person told the others, how they experienced themselves in the group and what their thinking is about the work in progress. Little by little, their way of meeting and forming relationships changed.

Conclusion

Self-organisation is not chaos, it's not unguided, it does not make everyone equal, it's not hierarchy free nor does it lack control. It does not make processes faster, and it's not easier to handle. It's not automatically serving democratic processes, nor does it increase employer's motivation. And it is not cost saving per se. And still, there are several reasons why institutions and companies introduce self-organisation nowadays. Ultimately, it is about making an organisation more successful at expert cooperation. It's about being more flexible in a volatile context and about gathering the resources and knowledge to deal with complexity.

Besides a clear task it is essential for self-organising teams to be set up in clear structures and to have a strong leadership who provides a suitable "container" for this collaboration and/or cooperation. This entails clarifying roles and responsibilities as well as competences. The contracts need to be negotiated on different levels. And to really get a shared understanding, a culture of respect and dialogue needs to be established. Leading a self-organising team is not a paradox, but a necessity.

References

Ashkenas, R. (2015). There's a Difference Between Cooperation and Collaboration. https://lp.google-mkto.com/rs/248-TPC-286/images/Google_6.23_HBR_article_Ashkenas.pdf?mkt_tok=3RkMMJWWfF9wsRojuK%2FNeu%2FhmjTEU5z16uQrWqCzgZh41El3fuXBP2XqjvpVQcRnMbjPRw8FHZNpywVWM8TILtQYt8FtKAzgAG0%3D (10.01.2020).

Balling, R. (2005). Diagnosis of Organizational Cultures. *Transactional Analysis Journal*, 35(4), 313–320.

Bauer, J. (2007). *Prinzip Menschlichkeit. Warum wir von Natur aus kooperieren*. Hamburg: Hoffmann und Campe.

Berne, E. (1963). *The Structure and Dynamics of Organizations and Groups*. London: Lippincott Company.

Berne, E. (1966). *Principles of Group Treatment*. New York: Grove Press.

Bohm, D. (2019). *Der Dialog. Das offene Gespräch am Ende der Diskussion*. Stuttgart: Klett-Cotta, 9. Auflage.

Buber, M. (1983). *Ich und Du*. Ditzingen: Reclam.

Clarkson, P. (1991) Group Imago and the Stages of Group Development. *Transactional Analysis Journal*, 21(1), 36–50.

De Graaf, A. (2013). The Group in the Individual. *Transactional Analysis Journal*, 43(4), 311–320.

De Graaf, A., & Levy, J. (2011). Business as Usual? Ethics in the Fast-Changing and Complex World of Organizations. *Transactional Analysis Journal*, 41(2), 123–128.

English, F. (1975). The Three-Cornered Contract. *Transactional Analysis Journal*, 5(4), 383–384.

Eoyang, G. H. (2001). Conditions for Self-Organizing in Human Systems. https://capitalrevolution.typepad.com/a_free_enterprise/files/conditions_for_selforganizing_in_human_systems.pdf (28.4.2019).

Erskine, R. G., & Trautmann, R. L. (1996). Methods of an Integrative Psychotherapy. *Transactional Analysis Journal*, 26, 316–328.

Fox, E. M. (1975). Eric Berne's Theory of Organizations. *Transactional Analysis Journal*, 5(4), 345–353.

Hackman, R. J. (1987). The Design of Work in Teams. In J. Lorsch (ed.), *Handbook of Organizational Behaviour. – HOB*. Englewood Cliffs, NJ: Prentice-Hall, pp. 315–342. www.uio.no/studier/emner/matnat/ifi/INF5181/h14/artikler-teamarbeid/hackman-(1987).design-of-work-teamspdf.pdf (3.12.2019).

Hackman, R. J. (2002). *Leading Teams. Setting the Stage for Great Performances*. Boston: Harvard Business School Publishing Corporation.

Hay, J. (1992). *Transactional Analysis for Trainers*. London: Sharwood Publishing.

Hengartner, M. (2012). Führung an Hochschulen. Professionelles Management und kollegiale Entscheidungsfindung ... aus der Sicht der mittleren Führungsstufe einer Universität. www.berinfor.ch/wp-content/uploads/2018/01/2012-Referat_Hengartner.pdf (21.6.2019).

Human Systems Dynamic Institute. (2020). www.hsdinstitute.org/resources/cde-model.html (10.01.2020).

Isaacs, W. (2011). *Dialog als Kunst gemeinsam zu denken. Die neue Kommunikationskultur in Organisationen*. Köln: EHP, 2. Auflage.

Janes, A. (2009). Wie Sie Mitarbeiter in Expertenorganisationen führen. www.janesconsulting.com/pdf/Wie_Sie_Mitarbeiter_in_Expertenorganisationen_fuehren.pdf (abgerufen am 6.8.2019).

Kaltenecker, S. (2015a). *Leading Self-Organising Teams*. Workbook for Lean & Agile Professionals. Published by C4Media, publisher of InfoQ.com.

Kaltenecker, S. (2015b). *Selbstorganisierte Teams führen: Arbeitsbuch für Lean & Agile Professionals*. Heidelberg: Dpunkt.verlag. www.dpunkt.de/common/leseproben//12397/3_Grundlagen%20selbstorganisierter%20Teams.pdf.

Kohlrieser, G., Goldsworthy, S., & Coombe, D. (2012). *Care to Dare: Unleashing Astonishing Potential Through Secure Base Leadership*. San Francisco: John Wily & Sons.

König, O., & Schattendorfer, K. (2016). *Einführung in die Gruppendynamik*. Heidelberg: Carl-Auer, 8. Auflage.

Krausz, R. R. (1986). Power and Leadership in Organizations. *Transactional Analysis Journal*, 16(2), 85–94.

Kreyenberg, J. (2005). Transactional Analysis in Organizations as Systemic Constructivist Approach. *Transactional Analysis Journal*, 35(4), 300–310.

Kühl, S. (2017). *Laterales Führen. Eine kurze organisationstheoretisch informierte Handreichung*. Wiesbaden: Springer.

Kühl, S., & Matthiesen, K. (2012). Wenn man mit Hierarchie nicht weiterkommt: Zur Weiterentwicklung des Konzepts des Lateralen Führen. In S. Grote (Hrsg.), *Die Zukunft der Führung*. Berlin: Springer-Verlag, s. 531–556.

Laloux, Frederic (2015). Reinventing Organizations. Ein Leitfaden zur Gestaltung sinnstiftender Formen der Zusammenarbeit. München: Franz Vahlen.

Landaiche III, N. M. (2012) Learning and Hating in Groups. *Transactional Analysis Journal*, 42(3), 186–198.

Lapworth, P., & Sills, C. (2011). *An Introduction to Transactional Analysis*. London: Sage.

Laugeri, M. (2010). Emerging Change and Transactional Analysis. *The Keys to Hierarchical Dialogue*. www.changementemergent.ch/sites/d/emergingchange_en_100820.pdf (19.8.2019).

Lee, A. (2014). The Development of a Process Group. *Transactional Analysis Journal*, 44(1), 41–52.

Levin-Landheer, P. (1982). The Cycle of Development. *Transactional Analysis Journal*, 12(2), 129–139.

Minuchin, S. (2015). *Familie und Familientherapie: Theorie und Praxis struktureller Familientherapie*. Freiburg: Lambertus.

Moreau, J. (2005). Using Transactional Analysis to Increase Organizational Performance. *Transactional Analysis Journal*, 35(4), 355–364.

Radatz, S. (2008). Laterale Führung – erfolgreich gelebt. *Lernende Organisation*, Januar–Februar, 41, 7–13.

Rosa, H. (2019). *Resonanz: Eine Soziologie der Weltbeziehung*. Berlin: Suhrkamp Taschenbuch Wissenschaft.

Rüegg-Stürm, J., & Grand, S. (2019). *Das St. Galler Management-Modell. Management in einer komplexen Welt*. Bern: Haupt, UTB.

Rybnicek, R., Bergner, S., & Suk, K. (2016). Führung in Expertenorganisationen. In J. Felfe & R. van Dick (Hrsg.), *Handbuch Mitarbeiterführung: Wirtschaftspsychologisches Praxiswissen für Fach- und Führungskräfte*. Berlin: Springer, s. 227–237.

Schmid, B. (2008). The Role Concept of Transactional Analysis and Other Approaches to Personality, Encounter, and Cocreativity for All Professional Fields. *Transactional Analysis Journal*, 38(1), 17–30.

Schmid, B., & Messmer, A. (2005a). On the Way to a Culture of Responsibility in Organizations: Concepts of Symbiosis Revisited. *Transactional Analysis Journal*, 35(4), 324–332.

Schmid, B., & Messmer, A. (2005b). *Systemische Personal-, Organisations- und Kulturentwicklung. Konzepte und Perspektiven*. Bergisch Gladbach: EHP.

Scholl, W. (2012). Machtausübung oder Einflussnahme: Die zwei Gesichter der Machtnutzung. In B. Knoblach, T. Oltmanns, I. Hajnal, & D. Fink (Hrsg.), *Macht in Unternehmen – Der vergessene Faktor*. Wiesbaden: Gabler, s. 203–221.

Thiele, M., & Korpiun, M. (2016). Wie Beziehungskompetenzen die Entwicklung von Kultur und damit von Organisationen prägen. In H. Raeck & L. Lohkamp (Hrsg.), *Tore und Brücken zur Welt. Willkommen in bewegten Zeiten. Reader zum 37. Kongress der Deutschen Gesellschaft für Transaktionsanalyse*. Lengerich: Pabst, pp. 400–416.

Thomann, Geri & Zellweger, Franziska (2016). Lateral führen. aus der Mitte der Hochschule Komplexität bewältigen. Bern: hep verlag ag.

Tuckman, B. W. (1965). Developmental Sequence in Small Groups. *Psychological Bulletin*, 63, 384–399.

Tudor, K. (2013). Group Imago and Group Development. *Transactional Analysis Journal*, 43(4), 321–333.

Links:
https://transferio.at/agile-coach/selbstorganisierte-teams-mit-dem-cde-modell-fuehren/.

5

FORCE FIELDS IN ORGANISATIONS

A new perspective on intervening in groups, systems and organisations

Jacques Moreau

Introduction

In the course of more than 500 assignments in companies across the entire business spectrum, I regularly observed how various situations, crises and periods of change in the workplace involved fields of tension (e.g. between production and sales or security and innovation).

It became clear that transactional analysis (TA) was an effective way of resolving these tensions, by helping people and systems achieve a new state of equilibrium. My colleague Véronique Sichem and I formalised this approach and called it "Force Field TA".

In this new perspective, I define groups as living organisms, propose a new definition of internal and external boundaries and tensions and describe the complexity of the environment in terms of the balance of three forces.

I also propose a way of examining the difficulties involved in management, humanism revived by OK-ness and the stances taken by the facilitator in Force Field TA.

Force field perspective

I was conducting some training sessions with a colleague, integrating our experience of intervening across various organisations and international contexts, and realised we were working on a different edge together. We decided to call our approach Force Field TA. This chapter expands on our initial work, laying the foundations for a new theoretical perspective and practice in transactional analysis (TA). I employ current TA concepts and take into account the influence of group-related and social aspects, and psychological and environmental (context) factors. The purpose is to facilitate successful intervention in groups, specifically in large social entities.

Force Field TA is founded on the principle that groups (families, teams, companies, multinationals, institutions, countries) are living organisms. They have the criteria required to be considered "alive", such as a replication system and the type of diversity that supports development (Le Drouin, 2017).

Force Field TA is a systemic, contractual and clinical approach:

- It is **systemic** in the sense that groups, like systems, involve a state of balance in a given space-time context. This balance stems from the interplay of tension between endogenous and exogenous factors and can be upset by unexpected events. When this happens, a new balance needs to be found taking into account the group activity, internal possibilities and external restrictions.
- It is **contractual** in that it involves seeking mutual commitment and agreements with respect to lawful objects, from the original "complaint" through to the desired outcome and effective contract. We pay close attention to ensuring the contract goal is realistic, by verifying that both the client and our intervention system have the required skills and abilities. Compensation is agreed on the basis of open, transparent negotiation.
- It is **clinical** in that our aim is to understand a specific system and the people it contains, who are unique and original. There is no ideal model of an organisation, just as there is no perfect person.

Finally, Force Field TA takes on a revised humanist perspective. We intervene with respect for living beings and the classical Bernian conviction that the "client" holds the keys to resolving any difficulty they may encounter. Among the various roles played by the transactional analyst that of catalyst is the most powerful to revive their potential.

A group is a living organism

A living system can be considered as "balanced" when the relationships between its internal components are stable over a period of time and in a given context. For example, a company achieves its targets through a combination of procurement, production and sales systems, which remain the same over a period of time. An increase in procurement costs could significantly impact its results and disturb the company's state of equilibrium (Von Bertalanffy, 1992).

Conventionally, the state of being "alive" is associated with the act of breathing. However, according to French developmental biologist and embryology researcher Nicole Le Drouin (2017), current scientific knowledge about living organisms indicates that life is the logical result of chemical (i.e. deterministic) forces. The evolution of living things is therefore considered a deterministic process, of which the required conditions are met each time.

Life can therefore be defined as:

- A system of identical reproduction (DNA), for example, human procreation results in a human embryo, not a bear or a cat.
- An infinite number of possibilities that statistics alone cannot predict.
- Extraordinary diversity in constant flux of the gene pool. The biodiversity of human beings, their cultures and their dwelling places are absolute necessities for human life.

According to Jacques Monod (1970), Nobel Prize for Physiology, goal-directedness or purpose is one of the fundamental properties of all living beings. As a highly organised complex system, life depends on the environment from which it draws its energy by absorbing the elements it needs and rejecting any waste, to continuously renew itself and its purpose.

As a doctor, Berne used this biological model as the basis for his conceptualisation of groups (Berne, 2005). Although research has made enormous progress since the 1970s, we can still say that:

- The nature of a group is reproduced through its set of cultural beliefs (etiquette, character and technicality). These constitute what I call its "founding myth".
- Groups are constantly readjusting their resources, weaknesses and skills needed to stay alive, even though they do not always succeed in doing so.
- Groups are driven to survive as a structure, relationship or idea.
- The structure of a group becomes increasingly complex when the environment changes if exchanges with that environment are fundamental to its survival.

My conclusion is that:

- A group is "alive" when it embodies a balanced system of forces.
- This balance can be upset by changes in the group's environment, in which case it must find a new state of equilibrium by preserving certain of its characteristics and readapting its resources in order to survive or achieve a developmental milestone.
- A state of imbalance is manifested in the discomfort felt by group members in relation to the meaning of their activity, the organisation, relationships and their feeling of belonging.

There is neither an ideal group nor a group ideal. Cultural diversity guarantees that a variety of solutions can be found for the problems facing our world and its inhabitants.

Key point

Group intervention must be focussed on helping the system reach a new state of equilibrium by addressing the tensions that emerge. This is what I call the tensional or Force Field approach in TA.

Large and small groups

Though groups have existed since the beginning of humanity, the notion of the group is relatively recent. It was imported from Italy (*"gruppo"*) in the mid-17th century and has its roots in the fine arts, meaning *"an assemblage of elements, a category of beings or of objects forming a harmonious whole"*. It entered general usage only in the sense of *"a coming together of people"* one century later.

Kurt Lewin was one of the pioneering researchers in groups and group dynamics (Lewin, 1946). Berne most likely drew upon Lewin's research and that of the systemic analysts of the era.

Another major contributor to the understanding of groups is French psychoanalyst and Emeritus Professor of Clinical Psychology, Didier Anzieu (1981, 1985).

A group needs to have at least three members: group phenomena become visible only with the arrival of a fourth individual.

Anzieu ranks groups according to their degree of organisation (and, hence, the level of commitment of its members) and by the number of members: *a crowd, a clan, a gathering, a primary or restricted group* (such as a family), or *a secondary group or organisation* (hospital, school, company, political party, etc.), much like Berne did in 1966. For convenience, the social sciences have studied "restricted" groups, which has meant that descriptions of large groups, such as countries or multinational organisations with economic, social or political mandates (such as NGOs), are often lacking. Yet it seems to me essential that groups like this be taken into account, as they not only impact the model and culture of more restricted groups (companies, families, etc.) but also feed into the social sphere. I propose a dual input diagram to map the different types of groups based on structural complexity and number of members.

Online groups and federations of countries are positioned on the boundary lines of this conceptual framework.

I propose to map both restricted and large groups based on structural complexity and number of members.

Key point

TA can be used to support not only systems like families and businesses but also countries and multinational organisations.

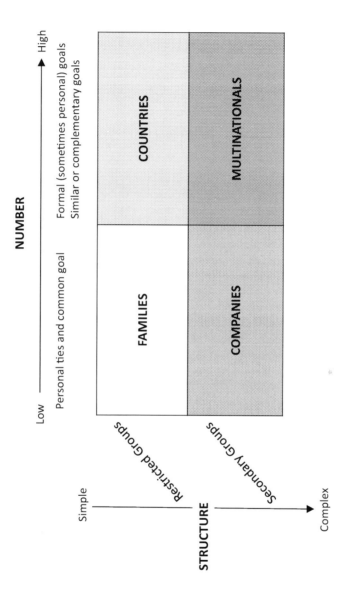

Figure 5.1 Group typology

Misunderstandings about groups

In TA our approach can at times place excessive focus on the individual. It is a bit like saying the history of France can be reduced to that of its kings and royal courts. While there is no shortage of novels telling stories about individuals, those featuring a group, family or people as the main character are few and far between. One exception is the novel *The Last of the Just* by André Schwartz-Bart (1959). The lack of stories also feeds some common misconceptions (what we refer to as "contaminations" in TA) about groups.

Professor Anzieu identifies the following misconceptions or contaminations about groups:

- *A group is a set of stable interpersonal relationships.*
- *A group protects but excludes the individual's personality (i.e. leads to psychological alienation).* In other words, a belief that the security afforded by an authoritarian system can deprive the group members of their individual freedom, and even result in self-estrangement. However, experience has shown that even the most authoritarian systems have never been able to prevent freedom of thought (when the Soviet system collapsed, for instance, priests reappeared within days, proving that they had never truly disappeared as such).
- *Human relationships in groups are limited to being a manipulator or being manipulated (sado-masochistic model).*
- *The group is a whole in which the individual does not perceive life in any other way (sociological biases),* that is to say, *it does not occur to group members that people may live or work differently in other groups (this is a frequent "contamination" of the Adult ego state).*
- *Small restricted groups are both an advantage and a threat to large groups, creating spontaneous distrust between the representatives of large groups and those of small groups. Anzieu notes that the size of groups can be a source of mutual distrust. For example, a small group of activists can be very dangerous for a large bureaucratic group. This distrust is based on conspiratorial fear (paranoid model).*

To which I would add:

- *Confusion arising from the application of psychological concepts to address group-related issues, and vice versa.*
- *Imagining that a single decision can change a group's entire culture.*
- *Mixing up problem, dysfunction and pathology. For instance, under "normal" health sector conditions, a shortage of face masks in a hospital may be treated as a* problem *that needs to be addressed. In the event of an influx of patients, the hospital's tendency to systematically reduce stocks could be analysed as a* dysfunction *(in which case the procurement criteria need to be changed). During a health crisis, the shortage of masks could prove* pathological, *as it would put the lives of the hospital's staff and patients at risk.*

- *Stating that an ideal group state exists and makes people happier or more efficient.*
- *Thinking that all bosses are abusive and irresponsible or the exact opposite.*

Key point

Facilitators have an impact on the success of a group's transformation plan. It may be a good idea to set aside time for our own personal reflection in terms of our beliefs and contaminations about groups and how these may influence the way we intervene.

Looking at recent protest movements in Europe, we can see that such prejudices are still playing a role in our groups today. The stance taken by governments and populations when faced with social realities, such as migration, demonstrates the fragile nature of our sense of identity and an underlying social violence. To give a concrete example, recent migratory flows in Europe have demonstrated differences in cultural tendencies in terms of closing or leaving their borders open, just like Sparta and Athens in ancient Greece. However, the political and popular discourse calling for exclusion or for unconditional acceptance that has accompanied these observations can be likened to the group contaminations described by Anzieu. It is an illusion to think that borders can be completely closed or even that they can be left wide open.

In addressing migrating issues, we have often confused problems (e.g. *how to facilitate the integration of a foreign community into a given country?*) with malfunctions *(the regulations in force are unsuitable, resulting in a solution that becomes problematic)* or even pathology *(the foreign community is installed in a village without preparing the inhabitants or the migrants, resulting in violence)*.

How can we define a group?

A group is typically defined as two or more people who interact, mutually influence one another and perceive themselves as "Us" for a given period of time. Four criteria can be used to identify group:

1 Presence of interpersonal relations
2 Pursuit of a common goal
3 Members mutually influencing one another
4 An organisational structure is in place

Berne states that a group exists when there are at least two boundaries (an External Boundary, Major Internal Boundary, and optionally Minor Internal Boundaries). A group needs to have at least three members. Group phenomena become visible only with the arrival of a fourth individual.

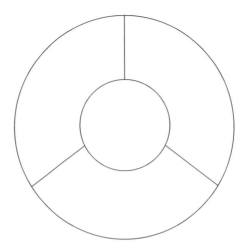

Figure 5.2 Berne's model of group boundaries

Key point

From a sociological and psychological perspective, a group is a living organism. This standpoint is supported by law, which recognises that a group may be subject to civil and criminal liability, beyond that of individuals and management.

From a sociological point of view, a group exists because third parties believe in it. For individuals, it is a place of belonging. In terms of the law, it is a responsible legal entity. For anthropologists, it testifies to the existence of a collective culture, with its myths, historical legends and rites.

I propose the following definition of a group:

- A group is an *aggregation* (of people, capital, means of production, know-how, etc.)
- That is recognised as an independent entity by its members and external partners
- From which they hope and expect to receive *material, psychological and symbolic benefits*
- In exchange for their *contribution to the life* of the group

I drew inspiration for this definition from José Grégoire (TSTA.P) and Isaac Joseph (2002).

What types of groups are there?

Berne (1963) identifies three types of groups:

- Work group: When the boundaries are in a state of well-established equilibrium, so that most of the group's energies can be devoted to its activity

FORCE FIELDS IN ORGANISATIONS

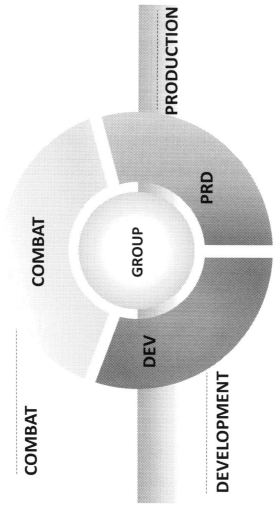

All groups have the potential to rally for action in a given mode according to the circumstances Jacques Moreau (TSTA-O)

Figure 5.3 Berne's three types of groups

- Combat groups: When internal group forces are engaged in conflict with external disruptive forces (external group process)
- Process groups: When the group's energy is chiefly involved in internal conflicts and concerts between forces (internal group process)

I prefer to call the latter **development groups** as, one way or another, the process results in the group's development.

I would add that all groups potentially contain these three characteristics and that these are activated according to changes in the internal or external circumstances.

In development (process) groups, a sense of "unconditional acceptance of others" will need to be instilled, as this is one of the conditions for individual growth within a group. In this type of group, we can observe the formation of a spontaneous, collective state of "flow" (Csikszentmihalyi, 1990). This "team flow" may seem strange but is consistent with the group's shared goal (e.g. in a supervision or therapy group, where the participants develop a sense of fraternity; during a show in which the public interacts with the performers; or even among members of a business team, committed to a development project).

In combat groups, members will need to learn how to act in conflict situations. We saw this at the start of the Coronavirus lockdown in numerous countries. People were used to functioning as part of a work group, which meant that the transition to a safe, protective stance was difficult for some, resulting in the introduction of legal restrictions.

Lastly, people in work groups can be seen to focus on their individual and collective efficiency. Problems can arise from the members' different mental representations of what constitutes "efficiency", but this can be easily resolved through group imago adjustment.

Forms of group organisation

Another key starting point for analysing groups is observing their main mode of organisation (Wilber, 2014).

Seven principle and emerging forms of organisation can be identified. Here, we propose an analogy; saying that the group functions like:

1   A herd
2   A tribe
3   A feudal clan
4   A hierarchical pyramid (as in a church)
5   A matrix
6   A regulated matrix
7   Ad hoc systems (or hybrid groups)

These forms of organisation arise in response to major changes in the group's environment and as a means of keeping the group alive. They therefore provide a specific reference framework that includes the group's founding myth, its beliefs and the ways it handles problems and grows.

While it is advisable to take a higher vision for the group's future, it is impossible to determine ideal ways of working outside the frame of reference used by the majority of the group's members.

For instance, take a family business that is run like a clan, with an authoritarian boss whose authority is inflated by a sense of ownership ("*this is my company; I'm looking after it for future generation*"). Initially, the easiest way to improve agility would be to help the leader adopt a Normative Parent OK/OK communication style, which would serve as a model for other members. Attempting to implement a "freedom-form" organisational approach would certainly not be advisable in this case, as the required changes would be too much for most people, particularly the person in charge.

In an organisation that functions as a bureaucracy (i.e. with a hierarchical pyramid), progress is achieved by removing barriers between the various departments. Here, introducing agility involves creating cross-company groups and agreeing upon a new way of defining efficiency. It would certainly not be advisable to propose improving agility by changing individual behaviour, although this may come later.

Key point

Groups are complex systems that can be addressed from various angles: their definition and social purpose, Berne's typology, their form of organisation and also the type of institutional power and governance at play (Mintzberg, 1982). The specific way in which all of these aspects combine is what makes the group unique.

C-group boundaries

The concept of boundaries is one of the major contributions from the application of transactional analysis to groups. In *The Structure and Dynamics of Organizations and Groups*, Berne writes: *A boundary is any factor, or set of factors, which, in the eyes of the observer, gives order to the group by delimiting a significant zone.* He adds: *Group dynamics may be defined as the study of the influences acting on and through the boundaries which are the foundation of the group's structure.* Finally, in the glossary, he states: *Boundary: Constitutional, psychological or spatial distinction between different categories of members – the internal boundary; or between members and non-members – the external boundary* (Evrard, 2017).

Berne gives a graphical representation which, in my experience, enables us to position 60% of the issues that need to be resolved within a group:

1   *Movements at boundaries*: pressure, agitation and tensions
2   *Belonging*: that which is "inside" versus that which is "outside" or what is "the same or different". *How members recognise one another as belonging to the group and how they form relationships within the group and with external groups.*

Developments

Berne's illuminating depiction of a group with three boundaries was consistent with the Westphalian perspective typical of his era. The Treaty of Westphalia, signed in 1648, laid the foundations of international law and nation states and put an end (at least in theory) to the survival of the fittest form of society. This offered a new way of apprehending the notion of sovereignty that lasted through until the bipolarization brought by the Cold War, and remains the legal standard today.

During this period, boundaries were primarily put in place to keep the peace. They had to be solid and serve as a more or less porous screening mechanism aligned with economic, political and military interests.

Boundaries have a greater impact on the inside than they do on the outside. They act to reinforce a nation's culture, with its sovereign state, language, memory, myths and national economy.

For example: The state structures society by imposing a national culture on minorities, eradicating local dialects, printing or devaluing money and opening

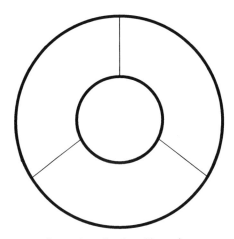

Illustration of a closed boundary

Figure 5.4 Berne's representation of a rigid (closed) external boundary

or closing its borders according to its economic interests. The French state was probably among those to push the furthest in building a homogeneous, centralised system, which is at least part of the reason for the difficulties it has encountered introducing progressive reforms to effect change.

Key point

This same conception prevailed in companies, with senior management imposing organisational decisions on the basis of its strategic objectives, with little regard for the professional view of its employees and managers and seeking to impose a business culture devised to facilitate cohesion.

However, the mounting number of boundaries at stake gradually called this model into question. For instance, in 1960, the United Nations consisted of 51 nation states. In 2019, membership reached 193. Whereas local tensions may often be resolved by taking into account the cultural, geographic, economic and religious specificities of each country in this way, new tensions may arise as a result of new boundary lines being drawn.

In the 1990s, Europeans were under the illusion that borders would disappear thanks to the single currency, the removal of border crossing points and the free circulation of people and goods, not to mention the opening up of travel to hitherto inaccessible destinations, such as China and South America.

However, in the 2010s, there was a return to so-called populist movements, all clamouring for borders to be closed. These movements are more or less in favour of a return to a strong nation state to protect its citizens against unfair competition from certain countries and the insecurity generated by immigration, terrorism and so forth. Racism and xenophobia are also on the rise in some countries.

This fear of a loss of identity, of being invaded and replaced, is indicative of archaic representations of the group and social imaginations. According to French researcher Jacques Fradin, the group imago is located in the decision-making centre of the paleo-limbic brain. Fradin, who is also a GP, therapist and lecturer at the University of Bourgogne, states that this part of the brain is activated when group-related issues arise (balance of power, self-confidence, aggressiveness, gregarious position, etc.).

This part of the brain sorts out "good" foreigners from "bad" foreigners, acceptable refugees from the others. Some movements go as far as to promote the idea of a community of "believers" as the only way of separating *that which is inside*, that is, "good", from *that which is outside*, which is by definition bad and to be conquered.

This call for a return to national borders is seen as "the only answer" to all different kinds of problems.

We are currently in touch with fears that were identified back in ancient Greece: *that of opening up our borders and ending up invaded (dissolution of identity) or building walls and ultimately choking to death.*

Little by little, independence movements have been sprouting up across the continent, all of which calling for new borders to be drawn, as in Catalonia, Scotland, Flanders, Northern Italy and Corsica, for instance.

Officially, what they want is recognition of their linguistic, cultural and economic specificities. However, experience has shown that separatism is doomed to fail in terms of international law. The results of the referendum in Catalonia, in favour of its separation from Spain, would also mean leaving the European Union.

However, separatist populations often have a strong sense of belonging: for instance, Scotland has been run by an openly pro-independence, centre-left party since 2007, one that has been re-elected three times. Despite this, successive elections have failed to give power to the Scottish National Party, which tends to confirm that independence is not the prime concern; rather, it is a drive for greater autonomy or what we in TA call "interdependence" (the ability to be oneself while belonging to a group).

Somewhere between the old model (in which borders are a permanent trait) and the temptation to turn inward (borders are walls), ad hoc boundaries of variable geometries are gradually emerging, setting up very different barriers and filters to those taught in 1950s geography books. These new kinds of borders make a distinction between the circulation of goods and the circulation of people, adjusting tax and social rights to the interest of those present (Dubet, 2018).

They also take into account the new state of play: borders are never entirely watertight. While the circulation of goods and people can be partly controlled, it is much harder to manage the flow of communication influencing our behaviour. Financial flows, communication via electronic media and the culture industry are forming a "neo-national" world just as the closure of national boundaries is making a strong comeback (Badie & Foucher, 2017).

The "boundary zone"

The idea of working in boundary zones came to me when I was putting together plans for analysing and intervening in various large organisations. I noticed how important it was to take a clinical approach, that is, one that is adapted to each system, which is unique, and that involves an empathic professional stance. Although there are a great many invariable factors, it is important to take into account the specific cultural and identity-related elements of each system.

Furthermore, when supervising my colleagues, I became aware that a high proportion of them were unconsciously convinced that the contract automatically made them members of the system, or that the fact of interacting with a system extending beyond their own led to a feeling of being used for other ends.

The boundary zone is a way of conceptualising boundaries that takes into account what really happens at the boundary lines. A boundary consists of both doors and bridges. Doors can be opened or closed and serve to selectively let people in and keep others out, while bridges are for forming ties. At boundary zones, we can therefore observe not just trafficking and illegal entry, but also meetings, trade and the construction of shared living spaces.

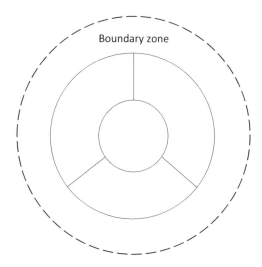

Figure 5.5 Berne's representation of a boundary zone

These "blurred" areas are necessary for our transition between two worlds or two limits. Travelling between them is not just a question of official maps. For instance, Lake Geneva is a natural boundary zone between France and Switzerland and its history is rich with legend and fantasy.

It is also the story of how fruitful collaboration was built. Similarly, the Mediterranean used to bring people together more than it kept them apart, before becoming a near-insurmountable border between Africa and Europe (2,260 migrants died in the Mediterranean in 2018 according to the UNHCR, of a total 115,000 who managed to make the crossing). Similarly, we can identify border zones between the Christian and the Muslim worlds, as symbolised by Turkey and Cyprus.

This prompted me to find out whether international organisations tasked with fostering cooperation between peoples and cohesion between multiple identities had ever "enacted" such boundary zones. I rapidly identified two examples:

The first example is the Erasmus system. Every year, the Erasmus scholarship programme enables students to complete part of their studies in another European teaching establishment, for a period of at least three months and a maximum of one year. The programme gets its name from the Dutch monk and theologian Erasmus (1465–1536). Erasmus travelled throughout Europe for many years to learn about different cultures and develop his humanist approach.

In 2004, the European Union's Erasmus exchange programme won the Princess of Asturias Award for International Cooperation, for being one of the biggest cultural exchange programmes in human history. The programme's importance extends beyond European academia and is recognised as fostering cohesion and knowledge-building among young people across the European Union. This has given rise to the term "Erasmus generation" when referring to university students who were able to form international friendships thanks to their experience on the programme and who are clearly aware of their European citizenship. The phenomenon was the theme of French film *Auberge Espagnole* (English title *Pot Luck*), about six Erasmus students from various countries sharing a flat in Barcelona, Spain. Looking beyond the personal ties formed during these exchange schemes, young Europeans clearly have greater potential to address the questions facing Europe from the perspective of cultural diversity than their elders.

The second example is the SEGIB. The SEGIB (Ibero-American General Secretariat) is an international support organisation for the 22 countries comprising the Ibero-American community. Its objectives include:

- Strengthening and fostering cohesion in the Ibero-American community and raising its international profile
- Promoting historic, cultural, social and economic ties among Ibero-American countries, while recognising and valuing the diversity of their peoples

Key point

We can see that, when it comes to nation states, borders are no longer just a line drawn on a map but a "boundary zone". This zone becomes necessary due to the greater complexity of affiliations, cultures and interests. The boundary zone acts as a buffer, in which to prepare, to conduct real-life tests, to bring together stakeholders' various interests before going on to develop a programme or make a decision affecting the real world. International organisations understand this only too well, setting up bodies, committees and schemes to help promote cooperation rather than confrontation.

Boundary zones: an attempt at a definition

A boundary zone is:

- An actual place (with symbolic meaning if possible) subject to a contract (meaning there are protections in place for those involved): alliance (A), confidence (P), and security (C)
- Subject to process analysis (transactional and group processes)
- Created like a programme, of which all the stages are important: complaint, initial request, formalised request, contract (Moïso & Guichard, 1988)
- Where the object is to create a training space for the client in which to cultivate transformation
- Led by a team of consultants capable of managing complex processes, who are attentive to defence mechanisms, and who are contractually committed to regulation/supervision between colleagues outside of their sessions with the client

Key point

The contracting process is often the most suitable for addressing such issues as it is based on the concept of boundary transgressions, which become "fodder" for analysis. In the boundary zone, this approach is more suitable and quicker to implement than that of "exploiting" the ensuing rise in anxiety.

The result is a concrete change in the group imago, with an impact on financial and technical performance and the co-construction of realistic and innovative options and solutions that would not have been envisaged without this creative process. To quote Mark Twain: "They did not know it was impossible, so they did it, differently".

Key point

Formally speaking, the boundary zone is a "bubble of OK-ness" in a world dominated by power plays and psychological games. While we may agree with Berne that human beings are born "OK", we can also observe that models of social relationships are often based on power struggles. It is an honour for us, as transactional analysts and other peacemakers, to participate in the construction of "OK-ness bubbles".

The boundary zone is a transitional space

French philosopher René Descartes (1823–1899) described space as a milieu in which observed phenomena occur, in other words a place in which *something happens*.

The term "transitional" was first coined by British psychoanalyst Donald W. Winnicott in 1951 (Winnicott, 2005). He talked about transitional space and potential space, from the Latin stem *transitio* meaning "going across or over". The boundary zone is therefore a transitional space, a training ground on which to prepare. It is a place of projection and introjection, thus requiring a contractual dynamic. Indeed, this is where a group can draw upon the "transmissions of information" it receives from its environment to foster the creativity needed for its autonomy and singular existence.

Winnicott's concept of *transitional phenomena* highlights the importance of observable facts as scientific matter, and also, as pointed out by French philosopher Paul Janet (1867), that of facts in motion, the shift from one fact to another. In reference to French philosopher Michel Foucault (1984), I also call these spaces "*transformation heterotopias*" that is, timeless sacred spaces juxtaposing with other spaces; places of expression and for inventing unexpected possible outcomes. They are not a utopia, of which none exists; rather, they are a place for determining what that utopia *could* be, like a forge in which to shape the future myth.

Like Winnicott, I see this transitional space as a place for fun, play and pleasure. Without this space, the group would be reduced to survival processes.

The boundary zone becomes a virtual space in which the group can test out its methods, processes and culture in contact with the outside world. It provides a sort of waiting area, a place in which to bring the inside and outside together. It is also a training space in which transmission is both visible (words, rules, lived experiences) and invisible (gestures, expressions, ways of resolving tensions, etc.), reminiscent of Berne's description of the script being passed down through the mother's breast milk.

Key point

*The boundary zone is a dynamic environment, an experience. The transitional object is not the contract we establish or a project to managed, but rather **the group itself**, the consultant's system and the system put together with the group, as a group.*

The importance of a transitional space in change management

My thinking about transitional space is the basis from which I began devising systems for intervening in companies.

Let us take the example of a mission conducted over a period of about 10 years in a semi-public company employing around 500 people. The aim was to get three types of employees working together: civil servants, entrepreneurs and technicians. The organisation was on the verge of dissolution. It was suffering from a very poor image within the profession and was producing negative professional and financial results. The staff spent their time in pointless competitions (psychological games and power plays).

We implemented a general framework based on the following pillars:

- *Creation of a "boundary zone"* for various groups tasked with working on the company's growth. It was decided that this zone would be located outside the company, in a neutral space, and suited to the type of work undertaken.
- *Definition of issue addressed*: various teams experimented with problem solving, the co-construction of innovative solutions, cooperating, developing professional managerial and interpersonal skills and developing awareness of group phenomena.
- *Implementation of modus operandi* (protection and permission)
- *Role definition:*
    - Members of the company were given responsibility for exploring, trying things out, making suggestions, receiving feedback, inviting external observers, making decisions and so forth.

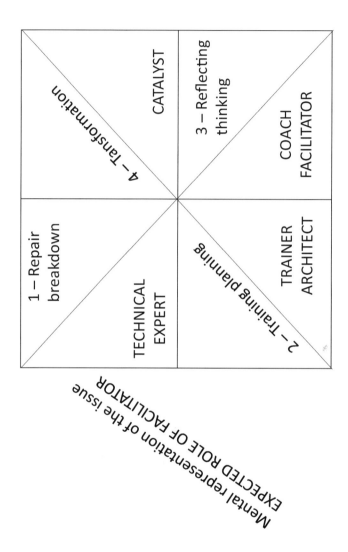

Figure 5.6 Different roles and related expectations

- Our team was in charge of conducting the sessions and, depending on the issue to be addressed, playing one of the roles defined in the adjacent matrix (expert, architect, coach or catalyst).
- Non-dogmatism: there is no ideal organisation; we intervene to support teams in building structures that suit their activity and level of development.

Slowly but surely this approach gave rise to a pretty amazing general state of mind in terms of OK-ness, with five concrete results identified by the company's management over the 10-year period:

- Business volumes doubled
- The company's market value increased by 50%
- Governance and teams were working as one, with a good level of cooperation (this point was recognised both internally and externally)
- Co-construction of an attractive project
- Brand image completely overhauled, enabling the company to win a contract with a prestigious client which would normally have been out of its league

Key point

Intervening in a system involves bringing two systems face to face (intervening as a team rather than a sole consultant). This is warranted by the ability of the consultant's system to take into account part of the complexity of the situation and to intervene with sufficient power to generate the right transitional space in which to resolve the issue at hand.

Observable tensions

When intervening in groups from a TA perspective, we have become used to working with boundary dynamics: pressures on External Boundaries, agitation around the Major Internal Boundary, and tensions at Minor Internal Boundaries. This chapter is not concerned with the treatment of such tensions.

I have noticed that tensions around the Major Internal Boundary may increase when members:

- Do not have a strong feeling of belonging
- Do not feel they are "well treated" that is, in a fair, equal, appropriate, equitable, acceptable manner, depending on the culture
- Do not feel they have enough individual freedoms to make up for social constraints

This is why group transformation requires that we first settle any issues that may stand in the way. Finding a new balance that allows tensions to emerge can be decisive in successfully effecting major change within groups. During an intervention in a multinational company, members of its French subsidiary found it very difficult to feel a sense of belonging. Targeted work, focusing on rituals at the boundary zone, enabled members to become more confident in each other and feel a greater sense of pride as a group. It also improved the atmosphere, enabled more vibrant communication and people gradually learned how to work together.

Tensions are not just a question of psychological equilibrium

German philosopher, Peter Sloterdijk (2011) draws our attention to the fact that expressions of anger and resentment can be a social and political driving force. Sloterdijk believes it was after the end of communism, and the fall of the Berlin wall in 1989 that liberalism began to spread across the world and economics became a vast competition leaving only winners or losers. How do losers spontaneously react to such humiliation? The answer is with anger, as expressed through terrorism and violence. This anger is no longer directed solely at the elite, but at the very rules of the "game". The Yellow Vests movement in France can be understood, in part, through this lens.

Social equilibria form a part of groupality and can be addressed using the various TA concepts. This allows us to take into account both psychological and social aspects, as well as the link between the two (we could call this a psychosocial approach). I have mapped out three drives in balance (erotic, thymotic and compulsive), which together help satisfy our need for meaning. The ancient Greeks believed the thymus gland was the seat of the soul. The urge for revenge is one of the most powerful feelings that exists: the recent anger-fuelled movements, from the Arab Spring to #metoo, all stem from this gland. They are all calls for dignity, demands both to be recognised and to be placed on an equal footing to others.

Key point

Berne believed the three keys to success in a team were the right equipment, an organisation structure adapted to the objective and team morale. We can also add the way in which the aforementioned drives come into balance in a given context and how members of the group are able, or unable, to satisfy their need for meaning.

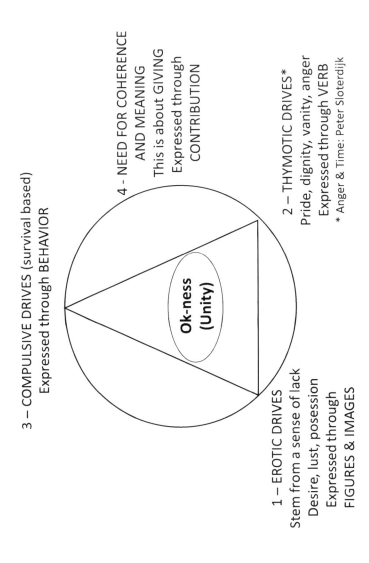

Figure 5.7 The need for meaning: three drives in balance

FORCE FIELDS IN ORGANISATIONS

An example of internal tensions: composite groups

Whether the group is large or small, we can observe the emergence of what I call composite groups. These are structures that form around different cultures and identities which, when they succeed in working together, provide a more relevant means of addressing change and the challenges arising in their environment.

In my experience, companies present both a collective identity, which is fairly easy to identify, and also sub-group identities, stemming from various occupations, past history, strategies for existing in a hostile universe and so forth.

The idea came to me when advising one of the world's leading producers of composite materials.

A composite material is made of a combination of two or more components which are immiscible (albeit presenting a high penetration capacity) and have mutually compatible properties. The new material created from this combination is heterogeneous, with properties that its components taken separately do not possess (e.g. cob, waterproof, reinforced concrete, laminated, thermoplastic materials)

This improves the quality of the material for specific uses (light in weight, resistant to strain, etc.)

A composite material consists of a **skeleton**, known as a brace *(to ensure mechanical resistance)*, and a **binding agent**, called the matrix *(to ensure structural cohesion)*. It involves the transfer of strain and, sometimes, of **loads** or additives to the brace *(to ensure a specific and necessary function)*.

Shedding light on the composite nature of a company both enables group members to feel a sense of recognition and gives them a form of permission.

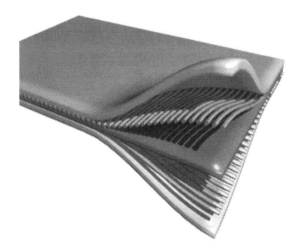

Figure 5.8 An example of composite material

Key point

More importantly, I have observed that this representation of the composite nature of groups helps focus work on the key issue: How do we work together when we are different?

Attention is turned to learning how to do something rather than on a presumed pathological "inability to conform". This confrontation mobilises the Child's energy while giving an invitation to work with the consciousness of the Adult.

Here is a representative example of a company in which we recently intervened.

Each colour represents a different reference framework (each with a specific organisation structure). In the case shown in the previous figure,

- Black (external circle) represents the very formal legal structure of the system, with a hierarchical organisation structure
- Dark-grey represents the "soldiers"
- Light-grey represents "strategists and developers"
- The two center circles represent a form of resistance to excessive formality, giving rise to organisation structures that are not necessarily visible but are very efficient in terms of cooperation and using resources

This company is now high performing and generates double-digit growth. Its employees feel relatively well treated.

Similarly, major groups, such as nation states, take in populations from various other cultures that both enhance the host country's capacities and sometimes raise questions about "how to live together with different identities". While migration is an obvious social fact, the expansion in means of transport and communications

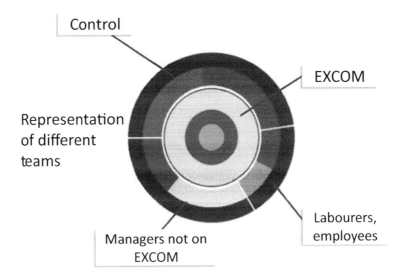

Figure 5.9 Different frames of reference in a company

during the last century enabled people to migrate on a much larger scale and still plays a major role in connecting geographies.

There are 200 million migrants worldwide, which is 3% of the world's population. The total number of international migrants has risen over the past 20 years, from around 150 million people in 2000 to 214 million people today. According to the United Nations High Commissioner for Refugees, the number of climate refugees is expected to rise 50 million in 2010 to 200 million in 2020.

Key point

More and more countries, companies and families are becoming composites. The same can even be said for people, due to the wide number of groups to which they belong. All of this is simply a drive towards biodiversity as a means to survive and develop in an increasingly complex world. Nothing will stop the trend. The key is to recognise this and work on answering the question: How do we live together when we are so different? The TAs approach is well suited to addressing this issue and can help formulate some answers.

Working with the environment

The environment is the milieu in which the group exists. It can also be referred to as an ecosystem.

In any given environment, forces are at play that both unite and disperse, concur and conflict; the ancient Greeks identified a balance of three inescapable forces.

The three components

- **Love**, in its four dimensions: Eros (sensual love), Philia (friendship, loving kindness), Storge (family love) and Agape (selfless, unconditional, universal love) (Comte-Sponville, 2013)
- **Conflict** (opposites generate fertility, creation) with four dimensions: opposition, competition, disagreement and war (when moderation is lost, man enters a state of pure violence with no respect for the rules) (Conche, 1986)
- **Destruction**, as embodied by the twins Thanatos (death) and Hypnos (sleep). Nothing is permanent, and death is an inherent part of all that is living.

All ecosystems are a balance of tension between these three forces, in which humans attempt to protect themselves from the havoc caused by predation, aggressiveness and excessive competition and also to stimulate associations and cooperation, in other words seeking what TA calls OK/OK relationships.

One way of maintaining equilibrium in an ecosystem involves creating one's habitat (one of the attributes of living beings): this enables life to unfold naturally. This is the case of groups, which are a form of human habitat (providing shelter for one's family, one's activity, etc.).

Key point

The group's environment is fragile by nature and imbalances can lead to hostile situations.
One possibility is to create "bubbles of OK-ness".
Conflict can be constructive if it is addressed within a set framework.
Destruction is inevitable because this is how life is regenerated through new structures.
The temporary balance of the three forces identified (love, conflict and destruction) needs to be regulated to ensure the group's survival and development.

Some sociological changes that have occurred since Berne

Berne practised psychotherapy in a post-World War II world. A lot has changed since then. In many western societies, a traditional tendency to submit to the group was replaced by a gradual shift towards taking individual needs into account, self-development and the idea that each person is unique.

What sociologists called *humanism* is a school of thought, feelings and related behaviours that give value to the individual by taking into account both their social needs and, as a corollary, their personal responsibility.

Conventional social matrices collapsed under the pressure of technological progress and globalisation. In France, there was a fairly clear distinction between the Christian social matrix and the secular Republican matrix. The collapse of these social matrices gave way to multiple protests in favour of individual needs.

This individualisation in society brought greater freedom of personal choice (of studies, profession, sexuality, way of life, etc.) and a corresponding sense of responsibility (I am responsible for the choices I freely make). This led people to compare themselves with others and the frustrations such comparisons may cause.

From a sociological perspective, this gave way to individual grievances: "**As a** *(woman, man, labourer, manager, farmer, therapist, etc.)* . . . **I need, I want** . . ." leading to major social tensions that sometimes resulted in collective expressions not just of jubilation and sharing but also of hate, contempt and indifference.

The ensuing loss of direction in terms of society and identity was used by certain "manipulators" to persuade those cut off from their affiliations, and from part of their consciousness, to slip into script patterns, some of which could prove fatal (Nathan, 2017).

These societal changes could also be observed to co-exist with conventional ways of life and hierarchical social matrices, fuelling tensions between world regions and even within countries, companies and families.

Indeed, many people believe themselves to be free and autonomous and yet seem drawn to this manipulative drive, which satisfies an unconscious desire to remain identical and to comply with repetitive patterns (i.e. keep the frame of reference unchanged).

The unconscious thus creates a kind of chasm in the Adult ego state, in an attempt to prevent the tensions emerging from *dialogue, debate and contradictions*, or from the expression of *an autonomous thought, justice or compassion*, from reaching conscious awareness.

The "technical" society

The loss of our traditional bearings gradually gave way to a "technical society" governed by experts *(executives and politicians don't understand technology and rely on the expertise of specialists)*, the aim being to make that society more efficient and keep it under control (Ellul, 1962).

The subordination of politics to technological expertise has meant that moral values now serve merely to hide this subordination and save face: the message is "We *(politicians, management)* still have control of the situation". The world has become increasingly dependent on new technologies, and we remain unaware of the fact that no-one has any control over the situation. The future has become truly unpredictable.

Key point

This trend is also one I have observed in companies, where managements struggle to show humility in the face of technological and societal change and instead seek the "right image" to save face and maintain the illusion of power.

An increasingly complex world

The rise in technology and its ensuing impact have helped build an increasingly complex world. The following points are worth noting:

- The wealth of information exchanged and in circulation worldwide
- Cultural minorities across the world have begun actively demanding the right to citizenship and recognition
- The existence of multicultural and multinational families
- The constant protests against governing authorities, the "elite" and even the system
- The abuse of power by certain leaders in sensitive areas (environment, health care, food, etc.)
- The disconnect between the authorities and voters (a poll conducted in France in 2019 found that only 38% of voters said they had a favourable opinion of elected representatives, while only 26% said they believed the latter took an interest in the concerns of the people)
- The action taken by lobbies to influence policymakers
- The creation of multinational companies with the power and financial reserves to match those of nation states

- The rising quantity of information accessible to people and their awareness of what is at stake (sociological development of the Adult ego state in step with higher levels of education)
- The sharp decline in economic inequality *between* countries, particularly between developed and developing countries since the 1990s (Bourguignon & Morrisson, 2002).
- Meanwhile, we have seen another major shift: after decades of stability, inequalities have been rising again *within* countries in a large number of developed or developing nations.

The world is changing, and this is affecting all of the groups and people living on our planet. The nature of these changes is far from clear, and we need to be very careful when listening to the *horribly simplistic view* taken by those who fail to see the real problems at hand, or the *utopians* who see solutions where there are none; they tend to prolong or exacerbate the conditions they are meant to improve.

Key point

The right attitude to take in the face of complexity is to observe the various influences and tensions at play in a given situation. Taken from the Latin, complexus, *meaning that which is weaved together, complexity is about connecting to something outside our usual perception. Complex thinking helps us understand things and people by considering them from every angle.*

"Impeded" management in the face of rising complexity

There is a strong tendency these days to treat authorities in charge of leading groups with suspicion. The abuses committed by some leaders have brought discredit upon all of the others. However, and while the unethical behaviour of some leaders is deeply regrettable, a large majority of them work to the benefit of both the group and its members: in my experience, they do their best.

As facilitators working in groups, we need to be careful not to "run with the pack" by taking a suspicious stance without first analysing the situation. Indeed, it has been my experience it is more the case that management is *impeded* from doing its job. Legitimate authorities must first negotiate their programmes and investments with the company's Board of Directors. After this often arduous phase, they need to get those in charge of conducting the plans to agree.

The first impediment lies with group members. Indeed, a whole raft of negotiations, consultations and associations are widely encouraged to ensure decisions are put into action. However, listening to the various points of view about how to do something, and the meaning of that activity, leads to frustration on all sides over at least part of the programme, and this feeling of dissatisfaction tends to become widespread. A second impediment stems from the fact that the group is confronted with an external administrative and legal system that slows decision-making to avoid legal challenges that may jeopardise the group. There is also a social injunction to conform. Many companies will say they are functioning at a level they have not in fact reached. Companies which claim to be agile, free, sociocratic and employing other sophisticated organisational structures are often employing a form of green washing. I sometimes call these groups "watermelons" (green on the outside and red on the inside). This too is a form of impediment.

Too often we forget that the authorities governing a group are in charge of its survival and that they must therefore ensure the economic and social model used is viable. This is the "accounts reporting test" to which all authorities are subjected, and which can potentially result in their dismissal.

Key point

I have observed a general sociological trend towards the mistrust of legitimate authorities, as if members needed to "keep tabs" on their behaviour. In reality, it seems to me that groups on the whole are instead experiencing impediments in making decisions and in putting these into action while paying a heavy price in terms of the energy spent conforming to social norms and to administrative and legal systems which at times set excessive regulatory milestones for societies, groups and companies.

Humanism revived by OK-ness

In light of these reflections, I would agree with Edgar Morin's thinking on *Revived Humanism* (Morin, 2019), in which he talks about "regenerated" humanism. While authorities and institutional rules may guarantee freedom and justice in general, there is no such provision for the OK/OK position and relationships, and yet these lay the foundations for the respect and acceptance of others that make Humanism a reality. OK-ness has its roots in the most intimate part of human nature, as Berne so well describes. It cannot be dictated. A fundamental sense of OK-ness allows us to forge existential, psychological and social stances over which we have a certain amount of power.

Revived Humanism goes beyond the declaration of human rights, which is necessary but insufficient. It means we have to steer human energy in four specific directions:

1 Awareness of one's self, one's dignity and one's *OK-ness*, so as to satisfy our hunger for stimulation, thus ensuring our own survival
2 Capacity to form privileged relationships: *I am OK, you are OK*, so as to satisfy our hunger for recognition and self-confidence
3 Awareness that we belong to a group that satisfies our hunger for structure: *I am OK/We are OK*
4 Awareness that we belong to the human race (the biggest system of all): *We are all OK*.

It is my view that these four pillars form an educational framework that serves all humans and that we should include them in school curricula and the inclusion programmes used for integrating new members into groups. Working on these pillars leads to an awareness of personal responsibility, just as children learn from their parents.

Key point

In preparing for successful intervention or work we suggest creating "OK-ness bubbles", either within a group or sub-groups or between groups and, obviously, people. This means spurring the members of a group to gradually take on board the four pillars described previously. The contract is indispensable but not sufficient: it needs to be supplemented with work on developing OK-ness.

The facilitator's stance in tensional TA

People often ask me *how* this is done. I will paraphrase Edgar Morin's maxim: *When we do not live the way we think, we condemned ourselves to think the way we live.*

Individual stance

Depending on the type of issues at hand, we can adopt various roles (experts, architect or trainer, coach or adviser, catalyst). In support of each of these roles, the facilitator can pay *special attention* to:

- *Results*, which means seeking to improve that which is produced, the group's financial results
- *Process*, that is, how these results are obtained and how to optimise this (e.g. addressing power plays to free up more energy, dealing with imbalances in boundary tensions to make them more secure)
- *Our inner stance* vis-à-vis the situation. A transactional analyst obviously thinks from an OK/OK position. This is important if we decide to look at the situation as an expression of tensions, that is, as a problem to be solved or a skill to be learned. For instance, a manager's domineering attitude is not necessarily pathological, even though it might be experienced as unpleasant.

In Tensional TA, I suggest exploring our frame of reference and our internal state with respect to the situation at hand. As Scharmer (2012) explains, we need to expand our internal awareness in three ways:

1 *Suspending* our usual thought patterns, just as when we sit down to mediate and watch things from a different point of view (nothing is happening in this case). This gives us a fresh outlook on the world, as one made up of objects which are external to us as an observer.

2   *Redirecting* our attention inwards instead of outwards, as if the observer is somehow caught up in what he or she observes. This opens up a gap in the boundary between the observer and the observed.
3   *Letting go:* when we enter the world of silence, we let go of our old thought patterns and begin resonating with that which could potentially happen.
4   I would add a fourth movement, one which is characteristic of OK-ness: *Wanting the best* for everyone (the group), both others and oneself, in other words, what we could call an internal empathic stance or an OK/OK position.

Adjusting the group imago: a question of communication?

Facilitating change in a top management team is a tricky exercise. There are a host of ways of doing so, depending on the contract, the level of urgency, the different intervention methods, the facilitators' personalities and so forth.

The main pitfall that must be avoided, in my experience, is what I call "star-shaped" working, where the facilitator works with each individual one by one in front of the rest of the team. While this way of working may be partially effective, it often triggers people's defence mechanisms and yields little in the way of collective results.

I have found that working "via the group" can be a more powerful solution. Each person works on a specific subject except that, here, the facilitator operates in a "circular" fashion, enabling underlying beliefs to emerge without castigating people and developing respect for their differences. This is a decisive stage in envisioning a way of working together beyond the social roles and behaviours expected of us (in TA, we call this authenticity and intimacy in professional relationships).

José Grégoire (TSTA-P) has written a summary of Eric Berne's first conference on Social Psychotherapy (1977) in which Barnes introduces Bateson's perspective (Bateson, 1997). He reminds us of the radical new epistemology brought by cybernetics, namely, circularity. G. Barnes invites us to resume the dialogue with cybernetics started by Berne in Paris (Bern, 1950).

The concept of circularity stems from systemic approaches and notably applies to complex systems, not to mention living organisms and human systems (political, economic, social, banking, corporate systems, etc.).

To paraphrase Alain Désert (2018), the presence of a large number of elements in interaction, of numerous feedback loops, makes it difficult to distinguish between the cause and effect of a phenomenon or of the change in a process. This is because the effect has a retroactive impact on the cause, thereby confusing these two factors and making it difficult, if not impossible, to say what was the cause of what. We are no longer dealing with linear or direct causalities but with circular causalities, reminiscent of a loop; there is no beginning and no end, cause and effect merge into one.

This is an interesting, useful and effective concept, enabling change to be effected starting from several opposing frames of reference and working towards a more global, co-constructed vision that takes into account dynamics, fluctuations, amplifications, perpetual change, cycles, disruptions, divergence and sometimes chaos. It provides a way to recognise human diversity and devise an ecosystem in which to host that diversity (what I call "bubbles of OK-ness").

Applying circular working in a team

Preparations

1. Let members get settled into the space provided, to get an initial mapping of the system. Only then do the facilitators sit down.
2. Session context and contract: Remind the group of the context bringing everyone together and of the "social contract" (simple rules and principles prevailing in the team).
3. Ensure contact is established with all three ego states of each participant: this takes more time during a first meeting and is necessary at every meeting.
4. Explore the issue to be addressed (problem):

    4.1 Is there a referring person (someone who recommended us)?
    4.2 Concrete search (for the symptom):

    - *What is happening?*
    - *How long has this been going on?*
    - *How did it start?*
    - *What was happening in your environment at the time?*
    - *What have you done about it so far? And with what results?*

5. Problem: symptom to problem

    5.1 *Ask each member: how is the symptom a problem?*
    5.2 *And how do you feel about it? What do you experience when it happens?*
    5.3 The facilitator asks questions and reformulates:

    - *As far as I understand it, this irritates you: is that right?*
    - *Yes, that's right.*
    - *How does feeling irritated pose a problem for you at this time?*

6. Objectives

    6.1 In terms of the problem identified: *what would they like to do and what would the team be like if the problem were solved?*
    6.2 *What would each member like to change to make things better?*
    6.3 *Are there things worth changing in the system?*
    6.4 *What was the system like before the problem arose?*

Key point

- *Everything we are working on here leads to assumptions about the system.*
- *One of the purposes of the symptom is to prevent us from "realising" what would happen if we dropped the underlying belief.*

Circular transactions

1. Invite the members of the group to talk to one another instead of to the facilitator.

    - *Could you tell him or her directly instead of talking to me?*
    - *How do you feel when you hear that?*

2. Act out the problem: play a part rather than talk about it.
Personally, I use sculpture-based techniques developed in family therapy. The aim is to put together a team in a given space.
3. The *pas de trois*.
Work with all members of the team, for instance:

    - *What is the director doing while his or her deputy is working with you and you are unable to gain their respect?*

We work with circular questions giving transactional answers.

Circular techniques

- **Each member is invited to talk about how he or she sees the relationship** between two other members of the group (this technique involves exploring all of the relationships in the group). One person discusses the relationship between two or more people. Example question:

    - *What do you think about the fact that Mrs X is still working with Mr Z?*
    - *How does the Chief Executive handle this problem?*

The questions imply a "broad" answer.

- **Specific behavioural transactions**

    A member is asked to discuss the relationship between two other members based on specific behavioural transactions (i.e. based on a specific fact).

For instance: *How does your colleague react when the CEO no longer wants to listen to questions that have not been prepared?*

- **Pluses and minuses**
  - *Who is the most affected by these issues?*
  - *Who is the least concerned?*
  - *Who can deal with this difficulty more easily?*

Key point

When a system's boundaries are blurred, members are unable to answer these questions because doing "that" would bring differences to light. This phenomenon therefore provides an element for analysis via a feedback loop positing the assumption of a boundary deficit.

- **Before and after**
  - *How were things before?*
  - *How will things be afterwards?*

Key point

These circular techniques put pressure on transactions and thereby shed light on the issues, and often the games, present in the system.

The information gathered in this way helps us prepare our intervention.

Our task will be to modify transactions by taking a co-construction approach. A solution generated by the team itself will have more lasting power: the facilitator will simply have played the role of catalyst.

Conclusion

Force Field TA can provide a useful perspective for those seeking to restore the balance of tensions within and between groups and enable people to work in the best psychological and social conditions possible.

This is possible with existing TA concepts and also with future theoretical developments. We have already devised a number of new concepts, such as the 12 tensions within groups, a questionnaire highlighting the composite characteristics of a group and exercises enabling facilitators to develop their Adult awareness and OK-ness during interventions. We can add the notion of a boundary zone and the conditions for its use, the seven factors impeding authority and so forth.

As we reach the end of this chapter, a host of outstanding questions remain:

- Can the notion of a boundary zone also apply to internal group boundaries?
- Can ego states also be said to have boundary zones?
- Is the TA approach useful in dealing with tensions within and between countries?
- Can the definition of groups as composite entities help pacify relations between a country's different sub-groups?
- Is it time to start teaching OK-ness in schools?

References

Anzieu, D. (1981). *Le groupe et l'inconscient. L'imaginaire Groupal*. Paris: Dunod.
Anzieu, D. (1985). *Le Moi-peau*. Paris: Dunod.
Badie, B., & Foucher, M. (2017). *Vers un monde néonational?* Paris: CNRS Editions.
Barnes, G. (1997). A Story About Telling Stories: Introducing Bateson's "Epistemology of Organizations". *Transactional Analysis Journal*, 27(2), 134–137.
Bern, E. (1950). Concerning the Nature of Communication in Intuition and Ego States. *San Francisco: TA Press*, 1977, 49–65.
Berne, E. (2005). *Structure et dynamique des organisations et des groupes*. Paris: Editions d'Analyse transactionnelle.
Bourguignon, F., & Morrisson, C. (2002). Inequality Among World Citizens: 1820–1992. *American Economic Review*, 92(4).
Comte-Sponville, A. (2013). *L'Amour en quatre leçons de philosophie*, Amour & Bonheur DVD. Paris: Editions Montparnasse.
Conche, M. (1986). *Héraclite, Fragments*. Paris: Presses Universitaires de France.
Csikszentmihalyi, M. (1990). *Flow: The Psychology of Optimal Experience*. New York: Harper & Row.
Désert, A. (2018). Agora Vox, May. www.agoravox.fr.
Dubet, F. (2018). Preface: Déclin et retour des frontières. In F. Dubet (ed.), *Politiques des frontières*. Paris: La Découverte, pp. 5–27.
Ellul, J. (1962). *Legal Historian, Sociologist and Protestant Theology. Propagandes.* Malakoff: Economica-Armand Colin Ed.
Evrard, B. (2017). *Question de frontières, AAT N° 157–2017/1*. Paris: Cairn Editions.
Foucault, M. (1984). Des Espaces autres, Presented at the Cercle d'études architecturales conference on 14 March 1967. *Architecture, Mouvement, Continuité*, 5, 46–49.
Janet, P. (1867). *Le cerveau et la pensée*. Paris: Ed. Germer Baillère.
Joseph, I. (2002). Erving Goffman et la microsociologie. *Philosophies*. Paris: PUF.
Le Drouin, N. (2017). *Dictionnaire amoureux de la Vie*. Paris: Plon.
Lewin, K. (1946). Frontiers in Group Dynamics: Concept, Method and Reality in Social Science; Social Equilibria and Social Change. *Human Relations*, 1, 5–40.
Mintzberg, H. (1982). *Structure et dynamiques des Organisations*. Paris: Editions d'Organisation.
Moïso, C., & Guichard, M. (1988). *Séminaire de Psychologie Clinique*. Besançon: Université de Besançon.

Morin, E. (2019). *La Fraternité, Pourquoi?* Arles: Acte Sud.
Nathan, T. (2017). *Les Ames Errantes*. Iconoclastes Ed.
Scharmer, O. (2012). *Théorie U, l'essentiel*. Gap: Colligence-Ed. Yves Michel.
Schwartz-Bart, A. (1959). *Le Dernier des Justes*. Paris: Points roman, Le Seuil.
Sloterdijk, P. (2011). *Colère et Temps*. Paris: Ed. Poche.
Von Bertalanffy, L. (1992). *Théorie Générale des systèmes*. Paris: Dunod.
Wilber, K. (2014). *Une théorie du Tout*. Paris: Almora.
Winnicott, D. W. (2005). *Jeu et réalité*. Paris: Gallimard, NRF (*Playing and Reality*, 1971).

6

MANAGING BOUNDARY DYNAMICS

Patrice Fosset

Introduction

The word "succeed" has its origins in the Latin word *uscire*, which has become *uscita* in Italian, a door, the one we open and close according to circumstances. Succeeding evokes a very important ability: to know when and how to open or close the door or, in other words, to know how to manage the processes that open and close a boundary.

Knowing how to manage the interactions between the different components of a system is a key factor to success in leading an organisation. In this chapter we will explore five aspects of boundary dynamics:

1. A quick presentation of the notion of Boundaries, according to Eric Berne
2. An explanation about the notion of Boundary dynamics
3. The characteristics of the healthy system in the light of this dynamic
4. Thoughts about how to intervene in a malfunctioning system
5. Some practical ideas about how to use a diagnosis to implement different types of intervention

The examples come from my 25 years of experience as a transactional analysis (TA) practitioner working in the field of organisations (companies, institutions, associations) particularly in the facilitation of change and the resolution of crisis situations.

Boundaries

In 1990, Iraq invaded Kuwait, which started the Gulf War. Kuwait did not have the means to push back the invader. An international coalition carried this out in order to recreate the original boundary.

Strikers block the entrance to an industrial site and block access to people and goods. The management call the police to free the passage.

In 1973, a "coup d'état" carried out by Augusto Pinochet brought down the Chilean government. The elected president Salvador Allende was killed in an attack on the presidential Palace. A military dictatorship was set up.

In all these examples, we are talking about Boundary dynamics.

The paradoxical dimension of a boundary

A boundary limits space (geographic, cultural, economic, social). It could be defined as a space which separates and differentiates. It indicates a distance between human, political and linguistic systems. It is a meeting zone, a place of exchange as well as a place where all kinds of tensions occur. It is a zone of contact between separate spaces. It can be open or closed, with several variables ranging from totally closed (a bunker) to totally open (a sieve), with different possibilities for entering or leaving. As a key stage in human development, separation is a founding act. It is the same thing in the case of systems or groups. It is also a way to reply to one of our fundamental needs, that of structure.

What is a boundary in transactional analysis terms?

In TA, we use the term "boundary" either for a person (the boundaries of our ego states) or for a system (the system's boundaries). It is a notion which refers to biology: Cells are surrounded by a membrane. A second internal membrane enables the nucleus of the cell to be contained. The membrane contains elements which form a living system which is complete and coherent and which interacts with its environment. The concept of boundary makes explicit what is inside a system and what is outside a system.

For example, in a company, what is "inside" is the management team but also all the employees in the company; what is "outside" (the environment) are suppliers, customers, partners, competitors. This concept enables us to study the exchange processes between what is inside and what is outside, taking into account that there are pressures which are exerted between the elements on the inside or on the outside.

Structural analysis: three types of boundaries

Eric Berne talks about three types of boundaries:

1 The External Boundary: it separates elements belonging to the group (the members) from the external elements (the environment).
2 The Major Internal Boundary: it distinguishes between the members who represent authority (the management) and the members belonging to working teams (the employees).
3 The Minor Internal Boundary: it allows us to identify groups living inside the system. For example, departments, teams or identity groups.

This concept of Boundary offers a representation of material or immaterial, visible or invisible realities. It makes it possible to clarify identities, important roles, places and functions in the heart of a system. Even when we are not a member of a system, we can feel we "belong" to this system. Or, we can be a member of a system, and not have any feeling of "belonging" at all.

A boundary can be visible and material

- The separation between two countries with a material boundary and the presence of customs officers
- An enclosure with walls in a medieval city, walls of a prison, the implantation of a factory, the closed space of a nuclear power station
- The location of the departments in industrial or administrative buildings, the different floors, the sales department, the accounting department, the production department, the dispatch department
- The walls separating individual offices, each person has their own office, their own cupboard
- The appropriate clothing according to different jobs or specific professions

Boundaries can be immaterial

- Languages, nationalities and race can create boundaries between people
- Social status: the boss/the management/the employees, with or without qualifications, origins and regional affiliation

Social advantages in one group of workers can be different from another group; for example, working hours, retirement age.

The system can be simple or complex

Figure 6.1 Examples of representations of a simple system

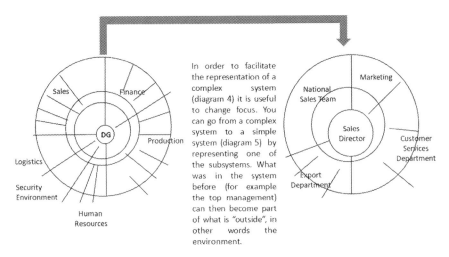

Figure 6.2 Examples of a complex system

Why are diagrams and visual representations useful?

Let's imagine a management team during a work session. One of the members presents his vision of a strategic project. The project is complex – it involves several members of the company but also exterior partners. The project will have an impact on the companies' strategic environment. The diagrams proposed by Eric Berne help to clarify individual representations when faced with the complexity of a system, to understand the different levels involved so that everybody can find their place in the system (inside or outside, in the leadership zone or in the members zone, in one department or another, in several places of the system). They offer the possibility to create and to share a common framework reference to the group. Are we talking about the same thing? Are we all in agreement about the vision of our company, of our organisation, of the places occupied by each person? Who is the sponsor? Where should we intervene? Who is going to do what, for whom? What are we going to deliver?

Marking boundaries is a process which helps to share representations between one person and another. It helps to clarify contents (what are we talking about exactly?). Problem zones will be identified more easily (who is concerned by what?). What are the pressures created by the resolution of the problem, and who will have to endure them? With this sort of approach, it is possible to construct a logical and coherent intervention programme.

The boundary dynamic

Building a wall to mark a boundary isn't a new concept. The Great Wall of China is nearly 2000 years old. On the night of August 12 to 13, 1961, what would become one of the physical symbols of the Cold War was erected in the middle of Berlin: the Berlin Wall. On the other hand, Europeans have worked hard to open their boundaries to facilitate free circulation of people and goods.

This brings us to the concept of Boundary dynamics. It is a question of identifying where and how information circulates. It gives us visibility about the quantity and quality of the energy being exchanged between the different zones. This concept also shows us what tensions and balances are in play: how easy exchanges are, or, on the contrary, what conflicts, cooperation or blockages, respect of specific spaces or, on the contrary, rejection of the latter, fights and different pressures.

Here are some examples of Boundary dynamics in a company:

- From the environment, customers put pressure on the group at the External Boundary in order to obtain better prices or delivery times.
- Employees put pressure on the Major Internal Boundary on members of the management team in order to obtain better salaries or better work conditions.
- The sales department can put pressure on the production department in order to obtain shorter delivery times (dynamic at the Internal Minor Boundaries).

Definitions of boundary dynamics

What we are talking about here is the adaptive response given by a group or by a part of a group to pressure. This definition is inspired by work carried out on stress by Hans Seyle, an endocrinologist who gave a description of the organism's adaptation in order to tolerate the consequences of natural or surgical trauma. The two keywords proposed by Eric Berne are Pressure and Response. It is also possible to talk about transactions (stimulus/response) of economy in the exchange sense – from the outside to the inside/from the inside to the outside. These processes create, de facto, a permanent power relationship, tension between elements inside and elements outside, with a circulation which is more or less free, with energies which are more or less controlled. The elements that circulate – information, stimuli, goods, riches, people, ideas, values, know how. The condition which makes exchanges possible is that the Boundary should be open enough. If the Boundary is too open, it is no longer possible to quantify exchanges and even less possible to control them. If the Boundary is too closed, there are no more exchanges and information no longer circulates.

Dynamic at the external boundary

I propose to look at three examples from the world of economics. In the first example, the company Textilo sees its market collapsing. Customers find equivalent products 30% cheaper from a new Asian competitor. Textilo's management decide to react: they find new investors, they invest massively in new material which greatly improves productivity, the research and development department proposes new materials which are more resistant and the logistics department sets up a plan to improve its services. The customers return and the company is saved.

In the second example, the Primo group launch a takeover to buy out a competitor. Primo's original shareholders join forces to stop the takeover of their company.

The third example comes from the paper industry: the invention of carbonless paper (introduction of beads of ink inside the paper fibres) lead to the closing down of the factories which manufactured carbon paper and the copy paper.

Completely naturally and almost continuously, the external environment puts pressure on a system's External Boundary. The group's job is to resist this pressure, at least in order to survive, otherwise to develop. The members' integrity must be preserved (their health and security) as well as the continuity of the group's activity (the reason the group exists). To do that, the group will build and maintain their team cohesion. The members mobilise their energy to serve the "common good". They have to find the most relevant adaptive responses to find the right balance between closing the Boundary, resistance and opening up to the environment. This can of course be applied to all human systems, including countries or nations.

For example, Brexit marks the decision of Great Britain to leave the European Union. The commercial agreements as well as free circulation of goods and people have been questioned. Lebanon opened its boundary to welcome hundreds of thousands of refugees coming from Syria. In 2005 Hurricane Katrina ravaged New Orleans. The region was flooded and the population was not protected quickly enough, which caused the death of 1836 people and the disappearance of 135 others. The survival of a human group (company, institution, nation) depends on the capacity that its members have to find cohesion through unifying projects.

One idea is to reinforce the External Boundary to stop all intrusions which could lead to the weakening of the group, to its deconstruction or even to its destruction.

Another idea: energetically push back any attack or intrusion of one's territory whether it be physical, psychological or symbolic.

Third idea: open up the External Boundary to welcome in riches, strength, support, alliances or resources which will contribute to the health of the system or to its development.

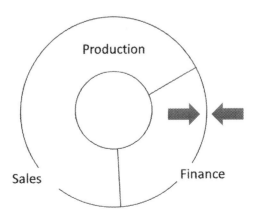

Figure 6.3 Dynamic at the external boundary

What is important is to find the correct way to adapt according to the situation: not too open, not too closed. This means that leaders need excellent knowledge of their environment. Resisting or closing the External Boundary can be either a healthy or a redeeming act. But it can be also very dangerous. Cutting off from the outside world, (rupture) based on a permanent fantasy of aggression, can lead to inward-looking attitudes which can then lead to a process of unsuitable defence against any foreign contribution.

Knowing how to practise a certain openness – at the External Boundary – towards the environment allows one to benefit from the riches from outside, in the same way that it is in the best interests of any national economy to export and import, even if it is more complex and difficult to manage.

The dynamic at the major internal boundary

Spring 2019: the Algerian people rose up against the decision of President Bouteflika to stand once again for election. Under pressure he finally resigned and new elections had to be organised.

In this case, the pressure is on the Major Internal Boundary. This pressure is exerted when members of the system need answers from the leadership. Demands can include subjects like security, the presence of leadership, the legitimacy of power, the buying power of the members, quality of services that they can use and their job security.

When the needs of members are not taken into account, agitation is the result. This agitation can translate into socio-political movements, which can be more or less violent. At Inferno, justified complaints about harassment led the shareholders to "let the leader go". A simple request can become a demand which can lead to a strike or even to violent acts against figures of authority, particularly when such a situation lasts for a long time, such as what happened in France with the Gilets Jaunes movement, a movement which led the government to take economic measures in order to reply to their demands. On the other hand, the leadership can also put pressure on its members across the major internal boundary in order to obtain a certain number of things: respect for rules, conformity to security norms, participation and commitment from the members to the life of the community, production activities. This happened in Textilo: after a series of accidents on the production site the management set up a security plan which imposed strict security rules which had to be respected by all the members of staff.

When the governing body is considered to be oppressive, after a period of over-adaptation, the members are also likely to become agitated, which will be more or less repressed depending on the determination of the power in situ. If the leadership does not react, the power can be overthrown. In the same way, a lack of presence of one or several leaders coupled with a lack of authority can generate agitation.

Agitation can also come from a group of managers, from a union or from members who want to take over from the leader or replace the present leader.

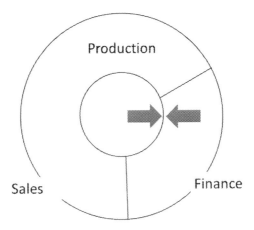

Figure 6.4 Dynamics at the Major Internal Boundary

On the other hand, when members feel secure, when they see their leaders as legitimate, present and efficient and with recognised authority, when there is a good balance between the capacity to take risks and the protection of each member and when the support departments carry out their role correctly, there will be a sense of cohesion.

Dynamics at the minor internal boundary

At Centralcom, a call center, planning holidays creates a lot of tension. There is a lot at stake. Employees who have children want to have priority over those who do not have any children. In this example, tensions arise at one of the immaterial minor internal boundaries, between two distinct groups. Each subsystem (unit, corps, department, clan) has to fight for its own demands and defend what is at important for its own role and place in the system. These issues can create tensions which are more or less strong (conflict of interest, conflicts about the direction to take, about deadlines, budgets, values, behaviour or results). These tensions can also come from the different cultures of the people involved or between professional cultures. A well-known example is the tension between the sales culture and the accountancy culture.

These dynamics can come from power games, from the intrigue between departments or between members of a department. When the sales department puts pressure on the production department in order to speed up deadlines, you might think it is a healthy intervention. But you have to be careful that is does not turn into furious, destructive competition. Engineers from a large university can be in conflict with engineers who have had only in-house training.

MANAGING BOUNDARY DYNAMICS

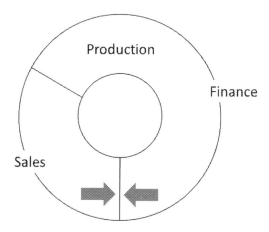

Figure 6.5 The dynamic at the internal miner boundary

The leaders' responsibility is to regulate such dynamics. Mediation is sometimes necessary as it reminds people of why they are there, of the rules, of contracts and of the other commitments they each have.

When these tensions are not regulated at all, or if it is done badly, the following phenomena are possible: criticism or attacks of one group or another. An absence of cooperation or retention of information. Closing down of boundaries and trench wars. Games of alliances, intrigues and conspiracies. On the other hand, when regulation is carried out well by the leaders, tensions are alleviated, and subgroups can put in place methods to cooperate efficiently.

The characteristics of a healthy system versus boundary dynamics

In the board of directors in the company Successtory, Mr. Boss, the leader, has been trained in TA for many years. When he welcomed new members onto the board, Mr. Boss wanted to remind everybody of the principles which led to the success of his company. And this is a summary of what he would say:

The dynamic (opening/closing) at the external boundary

Our success is directly linked to our capacity to identify, read and understand the strategic elements in our environment. This is how we build our vision, and therefore our short-term, mid-term strategy. We dare to fight back when we are under attack. At the same time, we have to make our offer understandable to our environment: Who we are, our values, our culture, our "savoir faire", our added value in the eyes of the environment.

Our practices are based on clear ethics and allow us to draw up clear contracts with the strategic elements in our environment, in other words, our customers, our suppliers and all other types of partners. We have determined the areas to which we are committed together. That is why we are able to use all our energy, assemble and organise our strengths, in order to respond in the right way, adapt to different kinds of pressure, and even to stand up to attacks and other attempts to destroy our group. Finally, we have shown our capacity to develop by creating added value and therefore creating riches (human social, technological or financial) for us and for our environment.

Key point to remember

Knowing how to match up what is on the inside (who we are) and what is on the outside (the strategic elements in our environment) to build a clear vision is essential.

The dynamic (opening/closing) at the major internal boundary

Inside the company, the same process of shared commitment (contracts) has been implemented between us (all the management) and the employees who are members of the company. Based on a clear vision, we have learnt to apply our strategy (whether it be short-, mid- or long-term). In real terms, these are action plans, with precise and shared objectives. We are proud to have been able to make our strategy visible and understandable as well as explaining what is at stake, to all of the members of our group.

We regularly adapt our organisation so that it can be efficient, we put in place the skills we need and we draw on our values, which are linked to the professional culture of our group.

We have developed tools so that the resources needed for each project are made available. We use the collective intelligence and the creativity of our employees.

We have the courage to listen to expectations and needs and we know how to say no, in order to say yes in a stronger way, to legitimate demands.

Key point to remember

Knowing how to embody the zone of authority in its different forms (institutional, organisational, operational, psychological) to allow the vision to be realised, by adapting the means by which this is done, in order to obtain the desired results, is important.

The dynamic (opening/closing) at the minor internal boundary

Regarding the dynamic between different departments, we are careful to apply the same philosophy regarding mutual commitment, using clear contracts and rules of conduct between members to make it easy to get on well with each other. We make sure that everyone knows the rules, that they make sense and that they are applied. We make sure that any infringement of these rules is followed by a sanction. We have set up a process to welcome new recruits to make sure they are well integrated. We try to eliminate superfluous meetings, but we encourage working time which favors cooperation and problem solving through creativity. The members should get to know each other, know who does what, and feel useful and recognized by the system. The management is trained to deal with the tensions than can arise between members (between departments, between entities in the system, between groups). Our support departments are essential for managing internal processes (how we work together) and external processes (how we work with the elements in our environment). They provide all the necessary means so that those who produce can work properly and they act as regulators and facilitators in the different processes.

Key point to remember

Knowing how to make contracts at all levels and regulate different internal and external processes, whether they be relational, financial or organisational, by relying on efficient support departments is a guarantee of success.

Questions to ask before any intervention

We will call "facilitator" any person who is responsible for dealing with one or more dysfunction in a system. When dysfunctional dynamics emerge, questions should be asked concerning **what to do** and **who is going to do it**.

I will now explain two types of facilitator: Mr. Externo and Mr. Interno.

The facilitator's position

The first question the facilitator may ask is linked to his place in the system: Am I inside the system, or am I outside?

Mr. Externo is a consultant who specialises in organisational change management. He uses TA as a tool to support his work. He has been contacted by Mr. Problemo, the owner of Textilo, and has been asked to intervene, in order to facilitate the resolution of several issues that are worrying Mr. Problemo. Mr. Externo is outside the system. He is part of the environment and has been called in as an expert. In his professional capacity, he might ask himself the following questions: Why me? Did someone recommend me? Am I here by chance?

As for Mr. Interno, he is part of the system. He is also an expert and he masters TA. The difference is that he is inside the system. He will be either in the leadership zone (the leader or a member of the management team) or in the membership zone. Several situations can arise concerning the Boundary dynamic:

- The problem exists in the system to which the facilitator belongs (e.g. a technical problem linked to computer software, pressure that the manager sees as excessive, a decrease in activity, tensions between people in the team, tensions between the manager and a team member, absenteeism).
- The problem exists in a department near Mr. Interno's department (e.g. lack of cooperation between departments, organisational changes in a department close by, tensions between departments, rumors)

In each case, Mr. Interno will be asking himself the same questions as Mr. Externo, concerning his legitimacy, his authority and the terms of his intervention. But belonging to the system can create particular difficulties for the person who belongs to the system in how to keep the right distance and a neutral position in order to carry out the intervention efficiently. This should lead to a certain vigilance before carrying out any intervention in a system to which one belongs.

The role of the consultant: in what capacity will he carry out this intervention?

Our two consultants could ask themselves the same questions concerning their role. What is expected of me? How am I perceived? Who are they asking to intervene? The technician, the expert (of what?)? The sociologist? The psychologist? The coach? The counsellor? The mediator? The doctor? The healer? The miracle worker? The rescuer? The guru?

The authority to intervene: in what capacity and with what legitimacy will he intervene?

This question demands reflection on the part of our facilitators (internal or external) on several levels:

- The level of *competence*: what sort of skills, what sort of know-how is needed?
- The level of *authority*: who has the power, and where is it situated, in order to take the necessary decisions about what is at stake? Will the person who has the power be sufficiently involved in the contract to take the right decisions each time it is necessary?

- The level of *legitimacy* in order to take action: what legitimacy does the consultant give to himself, and what legitimacy do the system and its members credit him with?
- The level of *energy*: the bigger the system, the more energy will be exerted at the Boundaries. A single consultant cannot "contain" all this energy alone. It is therefore important to face the system which is being accompanied with a "consultant's system", in other words, a team of consultants (one system facing another).

The intervention contract, or how to intervene on a contractual basis

Whether you are inside or outside the system, any intervention with the objective of resolving a problem linked to Boundaries will need the implementation of one or several, two party or three party or several party, contracts. The terms of the contract will define the perimeter of the intervention: the role and the position or the different actors involved, expectations, means.

Here are some examples of questions to ask, or to ask oneself, in order to set down clearly the ingredients in the contract:

- Who is complaining about this situation? In what terms is the problem discussed?
- Who is asking for the situation to be dealt with? What result are they looking for?
- What is at stake? What would happen if the problem is not resolved?
- What is the perimeter of the intervention? Is it a team or a department? (e.g. the sales team). Is it several departments (e.g. all the production departments)? Is it the whole organisation (the whole company)? The use of diagrams is essential at this stage of the intervention.
- Which actors are involved? If decisions have to be made that involve changes (organisation, recruitment, departures, investments), will the deciders be committed to doing so? How?
- What means will be attributed to this mission? (cost, length of the intervention, hours allocated, people mobilised, premises and material provided, all kinds of information supplied)

Here we can emphasise the conditions for a contract to be valid:

- The contractual object is legal and respects the laws which are outside and inside the system (including its culture).
- The different parties have the competence to engage in the contract.
- The payment is correct, which is reflected by deciding who is paid, when, how much and in exchange for what
- The different parties are all in agreement about carrying out the contract.

Where to start?

The first and most important task for the consultant is to carry out his diagnosis. This *clinical approach* comes from the theories of Juliette Favez-Boutonnier. In etymological terms, this means, *leaning over the patient*. Leaning over the *client's system* is essential in order to dissociate the symptom from the problem. What looks like a dysfunction is likely to be the symptom (the expression of the problem) and not the problem itself (the cause of the symptom). Organisations commonly tend to deal with the symptom.

The following are three typical examples:

In the last eighteen months, three human resources managers have been dismissed for incompetence or failing to reach results. The real problem is that the perimeter of the post has been badly defined, the human resources managers have not been able to find their real place and have not been able to succeed under these conditions.

A sales team is losing steam. The sales director, with good intentions, organises a team building event planned by an outside consultant in order to re-motivate everyone. Nothing changes. The real problem is that their products are facing competition from new technology which, in their client's opinion, is better and cheaper. Conclusion: dealing with the symptoms does not solve the problem.

Intervene with authority

In our experience, the authority of a transactional analyst resides in several key skills. He knows how to put into play all three ego states (Parent, Adult, Child). He knows how to change a complaint into a request which will then become a contract. He diagnoses the problem before intervening. In order to do that, he has several relevant guides at his disposal, one of which is Berne's theory of organisations. He tries to adopt and maintain an Ok posture towards the system and its members. His work and his different interventions are regularly supervised. He masters the different tools he uses in his interventions.

Intervene?

Imagine you are Mr. Externo. You are a consultant who uses TA. You are now facing Mr. Problemo who works for Textilo. Here we invite you to listen to how Mr. Problemo might present the difficulties he is facing. And to discover how Mr. Externo builds up his approach in three stages: the diagnosis based on the symptoms, the link between the symptoms and the underlying problems and finally the potential solutions that could be envisaged to solve the problems that have been identified.

To facilitate this presentation and clarify the methods used, we have divided it into three parts: the dysfunction linked to the dynamic at the External Boundary, those linked to the Major Internal Boundary and those linked to the Minor Internal Boundaries.

From the diagnosis to the problem resolution

In this part, I was inspired by Gilles Pellerin's article on rapid diagnosis. His work consisted of establishing a link between the works of E. Fox and the concept of time structuring. I use this to draw up a rapid diagnosis based on the Boundary dynamic.

The dynamic at the external boundary: too open or too closed

What symptoms might be presented by Mr. Problemo? *We are losing market shares, our turnover is decreasing, our Velour range which we have been so proud of for 15 years, is selling less and less, we are being suffocated by our competitors.*

Based on the symptoms presented, Mr. Externo will then explore several potential solutions (probable causes). All of them are linked to the dynamic at the External Boundary, therefore, with the company's environment.

- *"Head in the sand" policy*: Are Mr. Problemo and his teams refusing to see what is happening in the environment? When no system has been set up to keep an eye on the environment, the result is a lack of vision.
- *Entrenched military camp*: Is Mr. Problemo refusing any cooperation with other strategic elements in his environment? He might imagine that he has the capacity to master and control everything, remaining closed to any kind of alliance, exchange or partnership. Isolating himself in this way, he is depriving himself of precious information as well as of help and support. Is Mr. Problemo refusing to introduce new technology which is essential to the survival of his company?
- *To live happily, you have to hide away*: According to company culture, founded by Mr. Problem's great grandfather, this was the family motto. We do not show ourselves, which means that the company's skills, its specificities, are not known to the outside world.
- *The sieve*: Is confidential information about company life being communicated to the outside world? Mr. Externo will ask if the sales team sometimes talk to their customers about the difficulties that the company is experiencing, or if they complain about their management. Or does a department manager sometimes openly criticise another department in front of an institution which is exterior to the company?
- *The spinning wind vane*: How consistent is Textilo's strategy? A strategy which is inconsistent and constantly changing is likely to lose its partners, who no longer have a stable reference on which to base their own orientations.

Depending on his answers, Mr. Problemo could study different possible options which might lead to one or several corrective actions (ways to resolve the problems which were discussed). Let's start by identifying the strategic actors in your environment (who do you depend on and who depend on you?). Let's define the strengths and weaknesses of your organisation (using, for example, the SWOT model). What are the best ways to respond to the needs and expectations expressed by the strategic actors in your environment? How would you now define your vision, and what strategy will follow from this? Will it be important to build partnerships? How are you going to monitor outside developments? What kind of communication is needed to explain to your customers any important changes in your strategy? What rules of confidentiality are you going to put into place, and how are you going to guarantee that they are respected?

The dynamic at the major internal boundary: too open or too closed, too much or not enough pressure

In this case, here are the words that Mr. Problemo might use to talk about different symptoms linked to the dynamic at the Major Internal Boundary: *We don't seem to be able to retain our employees. Our HR department has noticed a high level of turnover. There is a lot of sick leave. We are having to face strikes. I have noticed the appearance of power games which are trying to overthrow the authority of the management. The decisions made by our staff are always being questioned.*

Together, Mr. Externo and Mr. Problemo will discuss some of the following hypotheses regarding the likely causes of these symptoms:

- *The absent father syndrome*: Is it possible that Mr. Problemo is too distant from his employees? Do they know him? Do they see him regularly, or his he always absent? Does he reply to messages? Does he communicate regarding his intentions, his strategy? Mr. Externo tells Mr. Problemo the following story: *Six months after the departure of a site director who was particularly liked by the workers, they went on strike. What had happened? The new director had never been to say hello to the workers in the production units. They had never seen him because he always used the "main entrance", whereas his predecessor used to come and say hello to them every morning, before "going up to his office".*
- *The tyrant syndrome*: Does Mr. Problemo have a tyrannical management style? Is he one of those people who always has to be right, who cannot stand being contradicted?
- *The Mr. Nice syndrome*: Is Mr. Problemo one of those leaders who always says yes to everybody and makes reckless decisions, then finds himself up to the neck in problems which are impossible to solve?
- *The ivory tower*: Does Mr. Problemo tend to isolate himself, close himself away in his office, managing alone? Does he keep his colleagues at a distance, with nobody knowing what he is going through, what he thinks or what he feels?
- *A lack of direction regarding the strategy or any changes*: The leader does not take care to explain decisions and strategy. The employees do not know the reasons for these changes.

- *Incongruity and incoherence*: Does what Mr. Problemo do contradict what he says? ("Do what I say, but not what I do") Do the answers that Mr. Problemo give "hold water", or do they change according to what the last person to speak says? In both cases, members lose confidence.
- *Withholding of information*: Is this process, which can be a kind of power game, in play between the leader and his teams and vice versa? When information, from the top down or from the bottom to the top, does not flow, the system's energy is blocked and the members cannot work properly. Power belongs to the one who has the information.
- *Lack of confidentiality*: Does Mr. Problemo or the members of the board tend to discuss serious confidential information in the corridors of the company, where everyone can hear them?

Accompanied by Mr. Externo, Mr. Problemo confirms some of the possible solutions discussed in order to get his company out of some of the difficulties he is fighting with.

He decides to be coached, to learn how to find the right dosage when putting pressure on the members of his teams. He understands how important it is to explain to his teams the meaning of his decisions, his choices and his strategy (25). He promises to listen to what is being said to him and take into account the remarks, suggestions and requests made by his members. Mr. Externo explains what the life position "I'm OK, you're OK" is. He wants to develop his ability to find and keep an OK position when he is with his employees. To achieve this, he decides to increase his level of awareness, of himself, of the other person or persons, and become aware of different situations, in order to show congruity and coherence in the way he communicates. He is going to check the quality and efficiency of the messages he sends out, by testing their impact on people he trusts before communicating directly with all his employees. Is it easy to understand what he means? Is the message coherent? Is the way the leader communicates his message congruent? He also realized the distance he keeps in his relations with his teams. He says he wants to be close to them, to respond to their requests and receive the messages that are sent to him. He has gained awareness of the importance of respecting confidential space and time regarding oneself, and to know how to respect them when they are essential. All these things are a way of developing what Eric Berne called the *"psychological leader"*.

The dynamic at the minor internal boundary: too open or too closed, too much or not enough pressure between groups

Mr. Problemo might talk about problems in this way: *As soon as there is a change of strategy, the implementation of a new technique or changes in our company culture, I notice that there are protests and the changes are systematically questioned. I see clans forming, those who are for, those who are against the new projects. Some teams don't want to speak to each other, and everybody does their own thing! I get the impression that the team spirit we had several years ago has disappeared and that any sort of cooperation is no longer possible. I get the feeling that I am in the middle of a school playground. I get the impression that there are sometimes power games, full of intrigue and trapdoors. I notice unhealthy competition; people want to hurt each other. And I also notice a lack of confidentiality in some situations. Some information should stay within the team. There are not many meetings, and when they exist, they are not very productive.*

Mr. Externo offers a few explanations.

You are talking about what Eric Berne described as "psychological games" (26). Three roles are being played: the Persecutor, the Victim and the Rescuer. The aim of a game is to obtain, in an inappropriate way, signs of recognition. Mr. Externo explains that this is very common behaviour: *when there is a change of leadership and/or strategy, each member works in their own corner, waiting for more information to be given about who does what and why (waiting to know "what the future holds").* One last point attracts the attention of Mr. Problemo: *psychological games will focus the attention of the leader on the fact that people's tasks have to be renewed, while at the same time making sure that they know the perimeter of the job, and telling them what the others do, too. In other words, team members will "play" in order to get their leader's attention in order to get answers to their questions, but without daring to ask directly!*

Based on Mr. Externo's analysis, Mr. Problemo will focus on the following improvements: *I am going to take time to check with each department manager that they have understood the reasons behind the changes and that they will be able to explain the organisation's general strategy coherently. I am going to clearly define the tasks that I give to each manager in the form of a mission statement, including clear specifications which will give legitimacy to members of staff to carry out their work based on the general interests of the company. Each time it is necessary, we will explain, or re-explain, the strategy and the meaning of different changes. This will apply to all modifications: the company name, the strategy, company orientations, objectives, internal rules, the organisation, changes in our profession, technology, materials or company culture. We will let people know about all measures that are taken. If it turns out that we have made a mistake in the decisions we have taken, we promise to recognise our mistake and we will rectify it. We will make sure that missions are clear, and we will reconfirm everyone's roles, especially if jobs evolve over time. Job descriptions will be drawn up and modified as soon as it becomes necessary. We will have the capacity to dismiss certain staff members if they do not adhere to one or several of the necessary evolutions we mention here. We will make sure to dedicate structured time and places to organise regulatory sessions to adjust our practices. These meetings will encourage exchange, enable staff to talk about "how we work together" and what each person needs to work correctly. We will make sure that the aim of these meetings is to draw up "cooperation contracts" between staff and between departments.*

Conclusion

What occurred to me while writing this chapter about the dynamics at Boundaries is just how modern Berne is, the founder of transactional analysis. Here, for example, are two examples:

It does not have the same name, but Berne's theory talks about the notion of **agility**, a concept which comes from the world of IT. The whole of Berne's theory on the pressure/response system, on adaptation, therefore on Boundary dynamics, refers to agility, presented as a continual search for a balance between what is active (do and prove that you know how to do), what is reactive (know how to react to changes) and what is proactive (know how to create value). The key is knowing *how to adapt*. This concept can be found in the *agile contract*. Berne had no way of knowing either, that the concept of **contract** which had become a determining factor in TA practice, would become the focus of research which would result, in 2016, in the Nobel Prize for economy given to Olivier Hart and Bengt Holmström for their work on contract theory. Here again, the idea of "incomplete contracts" (O Harts) connects with the concept of the amendment procedure evoked by Berne in his theory.

To conclude, I mention that Berne used the concept of the movement of energy to evoke the pressures and the exchanges which are in play at a system's' boundaries. There is a whole field, which has been little explored up until now, using energy as a specific approach of TA in organizations. Madeleine Laugeri talks about it in her article on emerging change by developing ideas such as planned energy and emerging energy, which lead to three types of contracts (contract of vision, mission and cooperation). But the idea of using energy in systems is a field which remains vast. In my view, this could be considered as a going back to the drawing board since the concept of ego states, born from Berne's observations of the movement of energy between the different ego states of his patients.

References

Berne, E. (1961). *Transactional Analysis in Psychotherapy*. New York: Grove Press, Inc.
Berne, E. (1966). *Principles of Group Treatment*, New York: Grove Press, Inc.
Berne, E. (1972). *What Do You Say After You Say Hello?* New York: Grove Press, Inc.
Berne, E. (1975). *The Structure and Dynamics of Organizations and Groups*. New York: Ballantine Books.
English, F. (1975). The Three-Cornered Contract. *Transactional Analysis Journal*, 5(4).
English, F. (1978). Potency as a Female Therapist. *Transactional Analysis Journal*, 8(4).
Ernst, F. (1973). The OK Corral. *Transactional Analysis Journal*, 1(4), 225–230.
Ernst, F. (2009). The I'm Ok, You're OK Classroom. www.listeningactivity.com/publications/The_I'm_OK_You're_OK_Classroom.pdf.
Goldman, S. L., & Nagel, R. N. (1995). *Agile Competitors & Virtual Organizations: Strategies for Enriching the Customer*. Kenneth Preiss.
Hart, O., & Holmstrom, B. (2010). A Theory of Firm Scop. *Quarterly Journal of Economics*.

Hay, J. (1997). Transactional Mentoring: Using Transactional Analysis to Make a Difference. *Transactional Analysis Journal*, 27(3), 158–167.

James, M. (1986). Diagnosis and Treatment of Ego State Boundary Problems. *Transactional Analysis Journal*, 16(3), 188–196.

Karpmann, S. (1968). Fairy Tales and Script Drama Analysis. *Transactional Analysis Bulletin*, 7, 39–43.

Mintzberg, H. (1979). *The Structuring of Organisations*. Prentice-Hall.

Reddy, M. La formation aux contrats avec le client. *Handbook of T.A. Users* n° 19–22.

Reddy, M. (1979). *Games: The New Approach. The Client*. Handbook of T.A. Users.

Selye, H. (1956). *The Stress of Life*. McGraw Hill.

Steiner, C. (1973). *Scripts People Live. Transactional Analysis of Life Scripts*. New York: Bantam.

Steiner, C. (1987). The Seven Sources of Power: An Alternative to Authority. *Transactional Analysis Journal*, 17(3), 102–104.

7

LEADING THROUGH PEOPLE – MANAGING VULNERABILITY IN WORKING RELATIONSHIPS

Graeme Summers

Introduction

This chapter bring a transactional analysis (TA) lens to the challenge of leading people in complex systems. Berne (1963/1973) defined three boundaries: the external, major and minor boundaries that delineate an organisation. The concept of boundaries provides a useful framework for understanding relationships within a hierarchical context. The overarching humanistic premise in this chapter is that every person brings a mixture of vulnerability and potential to their role and that the former needs to be accepted and managed for the latter to flourish. The nature and expression of vulnerability will vary depending on which boundary (or boundaries) are being navigated and in which direction. Building on Berne's idea of the psychological leader, the notion of the Leadership Vector is proposed. The intention here is to provide a framework for leading through building and maintaining effective relationships across different boundaries whilst accepting vulnerability in the process.

Leadership style downwards

For 21st-century organisations, the notion that leadership operates through centralised command and control has long been usurped by the rise of Transformational Leadership (Bass, 1998). Modern organisations now expect leaders to "engage" colleagues and external stakeholders through relational leadership skills rather than simply attempting to "control" people using positional authority and contingent sanctions or rewards. Involvement in cross-functional projects within highly matrixed organisations often require that the contemporary executive or manager must also lead others through vision, involvement, influence, persuasion and relationship rather than hierarchical position. Either way, the so-called soft skills of personal and professional relationships have moved to the foreground of leadership development to disrupt the idea that just being the boss and giving direction means that you are "leading".

Organisational complexity upwards

This change in leadership style is compounded by the degree of complexity a leader must manage. Often, the larger an organisation, the more complex it becomes. The public structure will usually show numerous levels of hierarchy and subdivisions within each level in addition to networks of cross-functional or regional connections and task groups. Additionally, these structures will dynamically change, with varying pace, in response to internal initiatives and/or shifting external factors. Within such complexity an individual may belong to several teams which will each have their own external work group boundary. In general, higher levels of leadership responsibility usually implies both a broader sense of group or organisational identity and a consideration of longer time frames for organisational development (Jaques, 1997).

Upwardly transitioning leaders often need to go through a process of "identity stretching" in order to step in and step up to the next level (Ibarra, 2015). This may involve moving from being a technical expert to a leader of people and may be especially challenging if those people have a higher or different technical expertise to their own.

Overlapping identities across

Most people also identify themselves, with varying strength of association, to other groups in addition to their job, profession or organisation. The myriad of possibilities, all deeply infused with meaning, include family, community, gender, class, race, political affiliation, national or global citizenship. We are constantly navigating these simultaneous, often overlapping and sometimes conflictual, identities and associated loyalties. If we over identify with one aspect, we may neglect another. We may also be impacted by changing social perceptions. For instance, following the financial crisis in 2007, several executives told me they felt social anxiety about "admitting" they worked for a bank. They experienced loss as their previous social status was now being perceived as a social stigma. These overlapping identities require an additional amount of sensitivity in leadership when managing across boundaries.

Global challenges outwards

A leader must also manage the external pressure and adapt performance to global trends. Zooming out to global trends we see increasing social inequality and looming environmental disaster, both of which will require radical re-organisation of our social and political structures in order to reverse.

Optimistically, if emerging artificial intelligence, robotics and related innovations can liberate us from "work" as we know it today, our sources of connection and purpose may become predominantly social rather than commercial – working for meaning and social contribution rather than money. High-profile business leaders have promoted the idea of universal income in anticipation of this shift (Clifford, 2017). If much of our current work becomes automated leading to mass redundancies, these propositions could be seen as an attempt to dignify equitable distribution of the benefits of our technological advances in contrast to the social stigmatisation currently associated with state handouts or charity. Pessimistically, if technology is used to create more profit for wealthy companies and shareholders with less human resources and/or social contribution, then our technology will continue to outpace our humanity.

Perhaps even more important than concerns about social equity is the pending environmental catastrophe propelled by economic models of growth rather than sustainability. The scientific statistics on this issue are frightening and, even if we get serious about fixing climate change, we may already be too late. Taming our consumer habits and fundamentally redesigning the political and economic engine that drives them may just be too much to bear. Whether organisations acknowledge the significance of these issues or not, they will be significantly impacted. If we do collectively turn this around it will not be without protest, in-fighting, struggle, uncertainty and loss. It will also require leadership that is disruptive, visionary, courageous and empathic.

Leading at every level

The development downwards, upwards, outwards and across boundaries leads to new insights about leadership. Let's zoom in to an individual perspective with the aid of a few theoretical "complexity reducers" (A. de Graaf, personal communication, April 2018) to consider how someone can lead within the context of their role while accounting for their particular opportunities, limitations and relational matrix. Oshry (1999) articulates a "total systems" view of power and suggests it can be exercised from any position in a system that is, top, middle, bottom and customer (or external stakeholder) and that each position will have a unique contribution to make. This echoes Berne's observation that in any given organisational context the psychological leader may not be the appointed responsible leader. Within this frame, using personal power from within or outside of the system to influence others is considered to be an act of leadership even if an individual does not hold an officially recognised leadership position.

For my purpose here, and utilising Berne's classification of boundaries, I will approach the challenge of leading through relationship within an organisational work group, represented in the following (over)simplified figure, largely from the perspective of the individual middle manager.

At the simplest level, Berne represented the public structure of a hierarchical group or organisation as contained within an outer circle (the external boundary) which in turn contains a concentric inner circle (the major internal boundary)

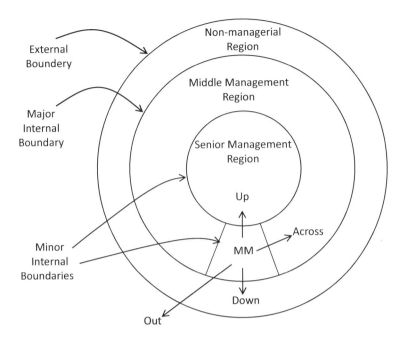

Figure 7.1 Leadership vectors in a work group

that differentiates between the (outer) group membership and the (inner) group leadership regions. He represented further levels of complexity by adding "minor internal boundaries". In the previous diagram, the inner concentric circle is a minor internal boundary that differentiates between senior and middle management. The straight lines either side of a hypothesised middle manager (MM) are minor internal boundaries that differentiate MM from his or her peers at the same management level.

For our fictitious middle manager, four leadership vectors will be considered, each indicated by the straight arrows. The vectors are leading up, leading down, leading across and leading out. Each vector will be explored with consideration of how human vulnerabilities may be experienced and navigated differently.

Leading up

John's contact with Sarah, his manager, was severely disrupted, as was the financial services industry in which they worked following the 2007 financial crisis. He experienced a double whammy of having to respond to chaotic events, some anticipated and others unforeseen, whilst feeling abandoned, as his boss was trying to manage chaos elsewhere. They were both struggling, but it was John who took the initiative to discuss the impact of events on his own sense of security and their working relationship. This small but significant leadership act helped them take stock and create improvised, albeit compromised, ways to stay connected that helped both of them ride the turbulence.

Andrea devised a low-cost technical fix for a machine in her local factory. Her simple innovation unlocked a bottleneck in production that had been creating recurring "downtime" costs that outsourced maintenance engineers had never been able to resolve. Despite her shyness, she documented the process, created a video and got her superior's support to distribute her solution to other factories across the world that were using the same machinery.

Delegates on a training program were outraged when their new regional manager publicly patronised, insulted and threatened individuals and the group as a whole. Concerned about their own negative experience as well as the integrity of the company culture, several delegates made a collective formal complaint which was thoroughly investigated. The new "leader" was subsequently dismissed.

Leading "up" means taking the initiative to innovate, challenge, raise questions or concerns and influence those above us in the hierarchy to change or improve a situation or process. Humans have a staggering capacity to passively obey authority, even when it violates our own moral code (Milgram, 1974). It is as though we are primed to see a "superior" as a nurturing or punitive parental figure rather than as a colleague further up the hierarchy. From a co-creative TA perspective (Summers & Tudor, 2000), our main upwards vulnerability is to act from Child ego states and Victim game roles. Along with Little (2006), I consider that an active Child ego state implicates the presence of an influencing Parent ego state. This occurs in reverse when leading downwards.

Leading upwards (from Adult) may therefore require significant courage to speak up and step up, depending on the circumstances, the issues at stake and "political" forces at play. It means being able to compassionately acknowledge our Child reactions (or potential reactions) and be willing to generate more effective Adult alternatives for engaging with presenting problems or opportunities as demonstrated in the previous examples.

Our sustained capacity to influence upwards also requires that we get respectfully curious about the perspectives and concerns of our "superior" counterpart(s) so that, where possible, our leading "up" initiatives can stimulate constructive dialogue and collaborative solutions through Adult-Adult transactions.

Leading down

A shrinking market due to new and disruptive competitors meant that Jean's company was now cutting costs and had abandoned several planned initiatives. Several of the best performers in Jean's team shared with her thoughts about leaving the company. Her openness in response had persuaded most of them to stay. She acknowledged the external threat and the problems this posed for her trusted employees and shared some of her own concerns about the uncertainty ahead of them. She also said, "I know things are bad but right now nowhere else in our industry is any better. I want you to stay and help us get through this".

Nothing stands still, and most leaders I speak to are initiating, implementing and responding to numerous changes simultaneously. What differentiates change leadership from change management is consideration of people as human beings rather than material resources that can simply be reallocated or dropped according to a change in organisational strategy.

The notions that "people don't resist change, they resist being changed" (Senge, 2006, p. 144) and "what people resist is not change per se, but loss" (Heifetz et al., 2009, p. 22) capture this human dimension. Rock (2008) provides a useful acronym – SCARF – that can help leaders consider the human impact of change initiatives. Even the most clearly presented vision, strategic rationale and positive intent will often be perceived (realistically or otherwise) as a threat to Status, Certainty, Autonomy, Relatedness or Fairness by those affected. These same vulnerabilities can also be experienced and manifest as ambivalence about desired changes. For example, a pending promotion may bring someone new opportunities but also a loss of relatedness to existing colleagues or a loss of identity, confidence and certainty derived from mastering their current position.

Leaders can help by acknowledging and assisting people to navigate these concerns through honest conversations about loss as well as opportunity. Engagement with the next organisational "project" and reorganised structure can happen only if we can let go of the last one. Claire leads a team of scientists in a company laboratory and is surprised at the strength of response she gets to implementing a new (regulatory) directive that test results must now be recorded using pens – "But we've been using pencils for years!" they protested. Obviously, at a technical level, this change is trivial but what Claire came to appreciate was that for this team it had become symbolic for the loss of "our familiar ways of working". This understanding enabled Claire to help people adjust by having conversations about the emotional meaning of this (and other) changes and what the team could do to integrate the new with the old.

In order to create engagement rather than passive compliance, many contemporary leaders are learning how to use a coaching approach with their direct reports. The purpose of coaching is to help someone create and use their own solutions to achieve their goals. The aim here is to stimulate ownership, initiative and accountability for the work someone does through skilful inquiry. Helping a person find or create a meaningful overlap between their personal and professional desires and the expectations, opportunities and limitations of their role is a powerful stimulus to the intrinsic motivation necessary for wholehearted involvement.

Leaders transitioning from a command-and-control mindset can feel vulnerable as they give up (or at least reduce) their more familiar patterns of giving advice or being directive. The main leading downwards vulnerability is to relate defensively using Parent ego states and Persecutor or Rescuer game roles. I encourage leaders to be non-defensive about their defences because this often leads to a paradoxical self-acceptance and willingness to experiment with leading differently. The key transformational difference is the openness to seek and explore the aspirations, thoughts, feelings and ideas of the people they lead. In co-creative TA terms this means shifting the leader-follower dynamic from Parent-Child compliance (or passive resistance) to Adult-Adult dialogue and engagement.

A common response to group coaching is an appreciation of not being alone with leadership struggles. Another is gratitude for respectful honesty. These responses reflect the ongoing need for leaders to maintain and use wide networks of support and feedback to feel both supported and usefully stretched beyond their immediate preoccupations. Reaching out with assertiveness and vulnerability is a key Adult skill that is learned and re-learned through ongoing experimentation.

Leading across

Don is sharing his learning from the leadership program. As a sales manager he talks about a recurring problem. Typically, a customer would request a customised variation to the product or packaging that he was keen to offer to seal a deal. He would then get frustrated when his operational colleagues presented reasons why these changes could not be made. Both sales and operational managers would escalate the problem within their own departments leading to convoluted and prolonged tussles; meanwhile, the sales opportunity was either lost or at least strained.

Both sales and operational managers are now on this training program where they have taken time to get to know each other's context and challenges. They have gained a deeper understanding of their different and common concerns. Don describes the significance of working with his non-sales counterparts in this way: "Now I pick up the phone and talk with someone I know instead of sending an email". In most cases he is creating quicker and good-enough solutions with his operational colleagues and is clearer about what he can feasibly offer in his sales negotiations. His counterparts are also finding more professional satisfaction creatively collaborating with sales colleagues rather than fighting with them.

Don is taking the initiative to lead "across" the internal boundary (rather than escalating upwards) to build solutions with people in a different but neighbouring function.

Another aspect of leading "across" occurs through mutual challenge. Coyle's (2009) research into talent "hotbeds" highlights the role of positive competition and accelerated learning that occurs in peer groups devoted to honing and developing their skills. You are therefore leading "across" when you take a risk to do or learn something new and this encourages your peers to do the same. The same is true of initiating and contributing to peer development through forums, team meetings, training events (like Don) or peer coaching.

We can, of course, lead well or badly using any of the vectors. Competing to work the longest hours or promoting yourself at the expense of your peers will damage a sustainable work culture and team synergy. Attending to our own performance anxieties and helping others with theirs will be more beneficial in the long run. Whilst leading up or down can invoke parental transferences, leading across may also evoke sibling transferences (Beekum, 2009) with peers in your own or an adjacent function. Perhaps Don was, at some level, fighting with his brother and sisters in his tussles with operational colleagues? Exploring ways in which his "recurring problem" is like a previous relationship pattern may have yielded insights that helped him decontaminate his Adult but the context here was not conducive to this line of inquiry. In this instance, simply getting to know a colleague as a person was enough for him to collaborate rather than fight.

High-performing teams are built on trust which in turn is built through working relationships that allow for mistakes and mutual vulnerability (Lencioni, 2002). Trust provides the psychological safety (Reynolds & Lewis, 2018) for taking risks to lead and innovate, evaluated through robust mutual accountability, in service of common goals.

Members of a somewhat randomly collated coaching group often declare how lucky they are to have connected with each other. I may acknowledge their satisfaction, but I will also invite them to dissect their "luck" in terms of the small acts of trust building that have preceded within the group. Who took a risk to be vulnerable? What happened next? How did that nudge others to risk being open? Shared visceral awareness that trust has followed from acts of courage and response in psychological safety often leads to asking, "so how can we do this back at work?" Taking, appreciating and encouraging Adult growth risks is a key trust-building skill in developing mutually affirming and challenging peer relationships.

Leading out

In a coaching session Ellen describes her situation. She has been tasked with coordinating numerous internal and external stakeholders to bring a new but unusual product to market. This involves mobilising diverse functions to collaborate in unfamiliar ways. Despite her best efforts at framing the proposition and persuading functions to get involved, progress has been slow. She thinks that one contributory factor is that function heads "don't know what to do".

This was a classically complex, matrixed challenge: so how did Ellen lead "out" to coordinate different stakeholders, each of whom had their own concerns and preoccupations?

As she explores her experience Ellen accounts for her anxiety which she has been expressing as frustration about the slow pace of the project. This was potentially a high-profile product and therefore an important opportunity for her progression. She realised that she was using her anxiety, coupled with her genuine excitement for the initiative, to push more than pull in her communications, perhaps evoking unintentional resistance.

Containing her own anxiety enabled her to get curious about the anxieties of her stakeholders in their subsequent conversations. Her intuition that "they don't know what to do" resonated with overworked function heads as they admitted it was easier to put resources into existing priorities where the variables and implementation strategies are more clearly defined. These conversations enabled Ellen to build trust and get faster progress by more openly appreciating the uncertainties for all involved and framing their collaboration with her as "helping each other figure this out as we go along".

Ellen had caught her contaminated belief that "I will be OK if I keep pushing" through her awareness that her pushy behaviour was counter productive. Instead, she opened up Adult-Adult conversations seeking collaboration based on understanding and framed a way forward that incorporated "not knowing" and the acceptance of associated vulnerability.

Other forms of leading "out" include finding external help, resources or ideas to support particular projects or professional development in general. External coaching, training workshops, mentoring, reading, online courses/videos, conferences, shadowing or swapping roles with someone in another function/industry are all possibilities.

Many people resist leading/reaching out because it is less certain than their prescribed role within their organisation and may justify such notions as "not my job". Jobs, however, keep changing such that even keeping a job, let alone progressing, requires ongoing learning. Additionally, networking for ideas and novel experiences are recognised as key behaviours of valuable innovative individuals within organisations (Dyer et al., 2011).

Finally, some of the most important external stakeholders in a person's working life are family, friends and community. For some of the people I have worked with, success at work has come at the cost of failing to attend to work/life balance. Alan is attempting to rectify this situation. His teenage son is asking in a tone of hurt and anger, "How come you want to spend time with me now?" Leading "out" is also, therefore, a critical vector for keeping working life in perspective.

Key "leading out" Adult skills include being able to take stock, spot trends, seek help, tolerate uncertainty, explore new situations, have new experiences and learn new ways of working and living.

Conclusion

Leading is both a personal and professional process. Using the four leadership vectors discussed earlier, different ways in which our own vulnerabilities interact with those other people have been considered. My intention here is advocate acceptance of our enduring vulnerabilities (Gottman, 2011) in the work place and to offer a framework for considering this in the context of leadership.

The shift to creating human "engagement" rather than demanding subordinate "compliance" means that leaders are asking people to risk bringing more of themselves to work – more passion, initiative, purpose, pride and ownership for the quality of service or product being co-produced. However, with increased personal investment comes increased exposure and vulnerability.

Vulnerability itself is not a problem. Indeed, it is a sign that people care about the work they do. What matters is how vulnerability is recognised, managed and co-regulated within a work group so that people can make their best contributions.

Cable (2018) articulates the important benefits for employees and business of creating work environments that stimulate our Seeking circuits rather than our Fear circuits (Panksepp & Biven, 2012). Attention to vulnerability can help us transition from the latter to the former by learning how to co-regulate rather than exploit our areas of weakness. Our vulnerability can then co-exist with our curiosity, creativity and potency to meet shared challenges.

References

Bass, B. M. (1998). *Transformational Leadership: Industrial, Military, and Educational Impact*. Lawrence Erlbaum Associates.

Beekum, S. van. (2009). Siblings, Aggression, and Sexuality: Adding the Lateral. *Transactional Analysis Journal*, 39(2), 129–135. https://doi.org/10.1177/036215370903900206.

Berne, E. (1973). *The Structure and Dynamics of Organizations and Groups*. Ballantine Books (Original work published 1963).

Berne, E. (2001). *What Do You Say After You Say Hello? The Psychology of Human Destiny*. Corgi Books (Original work published 1971).

Cable, D. M. (2018). *Alive at Work: The Neuroscience of Helping Your People Love What They Do*. Harvard Business Review Press.

Clifford, C. (2017). What Billionaires and Business Titans Say About Cash Handouts in 2017 (Hint: Lots!). *CNBC*, 28 December. www.cnbc.com/2017/12/27/what-billionaires-say-about-universal-basic-income-in-2017.html.

Coyle, D. (2009). *The Talent Code: Greatness Isn't Born. It's Grown. Here's How*. Bantam Books.

Dyer, J., Gregersen, H. B., & Christensen, C. M. (2011). *The Innovator's DNA: Mastering the Five Skills of Disruptive Innovators*. Harvard Business Press.

Gottman, J. M. (2011). *The Science of Trust: Emotional Attunement for Couples* (1st ed.). W. W. Norton.

Heifetz, R. A., Grashow, A., & Linsky, M. (2009). *The Practice of Adaptive Leadership: Tools and Tactics for Changing Your Organization and the World*. Harvard Business Press.

Hudson-Allez, G. (2010). *Infant Losses; Adult Searches: A Neural and Developmental Perspective on Psychopathology and Sexual Offending: Second Edition* (2nd Revised ed.). Karnac Books.

Ibarra, H. (2015). *Act Like a Leader, Think Like a Leader*. Harvard Business Review Press.

Jaques, E. (1997). *Requisite Organization: A Total System for Effective Managerial Organization and Managerial Leadership for the 21st Century* (2nd ed.). Routledge.

Lencioni, P. (2002). *The Five Dysfunctions of a Team: A Leadership Fable* (1st ed.). Jossey-Bass.

Little, R. (2006). Ego State Relational Units and Resistance to Change. *Transactional Analysis Journal*, 36(1), 7–19. https://doi.org/10.1177/036215370603600103.

Milgram, S. (1974). *Obedience to Authority: An Experimental View*. Tavistock.

Oshry, B. (1999). *Leading Systems: Lessons from the Power Lab*. Berrett-Koehler Publishers.

Panksepp, J., & Biven, L. (2012). *The Archaeology of Mind: Neuroevolutionary Origins of Human Emotions* (1st ed.). W. W Norton.

Reynolds, A., & Lewis, D. (2018). The Two Traits of the Best Problem-Solving Teams. *Harvard Business Review*, 2 April. https://hbr.org/2018/04/the-two-traits-of-the-best-problem-solving-teams.

Rock, D. (2008). SCARF: A Brain-Based Model for Collaborating with and Influencing Others. *Neuro Leadership Journal*, 1(1), 44–52.

Senge, P. M. (2006). *The Fifth Discipline: The Art and Practice of the Learning Organization* (Rev. and updated). Doubleday/Currency.

Summers, G., & Tudor, K. (2000). Cocreative Transactional Analysis. *Transactional Analysis Journal*, 30(1), 23–40. https://doi.org/10.1177/036215370003000104.

8
MANAGING FEAR AND ANXIETY

Anne de Graaf

Introduction

When I want to get the attention of an audience of managers, I like to provoke by saying things like: 'Most managers are more involved in managing their own fear and anxiety, than in managing their team or organization'. Some people are shocked by such a bold statement, while others listen and start reflecting on the level of fear and anxiety they feel in regard to their managing tasks. Managers should provide their teams with reassurance and calm. Reducing fear and anxiety is one of their main tasks.

On my desk is a book by the American family therapist and management consultant Jeffrey A. Miller titled The Anxious Organization, Why Smart Companies Do Dumb Things *(2008). Of all the emotions, Miller argues, fear and anxiety are the most contagious. So there is a lot to say in favor of managers who invest in decontaminating their Adult ego state in order not to infect other employees. Transactional analysis (TA) offers a profound theory and a helpful strategy for these managers to understand and deal with the fear in themselves and with the anxiety in their origination.*

Change of paradigm

I meet more TA professionals that are familiar with personal psychology than TA colleagues who are working with a more systemic, holistic perspective. My inspiration to think more systemically was Fritjof Capra. His groundbreaking book *The Web of Life* (1997) helped me to leave the mechanistic, reductionist or atomic view of organizations behind and develop a more holistic, organismic or ecological take on organizational life. I still work with Capra's definition of a system: 'A system is an integrated whole whose essential properties arise from the relationships between its parts' (Capra, 1997, p. 27). In other words, the whole is more than the sum of its parts.

Most TA concepts, certainly those of individual TA, fail to help us to a deeper understanding of how systems function. For instance, Berne's concept of imagoes (Berne, 1963) deals mainly with the intrapsychic structure of each individual and how that contributes to group cohesion. When Berne writes about group imago, he means 'each member's private view of who is where in the pecking order, and also includes where the members themselves are' (p. 28). It is the imago people hold of the web of relationships that stimulates and limits them in whatever they do. Fear and anxiety are often stronger than ambition. An imago reflects the thoughts that someone has about the informal structure of an organization or group and the feelings and emotions (fear and anxiety) that an organization or group evokes.

Another example is the concept of psychological games. Despite the attempt at a systemic definition of a game in *Games People Play* (Berne, 1964), the concept of games is mostly used to create insight in how gamy transactions lead to an individual payoff or goal. In the *Transactional Analysis Journal* article (de Graaf, 2014) 'The Group in the Individual', I proposed a view on the complex relationship between an organization or group and the individuals in it. The article shows a shift from relying on individual psychology to understand behavior in groups to an appreciation of systemic influences and unconscious dynamics within the group as a whole. Servaas van Beekum (2007) also shows that within the frame of reference of the psychotherapist or counselor, the relational dynamics are often individualized and related to the two individuals and their connection. With that they are isolated from the wider system in which the therapy takes place. One-on-one psychotherapy is usually not aimed at implementing broader system thinking. This is completely different when working as a professional in groups and organizations.

Let me quote Capra once more: 'Systems cannot be understood by analysis (alone)' (1997, p. 29). Analysis means taking something apart in order to simply understand it. Systems thinking means putting it into context of a larger whole. The latter solely demonstrates the enormous complexity of organizations and groups. I agree with Miller (2008) that it is the emotional system, the complex network of reactions, interactions and relationships, that determines much of what actually occurs on a day-to-day basis in groups and organizations. Here lies the source of the feelings and emotions I write about in this chapter.

A container of feelings

I invite everyone, who works in or with an organization, to notice how feelings influence their thinking, feeling and behaving. 'An organization can be seen as a large container with feelings that constantly fly through space' (John Bazalgette, personal conversation, 2003). The behavior that people display in an organization is related to the mixture of feelings they experience there. Within TA it was Carlo Moiso (1985) who showed how the frame of reference of all parties interacts to create a shared, often emotionally charged, reality. This applies to people in every position in the organization. Anyone who takes an initiative exposes himself or herself to the feelings of others in the collective. These can be pleasant feelings, like joy, gratitude and kindness. They can also be unpleasant feelings, like irritation, grief or scare. One thing is certain: organizations are not 'the iron cages of rationality', as Max Weber (1958) suggested.

Whoever is paid to manage an organization, whoever is involved in shaping organizational policy, whoever bears responsibility for the quality of the organization, must take into account that management of feelings is crucial. Effective managers are able to recognize that the feelings of others toward them often are related to what is going on in the system as a whole. And the other way around: their own feelings toward others might also have to do with what is going on in the system.

It is not the aim of this chapter to scapegoat managers. This chapter aims to explore feelings, mainly fear and anxiety, that managers need to deal with in order to take up their role, task and responsibility in the most effective and efficient way possible. Understanding feelings helps managers to use the energy that comes with these feelings in a way that is beneficial for the organization. Steiner (2003) explains that to be emotionally literate is to be able to handle emotions in a way that improves personal power and improves the quality of life. After all, emotion is motion (de Graaf & Kunst, 2010)! Both words come from the same strain linguistically. Emotions provide the energy to get moving in order to get what it is you need.

Feeling fear or being anxious?

When I use the words 'fear' and 'anxious' here, I realize that the English language has several words for this feeling or emotion. In this chapter I think it is important to differentiate between 'feeling fear' and 'being anxious'. Goulding and Goulding (1979) pointed out that anxiety, an emotion, is a response to something that has not yet happened, whereas fear, a feeling, is a response to a real or imagined danger. In my view anxiety is a fundamental expression of the survival instinct, an emotion.

Although the word 'emotion' and the word 'feeling' are often used interchangeably, I do think it is good to make a clear distinction. *Emotions* are lower level responses occurring in the subcortical regions of the brain, the amygdala, and the ventromedial prefrontal cortices, creating biochemical reactions in the body altering the physical state someone is in. They make it possible to activate fight-or-flight responses and are aimed at survival! Emotions are more or less instinctual and precede feelings (www.thebestbrainpossible.com, January 20, 2020).

Feelings are more personal. They originate in the neocortical regions of the brain and can be seen as mental associations. There is a tight connection between the script (Steiner, 1973) of a person and his feelings. Personal experiences, memories and script beliefs will determine if and to what extent someone will respond to an emotion or a cognition. I will refer to anxiety as an emotion and to fear as a feeling. In a simple one-liner neuroscientist Sarah McKay states: 'Emotions play out in the theater of the body. Feelings play out in the theater of the mind' (www.thebestbrainpossible.com, January 20, 2020).

The function of fear and anxiety

There is nothing wrong with feeling fear or with being anxious occasionally. Like all emotions and feelings, they have the function of warning us that something is needed. Like the red light on the dashboard of a car that tells the driver oil in needed, emotions and feelings tell us we need to make sure we get what we need in order to (eventually) survive. Whoever feels hunger, needs food. Whoever is tired, needs rest. Whoever is sad, needs comfort. Whoever is afraid or anxious, needs...

Paraphrasing Aristotle (from Goleman, 2009), I would suggest that anybody can become afraid or feel anxious – that is easy, but to be afraid or feel anxious to the right degree, at the right time and for the right reason, is not easy at all. It is my experience that managers who are capable of recognizing, exploring and acknowledging their fear or their anxiousness are more efficient and effective than the ones who get stuck in what they experience as 'a swamp of feelings'. Here lies the beginning of an answer to Miller's question (2008), written on the cover of his book, why smart companies do dumb things.

A personal example: three years before I joined a big consultancy firm in the Netherlands in 1997, the enterprise was on the edge of going bankrupt. At this time bankruptcy was a serious threat. The members of the board of directors collectively did everything they could to save the company, even 'taking a second mortgage on their private real estate to emptying their children's money boxes'. This organizational script was passed on to new employees of the organization by telling them stories. Every new employee knew this story, with this exact wording. The employees were being prepared for the far-reaching form of micromanagement they would be exposed to. I believe that the collective directors' behavior was driven by Child fear and anxiety as a result of insufficient Adult-driven research into the underlying dynamics responsible for the near drama of bankruptcy. Systemic risks, like going bankrupt, build gradually but materialize abruptly and, hence, are mostly neglected in the day-to-day considerations of those in charge. As far as organizations can be diagnosed with PTSD, this company experienced a constant level of post-traumatic anxiety. During the years I worked for this firm this was never successfully addressed, and it played a role in me leaving the company eventually.

The smell of fear and anxiety

Fear and anxiety are contagious. Kevin Dutton in his book *The Wisdom of Psychopaths* (2013) states that most people, except psychopaths, react to the fear and anxiety of people around them. He refers to a somewhat odd research project conducted by Lilianne Mujica-Prodi (2009). She collected sweat from the armpits of people who were about to make a parachute jump for the first time. In the laboratory, she transferred this sweat to a specially calibrated atomizer. She kept it under the nose of a group of volunteers in an fMRI scanner. Even though these subjects had no idea what they were breathing, there was a noticeably high activity in the anxiety-processing locations of their brains (amygdala and hypothalamus). Dutton (2012, p. 46) asks: 'Can we take on fear or anxiety from someone in the same way as we take on a cold?' Can emotional stress be contagious? A more important question might be if we can create immunity?

Let's have a closer look at how a lot of managers tend to contribute to their own scripty way of behaving and to the large container filled with feelings of fear and anxiety.

Script fear or real fear

Having worked with dozens of mangers over the last decades, it is clear to me that many of them create feelings of fear by holding on to their own script beliefs. What are some of these fears inducing script beliefs? Many managers become afraid because they believe that they should know the answer to any question an employee puts before them. Not knowing seems their worst nightmare. They also do not want a team member to know more about their field of expertise. A lot of managers are fearful of being left out. They do not want to miss out on a conversation on the job floor. That's why loads of them come in early and leave late. Others do everything to avoid having someone find out that they have insecurities too. A lot of managers suffer, to varying degrees, from the 'imposter syndrome' (Hillman, 2013). People who suffer from imposter syndrome set the bar high for themselves and underestimate their own performance. No matter how well they do their job, no matter how many positive strokes they receive, they are constantly afraid of being exposed because they persistently doubt their own qualities.

The relationship therapist John Gottman (2002) says that the subconscious, survival system in our brain is constantly evaluating how secure we feel. Unspoken questions like 'Do I matter?' and 'Do they accept me as I am?' are always being asked. If the answer is 'no', our survival system sets off an alarm. This alarm resides in the amygdala. When it rings it quickly pulls us into instinctual states of fight, flight or freeze. This occurs without our conscious permission, control or even awareness.

Most of these feelings can be seen as non-functional feelings. Thomson (1983) suggests distinguishing between functional and non-functional feelings. Functional feelings play a key role in identifying and solving problems. Feelings are functional when they are accompanied by functional problem-solving behavior. Non-functional feelings cause discomfort but provide little or no awareness about the nature of the problem, let alone that they contribute to any problem-solving activity. Managers not dealing with their feelings of fear contribute to a fearful atmosphere in their organization. Thomson goes even further when he writes that it is his contention that an important reason a person gets 'stuck' in one feeling is by not recognizing that other feelings are also present. For example, a manager might feel fear but actually experience his past (sadness), present (anger) and future (fear).

Organizational anxiety

Miller (2008) states that all organizations are anxious organizations. Any living organism that isn't anxious is on its way to becoming extinct. Anxiety – an emotion – is a fundamental expression of the survival instinct. Organizations are incredibly complex systems of interactions. Managing a team or organization most often is a very complex task. The essence of the problem at hand is that managers tend to discount (Mellor & Schiff, 1975) the anxiety that comes with being faced with this complexity. They are not aware that their behavior is anxiety driven.

What is meant by complexity? It is helpful to differentiate between simple, complicated and complex tasks. Not being aware of this difference means managers might apply the wrong approach to the right problem or the right approach to the wrong problem. Glouberman and Zimmerman (2002) use the following metaphors: *following a recipe* is a simple task, *sending a rocket to the moon* is a complicated one and *raising a child* is a complex task. In the world of recipes good results are produced over and over again when the recipe is followed. A simple task is also easy to explain. When things become complicated there still is a high degree of certainty of outcome. That's why rockets usually reach the moon. A complicated task however is difficult to explain. When the task is complex the outcome remains uncertain. A complex task cannot be explained.

How to manage an organization can therefore not be taught in a classroom. It can be learned though by doing it, including developing know-how and skills on how to deal with emotions and feelings of oneself and others. When Miller talks about managers using simple cause-and-effect thinking he argues that managers with a simple diagnose/recipe approach to an organizational context that is quite complex often add to the fear and anxiety 'in the container'. That's why for most tasks, a manager has to deal with the fact that there is no 'recipe'. Managing, most of the time, is also 'beyond rocket science'. Being in the midst of an emotional maelstrom, the management of emotions (their own and those around them) is a crucial part of the task of any manager. Reading, guidance and containment of emotions (positive and negative) should be a priority.

Individual psychology is not enough

Individual psychology is often rooted in a classical epistemology (knowledge theory). This classical way of answering questions like '*what* can we know and *how* do we know' is based on two inaccurate assumptions: (1) It is possible to isolate an element. Example: Let's send this dysfunctional employee to a coach! (2) That properties of the problem remain constant. Example: A dysfunctional employee is a dysfunctional employee, wherever, whenever.

Behind a more systemic way of answering questions like '*what* can we know and *how* do we know' there are two more accurate assumptions: (1) The doing and not doing of another does something to you. (2) Your doing and not doing does something to another. It is impossible to not have an influence, either pleasant or unpleasant. Example: The underperformance of an employee can be seen as the pay-off of a game (Berne, 1964) played by those involved and maintained by the large group of Bystanders, with all their Bystanders slogans (Clarkson, 1996).

On the edge of chaos

Miller (2008, p. 11) emphasizes: 'Simplistic cause and effect thinking, pointing fingers, fixing blame . . . may help us feel better for a while, but they rarely solve anything'. Simplistic cause-and-effect thinking are used quite often in organizations. There is a tendency to make life simple, easy and clear. Reasoning along lines of linear causality often seems an attractive alternative. Organizations however are never simple, often complicated and mostly far too complex to get to helpful interventions along this route.

Linear causality is something from physics that cannot be transferred to everyday organizational life. Linear causality, according to Bateson (1972), is the view that one event causes the next in a unidirectional stimulus-response fashion. He makes it clear that such an approach is woefully inadequate when dealing with organized complexity.

The analysis of the almost disaster of going bankrupt in the organization I worked for never progressed beyond establishing a simple linear relationship between 'too little control and financial disaster'. I heard the directors say things like, 'If we had been more vigilant, then. . .' and 'We cannot take any financial information for granted anymore' when term planning Afterward members of the board of directors checked the week-planning and the long-of all employees every Monday morning. Employees, including myself, were called to ask why the planned turnover for that week was not in line with what it should be. It evoked an anxious and money-driven culture in the organization. This micro-management from the top of the organization evoked a lot of fear and anxiety among the employees.

If you see only your own behavior, you see no more than a linear causality. Remember however that as soon as other people are involved linear causality goes out the window. There is an infinite coherence or equifinality, which means that an effect or result can be reached by many potential means. Bateson (1972) talks of circular causality. We do not know what the outcome depends on. One of my teachers from the Grubb Institute in London, John Bazalgette (personal conversation, 2003), tends to say that most organizations are constantly balancing on the edge of chaos. When chaotic, organizational behavior is so unpredictable as to appear random. That's really scary for most people. Managers and employees start walking on eggshells, owing to the great sensitivity of the organization to small changes in conditions.

How to manage systemic fear and anxiety?

Management training most of the time is not allowing managers to understand and work with the personal and relational skills of dealing with emotions. The training focuses primarily on economic knowledge and mechanistic skills. 'What is a solid budget?' 'How do you conduct an assessment interview?' 'How do you report to your manager?' And so forth. In 'Managers Not MBAs', Mintzberg (2004) challenges the validity of the perennially popular MBA program: a program that top-tier companies continue to rely on as essential to the creation of successful corporate leaders. Mind you, BA stands for Business Administration!

Managers who want to deal with systemic fear and anxiety better not ask themselves 'What should I do now?' This question allows most of the time for only one, script-based, option. They better ask the more Adult-based, question: 'How can I respond to this?' By asking 'What should I do now?' they activate the file 'action', within the Parental behavioral repertoire directory, within themselves. The command 'How do I respond to this?' activates, in addition to the file 'action', numerous other files, such as 'non-action', 'investigate the situation', 'wait', 'look', 'listen' and much more options.

Asking myself, for many years now, the question 'How can managers respond to the fear and anxiety in their organization?' leaves me with five main options: contracting, containment, language, focus and the practice of fearlessness. A short introduction to all five follows.

Stick to the contract

In the Netherlands twelve years ago there was a young woman, Laura Dekker, 13 years old, who planned to sail around the world. During the turmoil that emerged in the media, she answered a question about how she thought to deal with possible danger. She made clear that her father, a very skilled sailor himself, taught her how to sail at a very young age. The most important lesson, she told, was 'how to avoid fear by focusing on the task'. She learned that the best way to contain panic, anxiety or fear is to focus on the tasks in place.

When I talk with managers about how to develop skills for managing fear and anxiety, I suggest they use this mantra: 'stick to the task'. In order to stick to the task managers first of all have to know what their task is. To find the answer to this most important question, managers need to know 'what the organization is for'. It is not possible to effectively and efficiently take up a role, with the corresponding task and responsibility, if one does not know what the purpose of the system is. Thirteen-year-old Laura knew her purpose was to sail around the world, and the step-by-step tasks when the sea was rough and the waves enormous.

Besides purpose and task, any manager should be able to define the primary process: Who do we work for? Which products and/or services do we offer? The answers can be found in the multi-party and multi-level contracts (Hay, 2009) managers work with. It is my experience that if things go wrong, they mostly go wrong at the beginning. Lack of contracts or insufficient expectations-management will add enormously to the level of fear and anxiety that is in place already.

Contain fear and anxiety

Because organizations and groups are complex entities, often on the edge of chaos, and because as soon as people are involved there is no linear causality, most of the time it is not possible to determine whether change is the result of an intervention by the manager. The large number of variables makes linear causality impossible. A manager, who is made responsible for the outcomes of all kinds of processes, has to accept this Uncertainty. A painter at the end of the day can determine, with probability bordering on certainty, that the fact that the doors he painted have a different color is the result of his actions. Managing an organization is nothing like painting doors.

Managers, confronted with an emotional experience they can't control, benefit from developing so-called containment skills. The goal of containment, unsurprisingly, is to contain, to find a way to close oneself off from experiencing too much fear and anxiety at once. Some managers use a physical ritual to contain, for instance closing up their office in the same way every end of the day. Others meditate, for instance visualizing locking up a box with the organizational emotions inside.

Use linguistic interventions

Schiff (1975) talks about thinking disorders that evoke fear and anxiety. Managers can *overdetail* and overwhelm themselves and their employees with micromanagement. Or *overgeneralize* an issue in such a way that it becomes overwhelming. Managers can *escalate* or *discount* problems and cause more fear and anxiety.

Using linguistic interventions can be helpful to get a better grip on the complex reality managers have to deal with. Most of these ideas I learned from an inspiring teacher at the Belgian Interaction Academy in Antwerp, named Flor Peeters, between 1995 and 1997.

- Because generalization can be seen as an attempt to organize complex reality, the *differentiation of the generalization* can be very helpful to assist managers in dealing with fear and anxiety. Example: Generalization: You can't work with this team! Differentiation: What makes it especially difficult? When do you experience this the most?
- Helping managers to make a *difference between knowing and thinking* is also a very helpful intervention in order to bring down the level of fear and anxiety. Knowing after all is static, passive, factual. Thinking on the other hand is dynamic, active, possible. I use the word 'thinking' quite often when working with managers! Example: How does that influence your thinking? Help me think about this in a different way.

Be focused

From Mark Tigchelaar (2019), a Dutch psychologist and entrepreneur, I learned about the importance of 'focus'. The brain is very easy to distract. What Tigchelaar calls 'emotional shifts' cost our brain an enormous effort and make us postpone or not complete tasks. The emotional center of the middle of the brain is the amygdala. The more active this part of our brain is, the worse the cognitive, task-focused, brain functions.

The so-called amygdala hijack (Goleman, 1996) is an immediate, overwhelming emotional response, inappropriately strong given the trigger. Fear and anxiety can be major distractions from daily managerial tasks.

Tigchelaar argues that managers should realize that they have to organize their work in such a way that they make smart use of how their brain is built. He discovered four major concentration leaks. 'If you know what those leaks are, and how to close them, you will get your job done even on the most chaotic days' is his promise to managers. (NRC interview, May 24, 2019).

Too little time for too little reflection, no or not enough focus, partly answers Miller's question of why smart companies do dumb things. Dutch sleep-guru professor Kerkhof (2018) suggests taking so-called worrying fifteen-minute breaks, a simple and effective way to calm down. By writing down worrying thoughts, for no longer than fifteen minutes, you anchor them and prevent them from hijacking the amygdala. Focused managers become more resilient to fear and anxiety, more productive and more present in the here and now. They are able to use the main function of the Adult ego state: to create a moment of reflection between (emotion-driven) impulse and (cognitive-focused) action!

Practice fearlessness

One of my favorite thinkers about management and organizational development is the Dutch professor Yvonne Burger (VU, Amsterdam). She states that the solution for dealing with irrationality and complexity is awareness of the deeper grounds of self (p. 15): 'Self-knowledge is perhaps the most underrated source of good leadership . . . If you understand and accept yourself, then you can do that with others'. When she talks about how leadership requires courage, she introduces the term 'fearlessness'. Fearlessness does not mean that you no longer feel fear, but that you have the ability to recognize, acknowledge and explore your own fear as an opportunity for growth and development.

Cool, calm and collected managers invest in exploring the following decontaminating questions: What evokes fear or anxious in me? How do I behave when I am afraid or anxious? How does this behavior affect others?

Conclusion

Miller (2008) wrote his book *The Anxious Organization* in order to find an answer to the question of why smart companies do dumb things. I agree with him that it takes only one person to break the fear and anxiety chain reaction. To remain, calm, collected and clear in the midst of collective fear and anxiety is to take up the leadership role. Leading can be seen as showing the way by going first (de Graaf & Kunst, 2005). When any individual in the reactivity chain stops being reactive, the chain is broken. The ones who have the courage to work on the edge, to do the unexpected, to blow the whistle, can make the difference between an organization that thrives and one that does not survive.

If it takes courage to work with complexity and its emotions, which it does, managers above all need to be encouraged. Managers that, for instance, during management training had the opportunity to experience and explore what I call 'the behavior of a group' do better. They experienced different ways of understanding and making sense of what is happening in groups and organizations. This helps them to reduce and/or contain their fear and anxiety. They are encouraged to look at it differently. They are encouraged to stand for something. They are encouraged to maintain courage (even with headwinds). Encouraged to face their own fear and anxiety. Encouraged to maintain a relationship with very reactive people. And, finally, to take responsibility for themselves.

Assessing the nature and degree of threats and possible solutions, working in or with the complexity of an organization, also requires rational thinking. Using a very rudimentary concept of ego-states, Berne, in *What Do You Do After You Say Hello?*, makes it clear that the Adult ego state is the ego state where we appraise our environment objectively and calculate the possibilities and probabilities on the basis of past experience.

To finally paraphrase Miller (2008): why is there always a dying canary? The chronic fear and anxiety in the mineshaft is why! Canaries will keep dying until managers air out the mineshaft and address the systemic source of fear and anxiety. It is my experience that managers – like other people – benefit enormously from taking TA supervision, from following TA training and even from getting TA therapy. They'll learn some great ideas to air out their organization.

References

Berne, E. (1963). *The Structure and Dynamics of Organizations and Groups*.
Berne, E. (1964). *Games People Play. The Psychology of Human Relationships*. New York: Grove Press.
Bateson, G. (1972). *Steps to An Ecology of Mind*. New York: Ballantine Books.
Capra, F. (1997). *The Web of Life, A New Scientific Understanding of Living Systems*. New York: Penguin Random House.
Clarkson, P. (1996). *The Bystander. An End to Innocence in Human Relationships?* London: Whurr Publishers.

De Graaf, A. (2014). *The Group in the Individual, Lessons Learned from Working with and in Organizations and Groups.*

De Graaf, A., & Kunst, K. (2010) *Einstein and the Art of Sailing, A New Perspective on The Art of Leadership.* Hertford: Sherwood Publishing.

Dutton, K. (2013). *The Wisdom of Sociopaths.* New York (NY): FSG Adult.

Glouberman, S., & Zimmerman, B. (2002). *Complicated and Complex Systems: What Would Successful Reform of Medicare Look Like?* Commission on the Future of Health Care in Canada: Discussion Paper No. 8.8.

Goleman, D. (2009). *Emotional Intelligence. Why It Can Matter More Than IQ.* London: Bloomsbury.

Gottman, J. (2002). *The Relationship Cure, A Five-Step Guide to Strengthening Your Marriage, Family, and Friendships.* New York: Random House USA Inc.

Goulding, B., & Goulding, M. (1979). *Changing Lives Through Redecision Therapy.* New York: Grove Press.

Hay, J. (2009). *Transactional Analysis for Trainers* (2nd ed.). Hertford: Sherwood Publishing.

Hillman, H. (2013). *The Imposter Syndrome. Becoming an Authentic Leader.* Auckland: Penguin Random House New Zealand.

Mellor, K., & Schiff, J. (1975). Discounting. *Transactional Analysis Journal*, 5, 295–302.

Miller, J. A. (2008). *The Anxious Organization. Why Smart Companies Do Dumb Things.* Facts on Demand Press.

Moiso, C. (1985). Ego States and Transference. *Transactional Analysis Journal*, 15, 194–201.

Mintzberg, H. (2005). *Managers, not MBA's.* Oakland (CA): Berrett-Koehler.

Petriglieri, G., & Wood, J. D. (2003). The Invisible Revealed: Collusion as an Entry to the Group Unconscious. *Transactional Analysis Journal*, 33, 332–343.

Schiff, J. (1975). *Cathexis Reader, Transactional Analysis Treatment of Psychosis.* New York: Harper & Row, Publishers, Inc.

Steiner, C. (1973). *Scripts People Live. Transactional Analysis of Life Scripts.* New York: Bantam.

Steiner, C. (2003). *Emotional Literacy, Intelligence with a Heart.* Fawnskin (CA): Personhood Press.

Thomson, G. (1983). Fear, Anger, and Sadness. *Transactional Analysis Journal*, 13, 2–24.

Tigchelaar, M. (2019) *Focus Aan/Uit. Dicht de concentratielekken en krijg meer gedaan in een wereld vol afleiding.* (Focus On/Off. Stop the concentration leaks and get more done in a world full of distractions.) Amsterdam: Spectrum BV.

Van Beekum, S. (2006). The Relational Consultant. *Transactional Analysis Journal*, 36, 318–329 and (2007) Supervision as a Metamodality and Multiarea Activity. *Transactional Analysis Journal*, 37, 140–149.

Weber, M. (1958). *The Protestant Ethic and the Spirit of Capitalism.* New York: Scribner.

9

LEARNING PRACTICES AT WORK

A case for cognitive apprenticeship

Mandy Lacy

Introduction

Change is constant and occurs in all workplaces. Significant pressure and expectations are placed on leaders and project teams to have the same or similar levels of knowledge, experience and skills to deal with these projects. This is rarely the case. Boon et al. (2013) posit that "a collection of different individuals is not a sufficient condition to learning as a team". Organisations attempt various ways to develop teams in tandem with delivering projects. However, keeping staff, teams and ourselves up to date with new knowledge and processes can be overwhelming from a resource, cost and implementation perspective.

Rethinking learning at work from traditional training approaches has therefore never been more relevant. This is where the support for micro-learning has found a growing niche. Providing relevant bytes of new knowledge and skill development at the workplace, or within the workplace activity for immediate application, is proving beneficial for workers and organisations alike. Adjusting to these modern workplace learning practices is the challenge.

Background

Learning at work is an iterative process that is based on knowledge building, processing new skill development and integrating learning into practice. Learning requires space to integrate. Through the process of integration comes learning. Facilitating learning practices into the workplace requires a dedicated strategic approach. However, delivery and integration of learning practices requires operational planning.

This chapter introduces two planning methods for learning practices at work. The first is cognitive apprenticeship which offers four dimensions for designing and planning workplace learning that incorporates a pedagogical method to learning activities. The second is evaluating learning efficacy through the application and integration of new knowledge through collaborative reflection as a team. This method links planning with evaluation and deepens the individual and group learning experience through identifying improvement areas and noting integration that is working well.

At a strategic level transactional analysis (TA) offers humanistic and respectful fundamentals for teaching and learning in the workplace through Schmid's (2008) eleven TA principles. It has been my experience that when individuals and teams make a commitment and share the responsibility of learning, successful outcomes are more likely. From this perspective I added a twelfth principle "shared and equal responsibility for learning" (Lacy, 2012).

The Twelve TA Principles are:

1. Focusing on real people in real-life situations,
2. Acknowledging and understanding multiple background levels,
3. Accepting the necessary function of intuition in creating reality,
4. Acting from a position of OK-OK,
5. Being dedicated to how people find meaning in life,
6. Encountering others on an equal level,
7. Taking each other's autonomy and wisdom seriously,
8. Using concepts and procedures that can be understood and related to by everyone involved,
9. Keeping concepts as simple as possible yet profound on a deeper level,
10. Confronting each other about differences in perception and culture,
11. Building pluralistic and non-imperialistic association, and
12. Shared and equal responsibility for learning.

Operationally TA provides concepts and practical approaches for creating learning environments in the workplace. These include contracts for teaching and learning, engaging the Parent, Adult and Child ego states in learning along with permission, protection and potency for learning. TA also provides many theoretical concepts and approaches that can be taught in regard to leadership, communication, problem solving, culture, organisational development.

From my own experiences of learning at work and being a workplace trainer I have always been curious in understanding what makes a difference to professional development and personal learning. This interest deepened and further expanded through my training as a TA practitioner and becoming a teaching and supervising transactional analyst (TSTA) in the organisational field. It was here where I experienced the benefits of experiential learning and integrating theory into practice. Together with these, I have always felt inspired by Eric Berne's innovative open style of patient case management as a teaching and learning experience.

The impetus for this chapter stems from my PhD project where I researched learning, knowledge practices and group memory in team meetings (Lacy, 2018). I delivered two TA concepts designed as micro-learning units using a cognitive apprenticeship approach and collaborative reflection methods.

The structure of the chapter starts with the main TA approaches that have influenced me in relation to learning. I then provide an overview of the cognitive apprenticeship model. This is followed by an outline of my PhD project in relation to team meeting and the micro-learning TA topics that I have adapted to include practice and integration of previous learning. Collaborative reflection is the last concept introduced which is a reflexivity practice of continuous learning and improvement that I have developed. The chapter concludes with a summary.

Organisational TA overview

TA is both a theory and a system for the improvement of human relations. Its application to learning in organisations provides an approach to understanding the links between human needs and behaviours. Organisational TA offers ways that organisations, leaders and teams are effective or ineffective in solving their problems and providing services.

Organisational consulting and workplace training based on TA is a contractual approach. Workplace trainers facilitate and teach understanding and skills in communication and problem solving in organisational life. Organisational TA consultants and trainers are qualified to have insight into group dynamics; how groups work; who, in practice, will lead them; the organisational context within which they function.

Although TA was developed as a psychotherapy there are sound principles that have been used for many years in the fields of education, counselling and organisations. TA theories and models are readily understood and applied by people at all levels of an organisation. TA also provides many concepts related to specific aspects of organisational life, such as working styles for time management, cycles of development for handling change, and the analysis of organisational scripts to add clarity and direction to leaders, teams and organisational development. By observing limiting beliefs and ingrained behaviour patterns, the consultant and workplace trainer can offer guidance about how to create healthy organisational cultures in which individuals can function effectively and meaningfully.

Underpinning all workplace learning regardless of topic is the emphasis on finding choices for avoiding non-productivity and conflict, developing more effective communication and problem-solving strategies. In settings as diverse as health, banking, airlines, retail, manufacturing, government agencies, family businesses, local authorities and many others, TA has proven its value as a grounded approach to interpersonal skills, communication, leadership and management development and culture change.

Learning

Specific to learning Newton (2006) discusses Kolb's (1984) learning cycle of reflect, conceptualise, experiment or as adapted by Newton and Napper (2000) to 'experiential learning cycle' of do, look, think, change styles and postulates 'that our behaviour is changed as a result of reflecting on and drawing conclusions about the experience'(p. 189). The work and roles of trainer and learner include reflection and drawing conclusions.

Directly related to workplace learning van Poelje's (2004) research found that learning occurs in real-life work situations and "from key learning events, despite ingrained success formulas or scripts" (p. 225). This research has validated my own thinking and experience. So, too, has Goodyear's (2000) advice in not adopting exaggerated positions about knowledge, rather to remember that the essence in knowledge and skill development lies within the human experience.

The "experience principle" is a term referred to by Spector (2000) when applying learning to real-life work situations and activities where understanding begins in and is based upon human experience. The following quote has always warmed my heart, and it guides me as a reminder about the importance of the experience principle. Tyrangiel (2011) tells of his TA learning experiences, and that while much was gained from the theories that were taught, the most memorable learning experiences were through his experience of the people themselves. He said, "I hardly recall any specific interventions, but I am still touched by the meaningful encounters". The human experience and the experience principle bring in the relational aspect of learning as outlined in the first principle, focusing on real people in real-life situations.

Cognitive apprenticeship – a pedagogy for workplace learning

Designing and planning workplace learning has many variations depending on the situation, types of knowledge needed, the immediacy, learning culture and methods within the organisation and the learners themselves. I have found that the cognitive apprenticeship model provides an effective framework for designing and planning. This model is a pedagogical approach in the learning sciences which is based on an apprenticeship model to support learning in the cognitive domain. Application of the cognitive apprenticeship model has been found to embed experiential instructional design to support all levels of learning (Wiss et al., 2018). Whilst peer mentoring aligned with cognitive apprenticeship approaches supported developmental learning and peer coaching as a relational process for accelerating career learning (Mullen, 2020).

The differences between cognitive apprenticeship and traditional apprenticeship are that traditional apprenticeship was set in the workplace which is limited by what it can teach and what is pertinent to that particular workplace or specialty (Collins, 2006). Whereas cognitive apprenticeship on the other hand emphasises "generalising knowledge so that it can be used in many different settings" and articulates the common principles, to learn how to apply newly acquired skills and knowledge in varied contexts (Collins, 2006, p. 49). In my 2012 article Learning Transactional Analysis Through Cognitive Apprenticeship (Lacy, 2012) I discuss this model in depth in relation to my learning experience as a CTA trainee being very aligned to the cognitive apprenticeship pedagogical model which I applied as a framework as a supervisor and trainer.

There are four principles of cognitive apprenticeship model as shown in the following table.

Table 9.1 Cognitive apprenticeship model

Cognitive Apprenticeship Model

Content	Method	Sequencing	Sociology
• Domain knowledge	• Modelling	• Increasing complexity	• Situated learning
• Heuristic strategies	• Coaching	• Increasing diversity	• Community of practice
• Control strategies	• Scaffolding	• Global to local skills	• Intrinsic motivation
• Learning strategies	• Articulation		• Cooperation
	• Reflection		
	• Exploration		

These principles provide a practical guide for preparing, planning and developing workplace micro-learning. In essence the four principles are:

1. Content: defining the types of knowledge and strategies required for expertise
2. Method: the ways to promote the development and expertise through the following learning activities:
    a. Modelling: performing a task for learners to observe
    b. Coaching: observing whilst learners practice
    c. Scaffolding: providing support to assist the learner perform the task
    d. Articulation: encourages learners to verbalise their knowledge and learning
    e. Reflection: enables learners to contrast and review their work
    f. Exploration: invites learners to pose and solve their own problems
3. Sequencing: the planning and the key to ordering and pacing learning activities where meaningful tasks gradually increase in complexity
4. Sociology: the social characteristics of learning environments for situated learning to work on real workplace activities

The cognitive apprenticeship method can be compartmentalised into three distinct phases as articulated by Seel et al. (2002) and is shown in the following figure. Highlighted is that the learning activities of modelling, coaching and scaffolding are receptive meaningful learning, articulation and reflection are the metacognition and exploration is the application and transfer of learning.

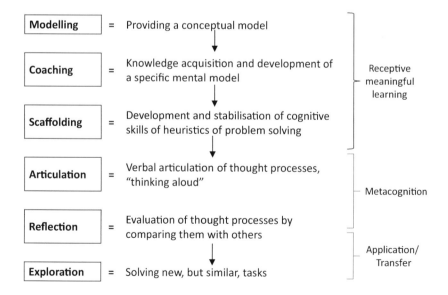

Figure 9.1 Cognitive apprenticeship method (Seel et al., 2002)

A brief example would be when teaching the TA concept of contracts: teaching TA contract theory, asking learners to think about and discuss examples and the facilitator demonstrating contracting with them and asking learners to practice amongst themselves making contracts within their workplace and role contexts are the receptive meaningful learning components. The metacognition components are inviting learners to discuss their learning and from their practice reflecting and contrasting the application of contracting practice. The final component is inviting learners to find other ways where contracting practice would be beneficial.

Why is learning in team meetings important?

The number of meetings in organisations has increased substantially over the last few decades (Rogelberg et al., 2007; Rogelberg, 2018). According to Kim and Shah (2016), "an estimated $54 million to $3–4 billion is lost annually as a result of meeting inefficiencies" (p. 625). This is based on meeting analysis findings from research and practice in corporate America. Kim and Shah also claim that the most common source of inefficiency is team members' understandings about the outcome of the meeting being inconsistent.

As we all know team meetings are a routine and major activity in organisations and typically have the tasks of sharing information, reporting, working on problems and making decisions. Today, team members often belong to several teams and attend regular meetings for each. Communication at team meetings is also changing, depending on the types of meetings, roles, meeting participant location, responsibilities and activities.

Many researchers argue that learning opportunities are missed in meetings and valuable knowledge is lost between meetings. Plus the systemic issues remain, such as the potential loss of project knowledge (Akgun et al., 2006), the sharing of information (Decuyper et al., 2010), sharing knowledge awareness (Dehler Zufferey et al., 2010) and team learning (Nisbet et al., 2015; Decuyper et al., 2010).

Ewenstein and Whyte (2009) claim that knowledge work should be at the core of team meetings. Learning in team meetings is defined by Van Den Bossche et al. (2006) as what allows the "building and maintaining of mutually shared cognition, leading to increased perceived team performance" (p. 490). Beautifully poignant is Boon et al. (2013) who argue that "a collection of different individuals is not a sufficient condition to learning as a team" (p. 360).

There is little debate about the importance of learning at work. My PhD research project on learning, knowledge practices and group memory in team meetings took place during 2016 with a telecommunications company senior leadership team. This company had experienced exponential growth over the preceding two years and needed to refresh the strategic vision along with reviewing senior management meetings and processes to be aligned with business demands and provide clear oversight. My contract was to work with the managing director and his senior leadership team to facilitate the strategic planning and prepare the change management project. The project took place through weekly meetings. These weekly meetings were a combination of strategic planning, change management preparation, micro-learning and reflection of meeting practices.

The research methodology was design-based research involving two phases. The first phase was an observational study, and the second phase was the research proper as outlined earlier. Video-ethnography and discourse analysis including conversation analysis were the research analysis methods. The research resulted in nine design principles and intervention guideline as a practical guide to improving meeting practices where group memory (intellectual capital), learning and knowledge building were paramount features.

Micro-learning

The definition of workplace micro-learning can be summarised as learning with micro content in small, fragmented learning units, which cause only "short-term interruptions to the actual working process" (Decker et al., 2017, p. 133). The definition from Hug and Friesen (2007) resonates with me where they describe micro-learning as "special moments or episodes of learning while dealing with specific tasks or content and engaging in small but conscious steps" (p. 2). It is not surprising that micro-learning has found a comfortable home in the workplace.

The two micro-learning sessions discussed next are those included in my research project with the senior leadership team. The TA topics are contracts and the change competence curve. Integration into work practices is the focus in regard to contracting and drawing on previous experiences and learning as leaders when understanding the stages and phases of change.

Contracting practice – the seventh P

When I am teaching the concepts and theory about contracts in workplace settings or to workforce groups, I typically use the term "agreements". From my experience, "agreements" is more easily comprehended in workplace activity and organisational contexts. The model I presented to the senior leadership group as a micro-learning topic was the six Ps of contracting (Hay, 2007, 2011). Within the presentation was the exercise to work through this model in order to define our own contracts as a group. This model stems from the well-known 3Ps of contracting (Crossman, 1966; Steiner, 1968).

However, it was through my work with the senior leadership team in using this model of contracting and my thinking about cognitive apprentices for new skills to be applied in various settings that it occurred to me that the group needed to work on an agreement for practicing and integrating contracting. Hence, I added a seventh "P": practice. Practice refers to deciding how the practice (the doing) of contracting will be integrated. This can be addressed through the answering the first six Ps questions. Practice is aimed at considering "how will we include the practice of contracting (agreements) into our workplace activities?" In this case: team meeting practices.

Table 9.2 The seven Ps of contracting

1.	Procedural	What attention is needed regarding dates, times, practical implications and administration considerations?
2.	Professional	What considerations are required regarding professional boundaries for each participant, including me as the facilitator?
3.	Purpose	What determinants are needed to be specific about the purpose of the project and the expected outcomes?
4.	Personal	What considerations are necessary regarding personal commitments and interactions within the group and to direct reports and others?
5.	Psychological	What unspoken things need to be brought to the surface for agreement?
6.	Physis	What commitments and actions need to be in place for learning and for professional and personal growth during this project?
7.	Practice	What ways will we integrate the practice of contracting into our work and workplace activities?

Source: (Adapted from Crossman, 1966; Steiner, 1968; Hay, 1995, 2012)

Through this consideration contracting became an integrated practice in determining the agreements not only at the beginning and at the end of meetings but also within meeting discourse and sub-meeting activities as well as outside the meeting work in their leadership roles. As the senior leadership team explored and practiced the concepts it became an integrated contracting practice that was often seen in the form of seeking clarity, checking out assumptions and seeking permission. See the following table for the seven Ps of contracting.

Previous learning experience

The next micro-learning topic was the change competence curve, wherein leaders integrate previous learning experience. Nowadays most leaders will have experienced and been affected by change whether personally and/or professionally. Understanding the human processes around change and transition are helpful both for understanding personally and when leading people through change. Taking time to draw on our experience of change and learnings can assist us in preparing ourselves individually and in our leadership roles for understanding and being empathically in tune with team members' responses.

The model I present is the competence curve which has been adapted from the Kübler-Ross (1983) grief model, Levin (1982) cycles of development, Newton and Napper (2000) developmental needs for adult learners and Hay (1991, 2011) which can be found in the first appendix at the end of this chapter. This well-researched model provides identifiable phases of change, learning needs and management strategies when leading people through change. Each stage of change has identifiable behaviours and reactions, the reasons for the behaviours and what is needed to support us and others going through change. Immobilisation, denial, frustration, acceptance, development, application and completion are the cycles of development. Being, exploring, identity, skills and integration are the competence curve and are iterative layers of experiencing change. There are also "spirals within spirals" (Hay, 2011) which are the experiential processes for both the cycles of development and the competence curve of experience and growth, learning new skills and proactive practical approaches to leading and managing change.

A week before the planned micro-learning session I asked people to think about and bring examples of past experiences and learnings of change. The experiences shared the following week were very meaningful and practical resilience strategies, learning, feelings and actions from a deep awareness and understanding of themselves in those past change environments and situations. Self-awareness was exemplified from taking the time to look back at previous experiences and draw on the learning, experiences and lessons. These insights were invaluable and provided thoughtful considerations when preparing and planning for how to best support themselves and then those in their teams, for the change. The following table shows the steps to include in previous learning, knowledge and experience at each stage of the competence curve.

Table 9.3 Steps to include previous learning at each stage of the competence curve

#	Stages	Steps to integrate your previous experience and learning
1.	Immobilisation BEING	• Think about previous work change experiences and context. • What was the context of the change? • Remember the range of experiences and emotions you felt. **What aspects of your being at this stage will be helpful to the current situation?**
2.	Denial EXPLORING	• What were the various roles you held and were involved with? • What is similar about the current change that is about to occur? • What is different? • What were your lessons learned about yourself, groups and organisations from what happened during the change? **What aspects of what you were doing will be helpful for the current situation?**
3.	Frustration THINKING	• What were your key frustrations and emotions at the various stages and phases of the change? • Do you remember repetitive themes of thinking (and feeling)? • What was other people's thinking? • How was this thinking differ from or the same as yours? **What aspects and kinds of thinking will be helpful for the current situation?**
4.	Acceptance IDENTITY	• List the key acceptance turning points. • What and who helped you through the change process? • How do you remember your identity from your own and others' perspectives? • How will your experiences inform your leadership during this change process? • What support will you specifically need? **What aspects about your identity will be helpful for the current situation?**
5.	Development SKILLS	• What types of learning served you well? • Where are the major learnings? • How will these benefit this current change? • Do you require further skills, and how can this happen? **What skills and knowledge could you pass on or recommend for the current situation?**
6.	Application INTEGRATION	• How did you integrate your new knowledge, skills and learning? • What did you notice about other people in relation to the integration of new skills, knowledge and learning? • What and how would you notice in your leadership for this change project that has integrated your previous experiences? **How will you integrate your past experience and knowledge for the current situation?**
7.	Completion RECYCLING	• How did you recycle the lessons learned from the past? **What are some ways you will note and capture your new learnings from this current change?**

It is from this experience that I have added a further column to the competence curve support strategies matrix in order to see previous learning at each stage, which can be found in the second appendix at the end of this chapter. This additional column is called "previous experience and learning". This step aligns to the cycles of development and competence curve by inviting leaders and managers to draw on and leverage from past experiences of change at work.

The purpose of this step is for leaders to identify emotions and learning from their past experiences that could be purposeful to understanding and preparing for the upcoming change environment and context in regard to their roles, working with team members and the organisation generally. Further, that through this preparation plans can be made to ensure they identify and meet their own individual needs and then that of their team members' as shown in Individual Needs (6th) and Leadership Strategies (7th) columns. In relation to the cognitive apprenticeship method building on and relating existing knowledge and learning generates further skill development and deeper learning.

Collaborative reflection

The final research project intervention took place at the end of meetings in the form of a collaborative reflection about the meeting practices. Before I discuss this in more detail it is important to highlight the phenomena found within the research. Looking back acts emerged as a key phenomenon from the video ethnography and discourse analysis. There were two types, 1. Naturally occurring and 2. Structured. Naturally occurring was when meeting participants would informally "look back" about the previous meeting to either confirm their own memory of events, to seek to be reminded or to find structure in what was agreed.

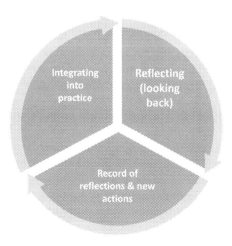

Figure 9.2 Collaborative reflection

Collaborative reflection was a structured formal looking back act of deliberating reviewing the previous meeting. This exercise had three distinct steps as shown in the following figure.

One of the key elements of the contract with the senior leadership team was to improve team meeting efficiencies. Therefore, reflection of current practices was important. Also important was a collaborative approach for the purposes of the team engagement, discussion, decisions, agreements and ownership of new ways of doing things. The first step was to look back on meeting performance and outcomes directly after the meeting had ended. This reflective practice was a very short learning intervention lasting no more than 10 minutes (5 minutes at best). The group agreements (contracts) for this exercise were being solution focused, making "I" statements, listening to understand and every challenge/critique being coupled with an improvement suggestion for discussion.

The reflection exercise commenced at the end of a meeting where participants were invited to stand up from the meeting table and move over to two posters on the wall (or a whiteboard). The purpose of this was to engage people in physically looking back at the meeting table and the meeting itself. The act of moving from sitting to standing took people from being in the meeting to taking a reflective view of looking back as observers. Once standing, participants were then invited to note onto the poster their perspectives of what worked well (WWW) and what learning (lessons) occurred (WLO) either for themselves or as a group. This included meeting practices and the meeting work.

Once all comments had been placed on the poster a participant was asked to read out the comments to the group. This created general discussion about whether there was agreement or challenges about the items raised. The second step was that agreements and outcomes were recorded and photos taken of the posters which were filed in the group memory online central repository and shown in the rich meeting summary at the beginning of the next meeting. The third step was integrating the improvements and changes agreed into practice at the next meeting.

The first reflection session items listed were more in relation to the meeting work. In the second session there is a combination of reflection on meeting work and meeting practices. By the third session, the feedback is mostly about actual meeting practices. Even though at that last session there is some discrepancy about time management there was an awareness of needing to improve timing.

My observations were that the leaders grew in trust and confidence as a group to then name specific meeting practice improvements which generally involved individual performance and actions. From a cognitive apprenticeship perspective this exercise was scaffolded through my leading and facilitating the processes in the first instance, and over time the leadership of the exercise was rotated between team members and I covered the notations and held the role of the observer. The group was completely self-managing of the exercise by the end of the project.

Summary

TA principles underpin my role and practice. They were instrumental as a guide and an evaluation process for myself personally and professionally. In the closing of this chapter I briefly discuss each principle. The project was with a real workplace situation of team meetings and participants from multiple background levels. Each meeting participant was a department manager representing all areas of the business which meant it was a team working together from not only different business leadership responsibilities but also different backgrounds. Time at the beginning of the project was spent understanding each participant's frame of reference.

I observed intuition emerging through the individual and collaborative reflection activities both for myself and the group which enabled discussion for creating a new reality. Contracting set the expectation for everyone to operate from the position of OK-OK, especially when confronting each other about differences in perception and culture. Specific agreements incorporated being committed to listening to each other's perspectives, encountering each other on an equal level and taking each other's autonomy and wisdom seriously and as an asset to the group knowledge.

TA offers many concepts that can be designed as micro-learning and applied directly into workplace practices as demonstrated from this research project. The practice of contracting sought to articulate the ways in which contracting (agreements) will be practiced in workplace activities. Integrating previous change experience and learning as a preparatory exercise into the competence curve supporting strategies offered a leveraging step to draw upon previous knowing before addressing the here-and-now support of self and others.

Integrating new learning into immediate practice in real workplace practices I observed increased leader understanding and purpose of the TA concepts. Regular reflection developed collaborative responsibility for ensuring team meetings were continuously effective. Finally, it was through the pedagogical method of cognitive apprenticeship which provided a practical scaffold from which to design, plan, reflect and evaluate the workplace learning activities.

References

Akgun, A. E., Byrne, J. C., Keskin, H., & Lynn, G. S. (2006). Transactive Memory System in New Product Development Teams. *IEEE Transactions on Engineering Management*, 53(1), 95–111. doi: 10.1109/TEM.2005.857570.

Berne, E. (1963). *The Structure and Dynamics of Organizations and Groups*. New York: J. B. Lippincott.

Boon, A., Raes, E., Kyndt, E., & Dochy, F. (2013). Team Learning Beliefs and Behaviours in Response Teams. *European Journal of Training and Development*, 37(4), 357–379. doi: 10.1108/03090591311319771.

Collins, A. (2006) Cognitive Apprenticeship. In K. Sawyer (ed.), *Cambridge Handbook of the Learning Sciences*. New York: Cambridge University Press, pp. 47–60.

Cornell, W. F. (2011) Keeping Our Work Alive: Reflections on Writing Upon Receiving the 2010 Eric Berne Memorial Award. *TAJ*, 41(1).

Crossman, P. (1966). Protection. *Permission and Potency Transactional Analysis Bulletin*, 5(19), 152–154.

Decker, J., Hauschild, A. L., Meinecke, N., Redler, M., & Schumann, M. (2017). *Adoption of Micro and Mobile Learning in German Enterprises: A Quantitative Study*. Proceedings of the European Conference on e-Learning, ECE 2017, Porto, Portugal.

Decuyper, S., Dochy, F., & Van den Bossche, P. (2010). Grasping the Dynamic Complexity of Team Learning: An Integrative Model for Effective Team Learning in Organisations. *Educational Research Review*, 5(2), 111–133. doi: 10.1016/j.edurev.2010.02.002.

Dehler Zufferey, J., Bodemer, D., Buder, J., & Hesse, F. W. (2010). Partner Knowledge Awareness in Knowledge Communication: Learning by Adapting to the Partner. *The Journal of Experimental Education*, 79(1), 102–125. doi: 10.1080/00220970903292991.

Ewenstein, B., & Whyte, J. (2009). Knowledge Practices in Design: The Role of Visual Representations as 'Epistemic Objects'. *Organization Studies*, 30(1), 7–30. doi: 10.1177/0170840608083014.

Goodyear, P. (2000). *Environments for Lifelong Learning: Ergonomics, Architecture and Educational Design*. In J. M. Spector & T. M. Anderson (eds.), *Integrated and Holistic Perspectives on Learning, Instruction and Technology*. Ordrecht: Kluwer Academic Press, pp. 1–18.

Hay, J. (1991). Choice, Chance, Change: Creating Future Realities in Organisations. In R. Bruce (ed.), *The Stamford Papers Loria*. Stamford: Omni Press, pp. 162, 172.

Hay, J. (2007). *Reflective Practice & Supervision for Coaches*. London, UK: McGraw-Hill International (UK) Ltd.

Hay, J. (2011). Setting Up the Coaching Contract. *IDTA Newsletter*, 6(2), 5–6.

Hug, T., & Friesen, N. (2007). Outline of a Microlearning Agenda. In T. Hug (ed.), *Didactics of Microlearning. Concepts, Discourses and Examples*. Munster, Germany: Waxmann Verlag, pp. 15–31.

Kim, J., & Shah, J. A. (2016). Improving Team's Consistency of Understanding in Meetings. *IEEE Transactions on Human- Machine Systems*, 46(5), 625–637.

Kolb, B. (1984). *Experiential Learning*. Englewood Cliffs, NJ: Prentice Hall.

Kübler-Ross, E. (1983). *On Children and Death. How Children and Parents Can and Do Cope with Death*. New York: Touchstone.

Lacy, A. (2012). Learning Transactional Analysis Through Cognitive Apprenticeship. *Transactional Analysis Journal*, 42(4), 265–276.

Lacy, A. (2018). *Group Memory Enhancing Learning and Knowledge Practices in Team Meetings*. PhD Thesis. University of Sydney, Faculty of Arts and Social Sciences Centre for Research on Learning and Innovation.

Levin, P. (1982). Development Cycles the Cycles of Development. *Transactional Analysis Journal*, 12(2), 129–139.

Mullen, C. A. (2020). Practices of Cognitive Apprenticeship and Peer Mentorship in a Cross-Global STEM Lab. *The Wiley International Handbook of Mentoring: Paradigms, Practices, Programs, and Possibilities*, 243–260.

Newton, T. (2006). Script, Psychological Life Plans, and the Learning Cycle. *TAJ*, 36(3).

Newton, T., & Napper, R. (2000). *TACTICS for Adult Learning*. Ipswich: TA Resources.

Nisbet, G., Dunn, S., & Lincoln, M. (2015). Interprofessional Team Meetings: Opportunities for Informal Interprofessional Learning. *Journal of Interprofessional Care*, 29(5), 426–432. doi: 10.3109/13561820.2015.1016602.

Rogelberg, S. G. (2018). *The Surprising Science of Meetings: How You Can Lead Your Team to Peak Performance*. Oxford: Oxford University Press.

Rogelberg, S. G., Scott, C., & Kello, J. (2007). The Science and Fiction of Meetings. *MIT Sloan Management Review*, 48(2), 18–21.

Schmid, G. (2008). The Role Concept of Transactional Analysis and Other Approaches to Personality, Encounter, and Cocreativity for All Professional Fields. *TAJ*, 38(1).

Seel, N. M., Al-Diban, S., & Blumschein, P. (2002). Mental Models & Instructional Planning. In *Integrated and Holistic Perspectives on Learning, Instruction and Technology*. Dordrecht: Springer, pp. 129–158.

Spector, J. M. (2000). Towards a Philosophy of Instruction. *Educational Technology & Society*, 3(3).

Steiner, C. M. (1968). Dunnette's Games. *American Psychologist*, 23(2), 134-135, Washington DC, USA.

Tyrangiel, H. (2011). On Skype with Eric Berne: What Did He Say After He Said Hello? *TAJ*, Transactional Analysis Journal. (2012). 42(4), 265–276. 41(1).

Van Den Bossche, P., Gijselaers, W. H., Segers, M., & Kirschner, P. A. (2006). Social and Cognitive Factors Driving Teamwork in Collaborative Learning Environments: Team Learning Beliefs and Behaviors. *Small Group Research*, 37(5), 490–521. doi: 10.1177/1046496406292938.

Van Poelje, S. (2004). Learning for Leadership. *TAJ*, 34(3).

Wiss, A., DeLoia, J. A., Posey, L., Waight, N., & Friedman, L. (2018). Faculty Development for Online Learning Using a Cognitive Apprenticeship Model. *International Journal on Innovations in Online Education*, 2(1).

Appendices

APPENDIX 1: COMPETENCE CURVE

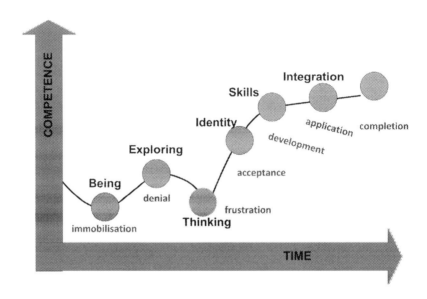

Competence Curve - Kübler-Ross (1983), Levin (1988), Napper and Newton (2000) Hay (1991, 2009).

APPENDIX 2: INTEGRATING PREVIOUS EXPERIENCE AND LEARNING – ENHANCING THE COMPETENCE CURVE SUPPORT STRATEGIES

1. STAGE	2. Behaviour Clues & Observations	3. Reason	4. Previous experience & learning	5. Individual Needs: Yours & Others	6. Leadership strategies to support Staff
1 Immobilisation **BEING**	We need time to absorb the change and to compare our expectations to the new reality. Can appear to be marking time, doing nothing, maybe not coping. **Competence drops** **Withdrawal** **Marking time**	• We lack information about the new situation. • We are concerned about doing it wrong and appearing stupid. • We may lack the motivation to make the change work.	• *Think about previous work change experiences and context.* • *What was the context of the change?* • *Remember the range of experiences and emotions you felt.* ***What aspects of your being at this stage will be helpful to the current situation?***	Time to get used to being in a new situation. We need reassurance and not to be pressured into starting the change too quickly. **Reassurance** **Time to get used to the change**	Provide clear and written information about change You're doing fine Ask me anytime. . . Contain anxiety **STAY IN FREQUENT CONTACT WITH INDIVIDUALS**
2 Denial **DOING**	We act as if our behaviour patterns and knowledge from the past will still be appropriate.	Problems can arise if: • We feel a threat to our level of competence and skill.	• *What were the various roles you held and were involved with?* • *What is similar about the current*	We want to explore at our own pace. We want others to be patient with us while we take time to describe	I like the way you ask awkward questions Provide clear boundaries including what is open to negotiation and what is a management decision

				STIMULATE STAFF – OPEN COMMUNICATION
	We hope our existing skills and knowledge will still be useful. **Can act as if nothing has changed** **Can waste time**	• We are reluctant to experiment. • We fear failure and rationalize that it worked okay for us in the past so why not now. • We can be unaware of our denial and continue to do and behave in that was previously successful. Slowly we allow our defence mechanisms to weaken and start to notice the need for change.	*change that is about to occur?* • *What is different?* • *What were your lessons learned about yourself, groups and organisations from what happened during the change?* **What aspects of what you were doing will be helpful for the current situation?**	and assess our situation. We may want to go off on our own to get more information, or to meet others and find out what they would do. **Patience** **Change to explore own way**
3 Frustration THINKING	We now recognize we need to do things differently and we don't know how.	• Potential overload due to our genuine need to learn new approaches	• *What were your key frustrations and emotions at the various stages*	We now want to do our own thinking about the change. We need tolerant listeners	Review information, timetables and roles Focus on individuals Invite feedback Listen to problem solving without judgment

(*Continued*)

(Continued)

1. STAGE	2. Behaviour Clues & Observations	3. Reason	4. Previous experience & learning	5. Individual Needs: Yours & Others	6. Leadership strategies to support Staff
	We can feel incompetent during our efforts to apply new approaches. Others may think of us as incompetent as we struggle with new skills, new knowledge and new situations. Sometimes we turn our frustration against others and see to blame them for our position. We can blame others for not helping us enough, not training us properly beforehand, even not warning	• Fear of losing status through decreased competence • Loss of our power base or our network of contacts • We struggle to work out how we should be and what to do different, what new skills do we need, what qualities are required in the new situation.	and phases of the change? • Do you remember repetitive themes of thinking (and feeling)? • What was other people's thinking? • How did this thinking differ or was the same as yours? What aspects and kinds of thinking will be helpful for the current situation?	to discuss our thoughts and opinions. We need models and frameworks, so we can understand what is going on for us. It will help if people ask us questions and listen to our ideas with interest. **Tolerance** **Test own Thinking**	Ask how individuals are feeling **PROVIDE CLEAR INSTRUCTURES**

		us against the problems we now face. **May want to manage the managers** **Know they need to change but not sure how**		
4	Acceptance **IDENTITY**	We let go of the attitudes and behaviours and skills that were comfortable and useful in the past. We can now start the process of acquiring new skills. We begin to test out our new ways of doing things. There will still be occasional moments of frustration, such as when our new skills are not quite practiced enough, or we identify	• We consider the differences and develop frameworks for understanding where we are now. • We begin to actively experiment. • We may still appear incompetent to a degree. • We are working out our identity in the changed situation, so although we have now accepted the	• *List the key acceptance turning points?* • *What and who helped you through the change process?* • *How do you remember your identity from your own and others' perspectives?* • *How will your experiences inform your leadership during this change process?*	We move into creating our revised identity. We need to believe that we have an element of choice and that others will be accepting of whatever we decide. At this stage we consider alternatives, so it will help if we have some knowledge of problem solving and decision-making models.	Invite staff to work out implications of options and prioritise effectiveness Give positive feedback about individuals in front of their peer group **GIVE RECOGNITION TO STAFF AND WORK**

(*Continued*)

(Continued)

1. STAGE	2. Behaviour Clues & Observations	3. Reason	4. Previous experience & learning	5. Individual Needs: Yours & Others	6. Leadership strategies to support Staff
	yet another area where we lack knowledge. This phase represents our move psychologically into our personal learning cycle. We review the situation and compare it with the past to identify difference. **Time to explore and select options appropriate to new situations**	change there will still be temporary problems as we try out new approaches.	• What support will you specifically need? **What aspects about your identity will be helpful for the current situation?**	**Acceptance** **Defining own identity**	

| 5 | Development SKILLS | We concentrate on developing the skills and knowledge required in the new situation. We become increasingly competent at operating in the changed environment. We make decisions about the most effective techniques and then become skilled at using them. **Acquiring new skills and knowledge** | Our knowledge increases so that others come to regard us as the appropriate expert in our field. | • *What types of learning served you well?*
• *Where the major learnings?*
• *How will these benefit this current change?*
• *Do you require further skills and how can this happen?*
What skills and knowledge could you pass on or recommend for the current situation? | We are now ready to learn the skills required to effect the change. Coaching and training might be required once we have determined our action plan. **Training** **Support** **Team Building** | Provide time for training and development including mentoring and coaching
Feedback to provide a sense of progress
Focus on developing teams and interdependence
FOSTER EXCITING ASPECTS OF WORK |

(*Continued*)

(Continued)

1. STAGE	2. Behaviour Clues & Observations	3. Reason	4. Previous experience & learning	5. Individual Needs: Yours & Others	6. Leadership strategies to support Staff
6 Application **INTEGRATION**	Most importantly we consolidate our identity in our changed role/ changed CRM. We develop our own views on how the job should be done, how we should relay this to others and how they should relay it to us. **Applying new skills** **Teams settle**	We resolve in our minds the questions about our status, our new skills, our beliefs about the situation, and our view of the organization. In particular we work out how we fit in the new scheme of things.	• *How did you integrate your new knowledge, skills and learning?* • *What did you notice other people in relation to integration of new skills, knowledge and learning?* • *What and how would you notice in your leadership for this change project that has integrated your previous experiences?* ***How will you integrate your past experience and knowledge for the current situation?***	We want to integrate the previous stages. We start pulling together our prior efforts of exploration, decision making and learning. Gradually, we begin to feel that we are performing as we should. We may rework some of the earlier stages to cover parts we missed. **Encouragement** **Delegation**	Compliment staff on how they are integrating change Be clear about future change, budgets, timetables Review strategic plan Revise objectives for the year **ENSURE ENDINGS OF PROJECTS & MOVING ON/NEW CHANGES**

| 7 Completion RECYCLING | We now feel comfortable and competent once again – so much so that we are no longer conscious of having experienced a transition. **Maximum competence** | We are really into the new situation and have ceased to compare it, favourably or unfavourably, to our position before the change. | • How did you recycle the lessons learned from the past? **What are some of the ways you will note and capture your new learnings from this current change?** | We have completed our transition and are on our way with a changed approach. Soon we will hardly remember how we were before we made the changes. **Interdependence** | Roles models, champions and leaders |

Source: (Adapted from: Kübler-Ross (1983), Levin (1988), Newton & Napper (2000), Hay (1991, 2011))

10
ORGANIZATIONAL CULTURES AND CHANGE INTERVENTIONS

Ugo De Ambrogio

Organizational cultures

In the sociological literature and in social psychology, organizational cultures have been widely addressed. This concept has become part of the common language of consultants and organizational analysts.

In transactional analysis many authors have also written about organizational culture, starting with Berne.

Berne describes three levels of organization: the structure and interpersonal levels in the public domain and the psychodynamic level, which is private and subconscious. Berne places organizational culture in the psychodynamic level. He says that an organizational culture is influenced by a Parent component, which he calls etiquette, Adult technicalities and a Child component, which he calls Character.

If we adopt this definition we think of the organization as a subject that has its own personality that is different from the sum of the personalities of the people who compose it. The organization has its own character, and this character is its culture. Therefore, in TA we could also say: "The ego states of the organization define the personality of the organization" (Berne, 1963, p. 112).

Rolf Balling states:

> Organizational culture is a set of habits and behaviours of organizational life that are typically exhibited by the members of the organization. They are accompanied by specific values, feelings and beliefs. Together they constitute the "personality" of the organization which is considered a living system.
> (Balling, 2005, p. 15)

Schein defines organizational culture in a very similar way:

> It is the total sum of all the shared and given for granted assumptions that a group has learned along its history . . . a particular symbolic universe that derives from interpretations, opinions and representations of reality, exchanged daily by the individuals who work there.
> (Schein, 2000, p. 23)

According to Mintzberg, there are five types of organizational configurations that have many similarities with the organizational cultures we are talking about in this chapter. Mintzberg claims that there is no unique and optimal way to build an organization, be it a factory, an office or something else. Instead, there are different ways, and the optimal choice depends on the circumstances or on the "contingencies in which the organization operates, which determines its uniqueness and culture (Mintzberg, 1993, p. 70)."

Typology of culture

Many types of organizational culture or analytical models can be used to understand the unique character of organizations.

Balling (2005) identifies three types of organizational cultures to which, according to the characteristics of the different professional worlds, organizations, despite their uniqueness, approach each other. I will add two models that I developed which are related to my experience as a consultant engaged mainly with non-profit organizations and public organizations (De Ambrogio, Dondi, Santarelli, 2017).

Organizational cultures are not good or bad. They can be functional or dysfunctional, effective or dangerous, just like people, depending on whether they are balanced, excessive or extreme. Generally, if they are conscious and balanced, they represent real or potential. Ahead they are described through analytical models that we can find more or less close to the various dimensions of reality.

The five models of organizational culture are:

1   Culture of Cohesion (paternalistic)
2   Culture of Order (hyper-efficient)
3   Culture of Challenge (spontaneous)
4   Culture of Rules and Procedures (hyper-bureaucratic)
5   Culture of Obedience (closed)

The first model is called the "Culture of Cohesion". It can become a paternalistic culture if exaggerated. Many non-profit organizations, characterized by charismatic but directive leaders, come close to this model, but it can also be found in small and medium-sized enterprises. For example in the Northeast or Central Italy, companies that have many organizational characteristics of a family, sometimes with a father-master who makes most decisions.

It is a cultural model rich in resources and potential, which creates belonging in its members, motivation for "productivity" and satisfaction in the various subjects involved (operators, beneficiaries). The main risk that Balling himself identifies is isolation.

Balling points out that when this very rich cultural model assumes rigid and negative traits, becoming exaggerated, it places the organization in an attitude of devaluation of the external world, which triggers behaviors that exclusively

Table 10.1 Characteristics of a culture of cohesion

Characteristics	Culture of cohesion
Image	Family
Typical ways of thinking	How can we develop a community in which employees like to cooperate and align their visions?
Fundamental issue	Emotional cohesion, shared visions
Beliefs	If we are together and are faithful to our values, we can overcome all difficulties
Prerequisites of the organization	A positive image of the organization in society that invites workers to identify with "family"
How the organization typically works	People position themselves as "spiders in the web", board members live (embody) the organizational culture
Type of people involved	Harmonized values and beliefs; strong demand for identification with something good
Resources inherent to organizational culture	Emotional bond and alignment of a common vision: the feeling of being at home; the common interest prevails over the interest of the individual
Risks when the organizational culture is exaggerated	Isolation, devaluing the outside world, symbolic loyalty requested by employees

Source: Translated from Balling, R. (2005). Diagnosis of Organizational Cultures, TAJ, p. 35.

highlight the symbolic fidelity required of members and in fact they lose the potential of effective intervention and interest for the community.

Goleman, in his text *Leadership: The Power of Emotional Intelligence*, identifies six leadership styles:

1. Visionary leader: he is able to share a dream and an objective with his employees and creates a particularly positive climate in the company. It is essential to use this style when the company is going through a moment of change.
2. Leader coach: he is able to create a link between the corporate objective and the aspirations of the individual worker. It is good to use this style to help employees improve their performance.
3. Affiliate leader: he is able to favor interpersonal relationships with his own actions, creating good company harmony. The approach is useful for creating a compact team.
4. Democratic leader: he enhances employees by seeking support before making decisions, creating a participatory environment. This style is useful for maintaining a productive work environment and getting good feedback.
5. Tread leader: he is able to reach the imposed targets first, precisely by treading. This style when used has not given excellent results since an abuse of the approach creates anxiety on the part of the employees. It can be used when facing new situations and markets.
6. Authoritarian leader: those who use this style send directives that do not include replication. Normally he motivates the staff with the fear of the consequences that will happen in case of failure, creating a difficult organization climate in which the individuals will hardly take responsibility. This style is recommended only in cases of emergency and financial crisis.

Using the leadership styles proposed by Goleman, we can see that often the organizations in which this character prevails are guided by **Affiliate Leaders,** who succeed in fostering interpersonal relationships with their actions, creating good harmony at the organizational level, or as **Democratic Leaders**, who enhance employees by seeking their support before making decisions, creating in this way a participatory and sharing environment.

This approach to leadership in cohesion-oriented organizations is useful for creating a compact team, but it may also require further attention to avoid isolation and self-referentiality, or to require leadership that also works to build collaborative relationships and network. This orientation toward leadership assumes a crucial importance in this vision, because it faces the risk of isolation and pathological drift of organizations in which the culture of cohesion prevails, whereas enhancing the aspect of effectiveness inherent to this cultural model favors the capacity for openness to cohesion understood as opportunities for cooperation and co-planning for the realization of efficient interventions and policies that create benefits for the community and satisfaction in the relationship among the subjects involved.

Table 10.2 Characteristics of a culture of order

Characteristics	Culture of order
Image	Machine
Typical ways of thinking	How can we build an organizational structure in which all functions integrate optimally?
Fundamental issue	Orientation to order the facts, strict definition of the objectives
Beliefs	Workers are like a machine gear: they have to work properly
Prerequisites of the organization	A certain level of business that justifies the effort to engineer all processes
How the organization typically works	Tendency to develop sophisticated structures, management by objectives, accurate description of tasks and duties.
Type of people involved	Good formal qualifications, when applied they show a pragmatic "mercenary mentality".
Resources inherent to organizational culture	Clear contracts on competences and objectives; whoever carries out is "free"; he or she can go home if the job is done; quick comparison when the plans are not satisfactory
Risks when organizational culture is exaggerated	Paralysis due to routine; human needs devalued or managed with technocratic distance

Source: Translated from Balling, R. (2005). Diagnosis of Organizational Cultures, TAJ, p. 35.

The second model is the so-called Culture of Order which can become, if exaggerated, of hyper-efficient type. This type of culture is strongly oriented to the result; it is frequently encountered in multinationals or in certain large, highly structured organizations, and it is also possible to meet it in companies that are also small in size but highly structured, which mainly have this type of cultural trait. Furthermore, even in public companies such as ASLs or hospitals, cultural traits of this type can be frequently found.

Referring to Goleman's leadership models, it seems particularly widespread and effective for organizations in which this trait of character prevails, the so-called **Tread Leader**, who is able to reach the imposed goals first by being a forerunner or tread for the other collaborators.

Also this cultural model is rich in resources and potential, it allows working efficiently to achieve appreciable results that create belonging in their members, linked to "productivity". The main risk that Balling himself stresses for the organizations approaching this model is identifiable in the devaluation of individual needs of the people who work in the organization, which causes dissatisfaction and frustration.

If in fact exaggerated traits of this culture prevail, there is the risk that tread leaders pay little attention to the needs of the people who work in their organization; they are leaders not inclined to exchange relational recognitions with their collaborators who are not gratified and often find themselves dissatisfied, becoming passive or looking at other professional alternative companies. An effective leader will also be able to assume other attitudes: he takes care of the relationships among people and of the exchange of recognitions as a driving factor that develops in the organizations of this type, and also elements of a culture of cohesion, to be integrated as complementary to the culture of order and at the same time to stimulate the development of creativity and individual motivation in order to enhance elements linked to the culture of challenge.

The third model is the so-called Culture of Challenge, which can become, if it assumes excessive characteristics, too spontaneous and almost "anarchic".

It is a frequent model found in certain social movements or in certain newly founded political parties but also in voluntary associations or organizations closely linked to product innovation, such as those operating in fashion or advertising sector where it is strongly motivated the dimension of creativity and professional freedom of the subjects that are part of it.

The leader of organizations with a prevailing orientation toward the culture of challenge often has the characteristics of the **Visionary Leader** described by Goleman: he is able to share a dream and an objective with the employees and creates a particularly exciting atmosphere in the company, linked to the possible realization of the "dream". An effective leader allowing the effective realization of the objectives may, however, combine the characteristics of the "visionary one" with the attention to motivational and value aspects (cohesion) as well as with aspects linked to the more defined structuring of roles, tasks, rules and

Table 10.3 Characteristics of a culture of challenge

Characteristics	Culture of challenge
Image	Playground
Typical ways of thinking	How can we build a platform where our professionals can realize their ideas and have fun at the same time?
Fundamental issue	Get a kick out of work, individual freedom
Beliefs	Beautiful people and beautiful ideas will win; roles and hierarchies are obstacles to flexibility
Prerequisites of the organization	Position in the market and in the technology that leads to professional challenges and the freedom to implement them in an innovative way
How the organization typically works	"Street gang" mentality, people organize themselves around natural problems, activities and leaders
Type of people involved	Motivated and competent for the task; they possess proven initiative and creativity
Resources inherent to organizational culture	Common questions, support for creative innovations; Fun and "easy-going" attitude supported by a lot of energy
Risks when the organizational culture is exaggerated	No protection in case of mobbing, "inventing the wheel again every day" order devaluation and leadership

Source: Translated from Balling, R. (2005). Diagnosis of Organizational Cultures, TAJ, p. 35.

procedures. Even this potentially rich and effective cultural model presents a threat if it is taken to extremes: in these cases, the fact that energies are concentrated mainly in always looking "forward" by promoting creativity and spontaneity leads the organizational structure not to be consolidated and spontaneity prevails, and excessive autonomy and separation between individual professionals or work teams can cause even high conflict with consequent drift up to possible separations.

It seems appropriate to add two more cultures to the three organizational ones proposed by Balling.

I think they are in some ways complementary to the three described so far and allow us to broaden the spectrum of models to which we refer.

The first of these is the Culture of Rules and Procedures which potentially contains important resources and values, such as the pursuit of fair treatment of citizens in front of a service or public policy.

However, if this type of culture develops in exaggerated terms, it can become "bureaucratic" in the negative sense of the term. It is a quite frequent drift of this model in public administrations that have in their organizational DNA a strong attention to the "declared", to how things have to be done, which sometimes colludes with what is actually requested by customers or by citizenship. The risks, when this culture is exaggerated, are that there is low productivity or that poor quality products or services are produced and they are not very efficient and effective for citizens. Compared with the internal dynamics these risks can induce behaviors such as absenteeism or the exit of people, because "there is always a person at the top to blame". On the subject, A. O. Hirsman talks about possible strategies of consumers, but also of members of organizations, to deal with conflicts and disagreements, the exit and the voice and considers loyalty and the sense of belonging as a crucial variable in orienting the choice toward one or the other direction (Hirsman, 2002).

Finally, the last culture proposed is the Culture of Obedience, frequent in organizations such as armies, monasteries, law enforcement agencies or, in some ways, prisons. A certain degree of obedience and discipline is functional and essential to organizations that have specific objectives such as having to guarantee the social order in situations of turbulence or participation in war conflicts, or the control of people who are expiating a sin. However, this culture can also be found exaggeratedly expressed in corporate organizations, especially in times of crisis, which used the culture of obedience, relying on precarious contracts and threats of dismissal, a strong argument to stay on the market.

In a recent Italian film by Paolo Virzì entitled *Tutta la Vita Davanti*, the life of a call center is represented very close to the model of the culture of obedience. In it, behind an apparent calm and healthy competition climate is hidden a climate in which ties and high productivity are guaranteed by the fear of job loss, and for this reason employees obey until they become excessively overworked.

Table 10.4 Characteristics of a culture of rules and procedures

Characteristics	Culture of rules and procedures
Image	Tax office
Typical ways of thinking	How can we do what is prescribed by limiting the action to what is due?
Fundamental issue	To do (only) what is within its competence, respecting the rules correctly
Beliefs	Doing your duty means respecting rules and procedures
Prerequisites of the organization	Position of privilege or monopoly in the market, which allows a volume of work defined a priori with little or no competition
How the organization typically works	We work in response to prescriptions, fearing sanctions rather than sharing values and objectives
Type of people involved	Formally qualified staff (usually employed by competition) but poorly motivated
Resources inherent to organizational culture	Clear functions and strict division of tasks, strong hierarchy of roles
Risks when the organizational culture is exaggerated	Risk of low productivity and absenteeism (exit): "There is always a manager at the top to blame for dysfunctions"

In organizations of this type we inevitably find leaders that Goleman defines as **Authoritarian**: a style that gives directives that do not provide for replication. The staff is motivated by the fear of consequences in case of failure, creating a difficult business climate in which individuals will hardly take responsibility.

The leader of these organizations should not be conniving with the risky aspects of this model (bureaucratization), but they should value their positive and important traits such as the fairness of the treatment and the respect of the rules; furthermore, they can operate as Goleman suggests, as **Leader Coach**: they are able to create a link between the organization objective and the aspirations of individual workers and introduce elements of development of cooperation, creativity and motivation, which other cultural models suggest as complementary.

Goleman recommends this style exclusively for cases of emergency and financial crisis. We believe that in organizations where the culture of order prevails, the authoritarian leader is a natural complementary effect, but we think that, without devaluing the aspects linked to loyalty and obedience, leaders will also be able to use other levers (collaboration, motivation, recognition and respect for rules, development of work by objectives) to broaden the cultural horizon of these organizations.

As the following table on the characteristics of a culture of obedience shows the main risk when this culture develops in an exaggerated way is that of rebellion and mutiny; in fact, if the loyalty to the organization is lacking, a strong reaction by the participants is likely. Next, I present a table prepared by P. Cola where the five models are schematically represented.

As I said before, the models of organizational cultures must be considered as analytical models for which there is no culture that is good or bad, each can be effective and functional, or ineffective and dysfunctional, depending on the characteristics of the contexts, on the reference markets (there are markets where it is easier to move with a certain cultural model and markets where it is easier to move with another) and on more balanced or exaggerated ways in which these cultures manifest themselves.

In the previous pages I have already pointed out how the role of a leader can be who takes into account the prevailing organizational culture and enhances and integrates it for the development of one's organization.

Now I would also like to highlight the role of the organizational consultant who is called by the management of a company to intervene in order to produce improvements and organizational changes in situations of impasses.

The analysis of the prevalent organizational cultures in an organization allows us to deduce important elements of diagnosis that then allow us to intervene effectively.

Next I present two examples of organizational consultancy where I have been involved, in which I intervened to change or, better, to integrate the organizational cultures, improving the "character" of the organizations and consequently their work.

Table 10.5 Characteristics of a culture of obedience

Characteristics	Culture of obedience
Image	Army
Typical ways of thinking	How can we make a mechanism based on strict rules work?
Fundamental issue	Reaching goals by enforcing orders
Beliefs	Order and discipline are the operating factors of the organization
Prerequisites of the organization	Position return linked to the definition of business volume given a priori
How the organization typically works	We work in response to orders, fearing penalties rather than sharing values and objectives
Type of people involved	Obedient staff, looking for overprotection (hyper-adapted)
Resources inherent to organizational culture	Roles with rigid and controlling positions; strong identity linked to the idea of belonging to a "powerful" group
Risks when the organizational culture is exaggerated	Protest (mutiny) if loyalty and a sense of belonging are lacking

Table 10.6 Characteristics of all five culture types

Culture of Cohesion	The affective P prevails, the organization has the appearance of a family. Belonging to this reality is a positive and protective factor, the invitation is to please, to adapt to the organizational culture. Examples are family businesses or non-profit organizations. There is the risk of isolating oneself from the external context and devaluing it, emphasizing internal loyalty. If one's model is exalted it becomes rigid and negative with paternalistic tendencies.
Culture of Order	The technical-scientific component prevails, the directives are at the center of the organizational activity and the life of the members and direct it. It is a reality that is often very sophisticated, well structured and organized, interested in qualifying and focused on the objectives to be achieved. This is the case not only of many multinationals or technology companies but also of the third sector public companies like ASL. If these resources are exaggerated, there is the danger of hyper-efficiency, of penalizing individual needs, in a climate that is lacking in recognition, so that members slip into passivity. We can speak in the most extreme cases of an Excluder Adult.
Culture of Challenge	The central value is the creativity of C, giving space to the potential and the resources of people committed to winning a challenge. Every time we start over: procedures and rules are put back into the background. This happens in spontaneous movements, in the area of associations and volunteering. The constant push forward is likely to make autonomy prevail and to loosen group and system cohesion, causing separation and in the most extreme cases anarchist attitudes.
Culture of Rules and Procedures	The normative component of the P prevails; there are important resources and values relating to the fairness of treatment and the importance of the rules. However, if these aspects are exaggerated, the members can only adapt; performing their task becomes a compliance with the rules. In this way the general and individual motivation is not fed. Membership in the organization can become adaptation or absenteeism and take the form of delegating responsibilities, as happens in highly bureaucratic situations and in some public administrations.
Culture of Obedience	It includes organizations that often have no competitors in their sector; they are closed realities. Obedience and discipline, however important, within certain margins, may risk replacing motivation and the sharing of values, even for the threat of sanctions. There is the risk of rebellion. This series includes armies, prisons and religious communities. Today certain realities in response to the current crisis tend to make the culture of obedience prevail with conditions of strong contractual precariousness and continuous hypotheses of restructuring (which involve dismissals).

Source: Casartelli, Cola,Merlini,2017, p.172.

From a methodological point of view I proceeded in both cases, adhering to the following paths:

Phase 1: negotiation with the board (**Preliminary meeting, dialogue, in-depth interview** with each of the players of the group of **managers**, aimed at identifying the different points of view on the current phase of the organization's life, on its current structure, and the expectations of change of each)

Phase 2: diagnosis (conduct an interview through a questionnaire) on organizational cultures to all operators – hypothesis of diagnosis highlighting strength points ("secure base" of the organization) and weakness transformed into improvement objectives – focus group with all the workers to compare hypotheses of diagnosis and collect possible strategies for change

Phase 3: co-design with the management a project of experimentation of the changes (e.g. realization of training courses of team building to develop cohesion culture, of co-designing of new practices to develop the culture of order)

Phase 4: experimentation and evaluation of the project of changement (launch of the experimentation – co-designing of the evaluation plan – data collection and evaluation (identification of the results achieved and assessment of strengths and weaknesses of the experimentation of the new organization) – development of a project to implement changes

The first example refers to a public company of personal services (of about 50 employees) which is expanding on the market of socio-educational services in its territory. This organization asked the company for which I work for an organizational diagnosis to understand in which direction to intervene to change the current organizational set-ups and how to accompany their own board in a delicate phase of generational change, since the historical leader was close to retirement.

The board was made up of a director and three area managers who also make up the board of directors and their operators (45 company professionals – these are social workers, educators, psychologists, social assistance auxiliaries and administrative employees).

In order to grasp the specific traits of the character of the organization with some colleagues (Federica Artiaco, Patrizia Cola, Andrea Dondi, Paola Fusaro, Davide Garofalo, Stefano Lauciello, Francesca Merlini, a.k.a. OrganizzAT supervision group) we developed a diagnostic questionnaire of the organizational culture that we subsequently submitted to the entire group of professionals (50 people).

The questionnaire, consisting of 30 items, asks for a score to be assigned to six sentences for each organizational culture, each of which represents an indicator of a specific organizational culture model contemplating its values, leadership style and prevailing relational modalities, or "how the organization typically works". (As an example, in the following figure, we present the two sections of the questionnaire related to the culture of order and the culture of rules and procedures. For each field, a score from 1 to 10 has to be assigned, in which *10* is completely corresponding to how your organization is and *1* is totally not corresponding to how your organization is.)

We then calculated the average of these scores and placed them in a graphical representation (the pentagon of organizational cultures) shown in the next figure.

Table 10.7 Sample from diagnostic questionnaire of organizational culture

Item	Score	Culture of Order
19		We are afraid of making mistakes
20		Orders are only given by the superior
21		If you execute the orders well, you are rewarded
22		Discipline is a value of this organization
23		Only what is said to do will be done
24		To obey protects responsibilities

Item	Score	Culture of Rules and Procedures
25		Bosses have the function of enforcing regulations and procedures
26		You do your duty and you are right
27		Rules are fundamental to guarantee fair treatment
28		You do not deal with issues that do not compete to you
29		You try to be unassailable
30		Fairness, transparency and equal treatment are guaranteed

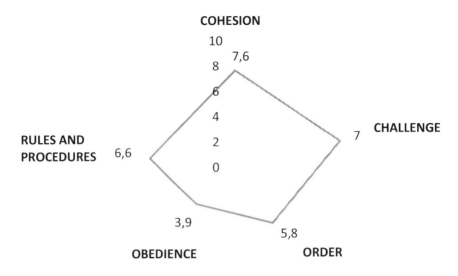

Figure 10.1 The pentagon of organizational cultures – public company of personal services (northwest Italy)

Reading the averages of the scores obtained allowed me to draw synthetic elements of organizational diagnosis by tracing the "character" of the organization on the basis of the mix of organizational cultures that are proper to it. This is an excellent starting point for the consultant to identify the possible strengths and paths for improvement that the consultant can suggest to the company management.

For example, in the case presented we can see that the organization has marked traits of cohesion, a certain orientation to challenge, median values related to order and rules and procedures, little propensity to obedience.

In this organization the leader, close to retirement, maintained a paternalistic spirit. He seemed good natured and we could say good looking, but in fact he was a top-down centralist, and in the organization there were few rules, little sharing and a father-master.

The change at the top (due to the retirement of the historical leader and also thanks to the reflections of the new director during his coaching with me) has allowed the generation of a more functional leadership to promote a change in terms of positive development of this cultural model. The new leader is committed to stimulating change, and in empathy with the organizational culture, he has shown good will in serving the organization without ambitions for power, keeping attention to the affective dimension of cohesion, which is crucial for the development of the organization, also supporting it with attention to the normative aspects, with an orientation toward more certain rules, attention and respect of the roles, more transparency in the modalities of taking decisions, which instead, often, with the previous leader, was lacking. Therefore the type of change that was

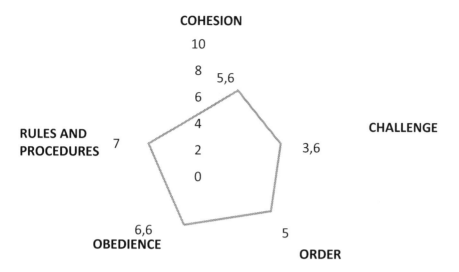

Figure 10.2 The pentagon of organizational cultures – public company of a municipality (northeast Italy)

proposed was not a revolutionary one but a "reformist" improvement in the life of the organization that remained with its main cultural character oriented toward cohesion. The organization began to set more operational objectives, to build a clear structure of roles and tasks, to provide for delegations and dissemination of leadership, to build clearer and more transparent spaces, places and decision-making procedures, to listen to and recognize disagreements and their collective elaboration.

This strategy has therefore made it possible to "rebalance" the character of this organization, enhancing the traits of cohesion and challenge and at the same time strengthening those of *order, rules, procedures and obedience.*

A second example concerns a public administration (the social policy sector of a municipality in a provincial capital town) which I followed for some years as a consultant. Here the pentagon has highlighted a prevailing culture of rules and procedures, followed by order, cohesion and obedience, with little inclination to challenge.

The historical leader (an administrative manager) used to write and rewrite procedures to find new and better ones with the illusion that proposing new prescriptive rules could produce change and satisfy the wishes of the various advisors. The result was immobility. They spoke about changing things, but things always remained the same. The mistake consisted, in my opinion, in insisting on the appearance of rules and procedures without seeing further.

The change was possible when the historical leader went in another sector and a new leader came. During the coaching (I was the coach of the new manager of the sector) we agreed on a functional strategy to stimulate workers to think about values, about the meaning of organizational action, without devaluing rules and procedures but going deeper, looking over rules and procedures, recovering the organizational mission. It was also useful to pay more attention to executives and operators considering their experiences and needs (the use of the Affective Parent, that is, strengthening the character of the cohesion), and paying more attention to the citizen client, working to satisfy his needs not as a response to prescriptions, but as the development of a planning and evaluation perspective that is attentive to the evolution of the needs of the citizens of the territory and to the identification of opportunities and resources to be mobilized to face them (enhancing *challenge*). The program of change (carried out through training for operators, initiatives to raise public awareness, etc.) made people who worked in the organization proactive by bringing out their resources in terms of planning skills, creativity and recognition of results.

Conclusion

In conclusion I would like to point out that the idea of knowing and analyzing the organizational cultures within which we find ourselves working can be useful to those who want to improve organization and consider them as resources. The "organizational culture" is in fact a resource of the organization that must be recognized and caressed and not opposed and fought. Consultants or leaders who put themselves in a revolutionary position saying, "I don't like this organization, it should be turned like a glove", would presumably be ineffective; they would not be able to play their role and probably would not do a good service to their company, because the culture, the organizational personality has been built up during the time and has good reasons for being consolidated.

However, it can be improved and enriched with new cultural elements, drawn from other models, which allow the organizational personality to become more integrated.

When we learn new things as individuals we maintain the beliefs and knowledge we previously had and expand them, so the personality of an organization is progressively enriched with new and further points of view.

To operate in this way it is good that the consultant and the leader can perform the various cultural models when the organizations develops in imitative and exaggerated terms.

Therefore, a good consultant and a good leader do not detract from the culture of the organization but enhance it and reinforce it by proposing wider and more integrated visions. It is a question of operating in a similar way to what (Erskine, 2018) suggests in his approach to psychotherapy called "integrative AT". In strictly analytical-transactional terms it means in fact that one work in an integrated way with the organizational personality, dialoguing with all the states of one's self and of the organization, without the prevalence of an ego state and the minor presence of another.

Bibliography

Balling, R. (2005). Diagnosis of Organizational Cultures. *TAJ* (35).

Berne, E. (1963). *The Structure and Dynamics of Organizations and Groups*. Philadelphia: Lippincott.

Casartelli, A., Cola, P., & Merlini, F. (2017). *Il servizio sociale incontra l'Analisi Transazionale*. Santarcangelo di Romagna: Maggioli.

De Ambrogio, U., Dondi, A., & Santarelli, G. (2017). *Analisi transazionale e cambiamento nelle organizzazioni*. IRS.

De Ambrogio, U., & Guidetti, C. (2016). *La Coprogettazione*. Milano: Carocci.

Erskine, R. (2018). *L'analisi transazionale nella psicoterapia contemporanea*. Roma: Las.

Goleman, D. (2001). *Leadership: The Power of Emotional Intelligence*. Best Bur: selected writings.

Hirsman, A. O. (2002). *Lealtà, defezione e protesta*. Milano: Bompiani.

Mintzberg, H. (1993). *Structure in Fives. Designing Effective Organizations*. Englewood Cliffs: Prentice Hall.

Schein, E. (2000). *Culture d'Impresa. Come affrontare con successo le transizioni e i cambiamenti organizzativi*. Milano: Raffaello Cortina.

11

BERNE'S ORGANIZATIONAL THEORY APPLIED TO THE PREVENTION OF PSYCHOSOCIAL RISKS

A European phenomenon

Marleine Mazouz

Introduction

The aim of this chapter is to provide managers with simple and powerful tools for understanding and applying the organizational theory of Berne in the prevention of psychosocial risks of employees.

The WHO (World Health Organization) reminds us:

> *Mental health is not just the absence of mental disorders. It is defined as a state of well-being in which the person can fulfil himself, overcome the normal tensions of life, perform productive and fruitful work and contribute to community life.*

This definition alone sums up the central role of the leader toward his team and the environment.

Indeed, work situations involve and/or induce psychosocial risks whose causes are multiple:

- *Organizational constraints*
- *Demanding human resources management methods*
- *Managerial drifts*
- *Bullying*
- *Stress*
- *Burnout*

In addition, there are non-work causes that can have triggering or simply aggravating effects (ANACT, n.d.).

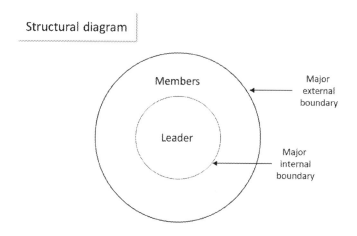

Figure 11.1 Structural diagram

Structure and dynamics

Eric Berne (1963), a psychiatrist, wrote a major book of transactional analysis (TA), *The Structure and Dynamics of Organizations and Groups*. In this work, he relies on his observations and his analysis of the functioning of a hospital type of organization.

This book also provides many avenues to enable the leader to exercise greater vigilance and help him understand the necessary actions to implement in terms of prevention of psychosocial risks and, the employees, who, when they undergo a managerial pressure which is too strong, tools allowing them to protect themselves and participate in the "healing" of the considered organization.

The following diagram visualizes the roles and missions as well as the dynamic that the leader implements to exercise his authority and power.

What is a boundary?

Definition from Wikipedia: *a boundary is a space of variable thickness, from the imaginary line to a particular space, separating or joining two territories, two sovereign states. The functions of a boundary can vary greatly according to regions and periods.*

At the level of a nation, the boundary indicates the boundary between two states and separates two regions within a state. It can be compared to thick and solid or porous and fragile skin. These limits therefore fulfil two functions for a nation:

- A protection, a security
- A confinement and prohibitions

Like, for example, the Berlin wall. Other boundaries also exist:

- Maritime boundaries
- Airspace boundaries

And, for this second example, we were able to witness dramas when an airplane crossed the airspace of a country without authorization.

The boundary therefore guarantees the space within which employees benefit from all the protection necessary for their physical and psychological well-being for better productivity.

Here the boundaries are clear and healthy. The leader plays his role and assumes his responsibilities. Psychosocial risk is little or not present. The team works well. Productivity is there.

Organizational structure: three types of structures

- **Simple structure**: a leader and his team whose major external boundary protects them from the environment. The psychosocial risk can be generated by the leader toward a member of the team or the whole team: it is a managerial drift.

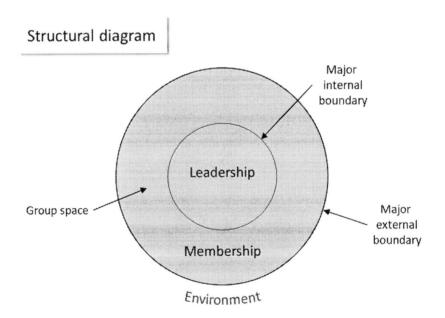

Figure 11.2 Structural diagram with environment

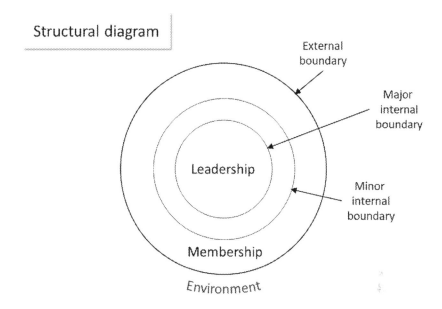

Figure 11.3 Three boundaries structural diagram

- **Composed structure**: several hierarchical levels. The psychosocial risk is present. The leader puts pressure on his subordinate who reproduces it with his team. In this hypothesis, in the event of a situation of ill-being at work, each hierarchical level can decline its responsibility and discount the reality of the situation (*Unconscious omission of information useful in solving a problem*, Schiff, 1971) with a passive behaviour: "*I am not responsible since I am not the one who originated it*".
- **Complex structure**: leadership and several teams. Each team is delimited by a minor internal boundary. Conflicts of interest arise from the difference in the needs of each team. There is potential for psychosocial risk and can arise if the leader does not exercise regulation between teams.

Of course, the *boundary* is a virtual concept. Its function is to bring security to the team. We observe that, in an organizational structure such as the previous three boundaries example, boundaries allow each team to work in its space. It protects all the members of this structure.

The *internal boundary* separates the leadership from the membership and makes it possible to distinguish who takes the initiatives, decides and gives instructions so that the team functions and produces.

The *minor internal boundary* separates the different categories of members (different departments, executives, employees).

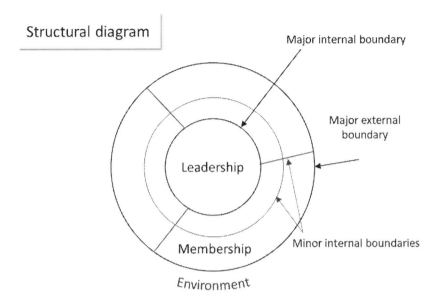

Figure 11.4 Three boundaries structural diagram with another sort of minor internal boundary

When leadership is exercised in a "healthy" way, it allows the team to avoid tensions and conflicts of interest. There is little or no psychosocial risk. There is energy, and activity is high.

How are the energies organized?

Balance between two energies

Easy to understand and diagnose, Berne evokes two types of energy:

- **Planned energy**: emanates from the leader, hierarchy, structure, missions

- **Emerging energy**: emanates from the members of the team, the working methods and the experiences of each

Each of these energies can have positive or negative effects on the leader and on team members, and in some cases can lead to dangerous situations with high psychosocial degrees.

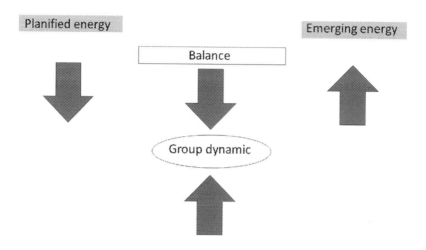

Figure 11.5 Two types of energies

This figure shows the balance between planned energy and emerging energy. The dynamics in this team neutralize any psychosocial risk.

The two energies, planned and emerging, are equal and maintain balance in the dynamics of this group. The quality of management is there. The well-being of employees is taken into account.

What are the risks in the event of imbalance?

Planned energy too low

When the leader is faced with a crisis within his team, if the planned energy is too low, that is, if the leader does not have the means to manage this crisis, then the emerging energy, the one that comes from employees, unbalances this dynamic and causes crises that can be dangerous for the company.

Indeed, if the leader does not assume his role and his responsibilities and does not exercise his authority, "the place being free", it is the emerging energy, that is, the one which comes from the bottom, which will take power. Leadership is in danger.

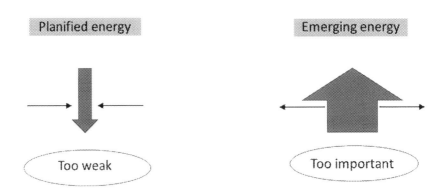

Figure 11.6 There is a dysfunction, when . . .

Example

A company fires an employee for gross misconduct. Teams are not informed of this decision until after the employee has left. Without information on reality, this situation causes agitation and fear within the teams. A strike of employees accentuates the weakness of the Management Committee, which is losing ground and failing to re-gain the trust of the teams.

The emerging energy is too strong. Power is shifting from leadership to collaborators. The company is in danger. It must act quickly to avoid a serious conflict that could leave indelible marks. Specifically, in this situation, the Management Committee misunderstood and/or poorly evaluated the reaction of the employees. Their agitation resulted in passive behaviour of the leaders and fear petrified them.

Planned energy too high

When the planned energy is too strong, it leads to too low an emerging energy with high psychosocial risks by the end.

In this specific case, we can assume a directive, even autocratic management that leaves no space or autonomy for its team. The team's creativity, productivity and enthusiasm are largely limited: "*I do just what I am asked, and nothing more, for the thanks that I have in return*".

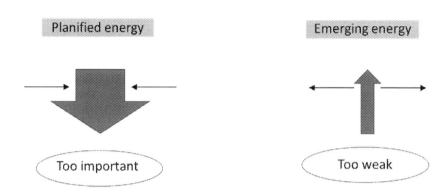

Figure 11.7 There is a dysfunction, when . . .

The leader does not benefit or does not benefit enough from the involvement of employees who do not receive positive strokes: "*We are not here for that; they must do their job!*"

The psychosocial risk has been proven and third-degree psychological games are indicated by:

- Human Resources management
- Employees
- Trade union organizations
- Occupational health
- Labour inspection

For Berne, a third-degree game ends:

- In court
- At the hospital
- At the morgue

Psychological games are part of the structuring of time which includes six, retreat, ritual, pastime, activity, game, intimity (Berne, 1964).

It is defined as *a **relational sequence** which consists of a series of transactions carried out in a given framework with a beginning and an end, which has a **hidden motive**, that is to say a psychological level different from the social level, which has as result the attainment of a **payoff** to each player.*

Most of the time, the proven psychosocial risk situation is due to:

- Work stress
- Moral harassment

Definition of moral harassment at work, as given by the European Agency for Safety and Health at Work:

- "Moral harassment in the workplace means repeated and abnormal behaviour directed against an employee or a group of employees while creating a risk to health and safety [physical or mental]".
- "Abnormal behaviour" means victimization, humiliation, decrease or threat, for example through an abuse of power.

Stress and moral harassment have devastating effects on those who experience them. These serious situations for the employee's health very often require the psychological support of a professional to enable him to get out of it.

In the case of moral harassment, the person presumed to be harassed has enormous difficulty in "returning to work". In many cases, a negotiation is made which leads to a contractual termination of the employment contract.

Increased vigilance is necessary. The employee – the victim – left the company. The presumed harasser is still in place. A high level of managerial discount or a refusal to take an objective look at the level of energy deployed by the leader can lead this same company to relive the same scenario.

How to restore the balance between two energies?

Three boundaries, three specific dynamics

- **Pressure/consistency**: when the environment puts pressure on the major external boundary, the leader's role is to provide energy of the same kind to bring consistency and maintain this balance.
  The environment can be represented by a person who is not part of the team and who plays second- or third-degree psychological games, which can undermine this balance.
- **Tension/regulation**: the leader faces two teams or two members of different teams who are experiencing difficulty and cannot find common ground in the organization of work. To restore balance between the two teams, his role is to regulate.
- **Agitation/security**: in this dynamic, the leader is faced with an agitation which comes from his team towards him. As we saw in the previous example, the leader must provide security to his team to avoid psychosocial risk.

BERNE'S ORGANIZATIONAL THEORY APPLIED

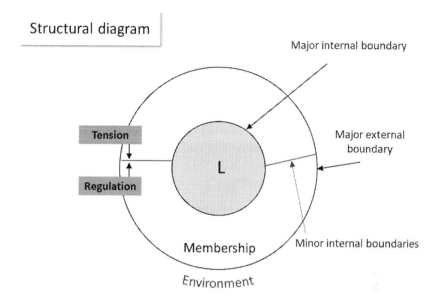

Figure 11.8 Dynamic diagram on external boundary

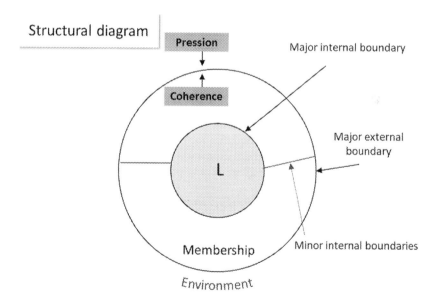

Figure 11.9 Dynamic diagram on minor internal boundary

183

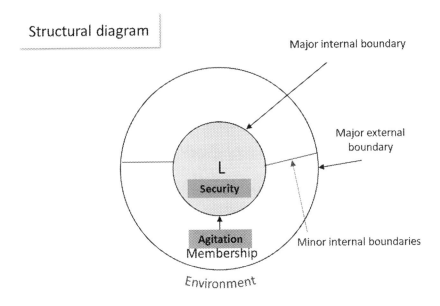

Figure 11.10 Dynamic diagram on major internal boundary

What is the role of the leader in preventing psychosocial risks?

The texts indicate that the effective responsible leaders are legally involved. As a reminder, the definition of the WHO: "*[A] state of well-being in which the person can achieve himself, overcome normal tensions of life, perform productive and fruitful work and contribute to community life*".

Doing "prevention" means anticipating risks and being attentive to the needs of employees, collectively and individually.

The company has an occupational health obligation and must organize information and training sessions so that all managers learn how to do these two actions:

1 **Detect the clues**: any fact, event, unusual attitude that is long-term or has a degree of seriousness in relation to a dysfunction.
2 **Adapt the official texts to a healthy, collaborative and participative managerial practice**: "Support managers to help them develop a culture of psychosocial risk prevention which has three levels:

   A **Primary level prevention**: identify risk factors to eliminate them or reduce their impact and develop a culture of prevention.

   • **The manager is aware of his level of responsibility** for the well-being of his employees. Everyone feels concerned and involved in the proper functioning of the team. Cooperation is a driver. Internal mutual support helps maintain a high level of collaboration and collective intelligence. The boundaries are clear. In case of difficulty, the team meets for its rapid resolution. There is a balance between planned energy and emerging energy (E. Berne, 1963). In this context of balance, everyone has his place and his role to play. The collaborators fulfil their mission and are autonomous.

The external consultant can intervene to maintain this high level of team cohesion.

B **Secondary level prevention**: develop the knowledge of employees, managers and key players and thus limit the exposure of employees to risky situations.

- **The manager acts through training and information** within his team. He looks after the resolution of the problem with which a member of the team was confronted to allow him to regain his productivity and his enthusiasm. In this step, he will be supported by an expert consultant in psychosocial risk prevention. He sets up a training and information action for the whole team. Objective: to allow each member of the team to better situate themselves within the team, which Berne calls "private structure": *"What members have in mind about their mutual relationships and their relationship to group activities and processes. The basic element of the private structure is the imago that each person has of himself in relation to the other members and especially to the leader; it is what allows him to orient himself when he commits to the service of the group's ideology and its cohesion, that is to say the force necessary for its survival"* (E. Berne, 1963, TAJ V, 4, october 1975, pp. 345–353).

  The consultant intervenes to help the team identify the malfunction(s) and implement corrective actions.

C **Tertiary level prevention**: support employees and teams in a major crisis; in reality, it is more about repairing than prevention.

- At this level, the manager cannot intervene. His role boils down to alerting the Human Resources department about the level of potential or proven danger. The aim is to take care of the weakened employee by setting up psychological support and protective measures for the team. The work is focused on the person and the management of his suffering. In some cases, setting up a listening unit may be necessary, or even essential, to support the suffering employee and support other employees.

Table 11.1 Manager's role and prevention levels

Levels	Manager's role	Limits of the manager's role
Primary prevention	• Define the objectives and organize the work in order to respect everyone's capacities, skills and expectations • Recognize efforts	• Diagnose the nature of the risks • Define a prevention policy • Deploy preventive measures
Secondary prevention	• Listen to employees' complaints in a risky context	• Train employees to manage stress, aggression or incivility
Tertiary prevention	• Provide initial moral support to the weakened employee • Organize the employee's recourse in the event of injury	• Provide post-traumatic psychological assistance

Conclusion

Three important things to remember

1. Psychosocial risks: this is a particularly important problem to fight, it is the law, otherwise risk of escalation
2. Two types of TA intervention which are also very important:

    - Managing boundary permeability: healthy permeability
    - Manage energies and dynamics

3. Create coherence within the structure

The three responsibilities of the leader in terms of process

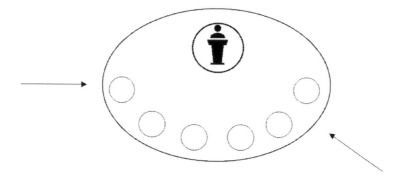

Figure 11.11 Pressures on external boundary

Guardian of the external boundary

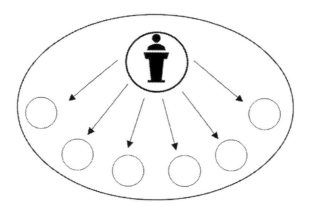

Figure 11.12 Security on major internal boundary

Equal treatment of members

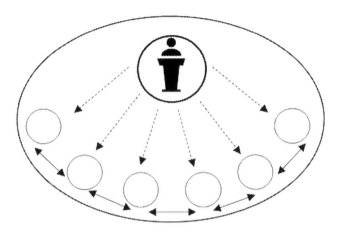

Figure 11.13 Equal pressures on minor internal boundary (De Miribel, 2016)

Generator of fluidity between members

Psychosocial risks: an organizational approach

In a report on psychosocial risks at work, Eurogip (1991) draws our attention to the fact that

> *their sources are not only in the individual, but also in the organization of work, the definition of positions and the physical environment. Comprehensive analysis of the workplace, in particular through the use of checklists, can help identify what, in the organization and work environment, can lead to psychosocial risk. The reduction of physical risks has an influence on the mental well-being of employees. Organizational prevention of Psychosocial Risks requires a global and systematic prevention policy for the workplace, taking into account all Risk factors.*

References

Transactional analysis

Berne, E. (1963). *The Structure and Dynamics of Organizations and Groups*. Philadelphia: J. B. Lippincott.
Berne, E. (1964). *Games People Play*. New York: Grove Press.
De Miribel, M. (2016). *Manage a Library. A New Leadership*. Paris: Cercle de la librairie.
Janvier (1971). Passivity. *Transactional Analysis Journal*, I, 1, pp. 71–78. TAJ, V, 3.
Juillet 1975. *Transactional Analysis Journal* pp. 295–302, V, 3.

12

TRANSACTIONAL ANALYSIS

A passport for the next decades

Rosa R. Krausz

We are now entering into the third era of automation, in which machines develop intelligence and start to make decisions.
Davenport & Kirby, 2016, p. 32

Very few organizations have defined and started to develop the organizational capabilities they will ultimately need.
W. Passmore et al., 2019, p. 70

The value of horizontal teamwork is widely recognized.
T. Casciaro et al., 2019, p. 132

A call for action

Companies and professionals in various sectors are struggling to develop new organizational models to cope with rapid technological, scientific and socioeconomic transformation, but many lack the knowledge, the agility, the workforce engagement and adequate structure to deal with an ever-changing environment.

Companies need a work force prepared to think, create, innovate, use new technologies, work in teams and cope with the growing instability and unpredictability.

To attract this kind of talent, organizations need to offer meaningful and challenging work, and humanistic values, in a healthy organizational climate and professional and personal opportunities for continuous learning and development.

Millennials and now Generation Z have been moving into leadership positions. Both desire space and options in their work environment and prefer participation and self-direction to being closely observed and controlled by management.

What is needed in organizations of the future?

In September 2017 STAR Lab invited (Passmore, 2019, pp. 76–77) 30 professionals to discuss the future of technologically enabled organizations. The participants' vision of the organizations of the future clearly contrasted with the dominant form of most of the existing organizations today.

Some conclusions concerning the organization of the future are:

- While in traditional organizations optimization is an *internal goal*, in the near future optimization will be focussed on the *external network and ecosystem*.
- Optimization between social and technical systems will require continuous change and adjustment.
- Advanced learning capabilities will redistribute power from the centre to the periphery, from internal to internal and external parties.
- The ability to change will become more important than stability for competitive advantage.

Participants also agreed that top-down leadership "will no longer be viable". Leadership will be broadly distributed rather than narrowly held (Passmore, 2019, p. 77).

Organizational functionality will require more and more autonomous individuals aware of the here and now, participating simultaneously in different teams, in different roles, prepared to accept challenges, share power and leadership positions and continuously upgrade the use of their potential.

This is why it will not be enough to attract and maintain the best professionals available. It will be necessary to connect them so that all, individuals, teams and organizations, will work in an interdependent network to reach organizational objectives together.

The survival of organizations will also depend on their capacity to embrace change and transform themselves into a "team of teams" (McChristal et al., 2015).

Transactional analysis can contribute

What contribution can transactional analysis (TA) provide in this context?

The *first contribution* is of a philosophical and humanistic nature.

TA is "a theory of personality and human relations offering systematic methods for personal growth and professional development" [Project Aristotle, 2017, *TAJ*, vol. 47(4), p. 325] developed concepts and ways of applying them to understand individual, collective and organizational behaviour." It "offers a systematic framework for the therapy of ailing groups and organizations" and considers "the real individual as a member of groups and organizations and his anxieties and operations when faced with the emotional complexities of personal relationships" Berne, 1963, p. vii).

As Stewart (1992, p. 17) underlines, the significant new step that Berne took "was to construct a theory that was psychodynamic in concept, yet which could be checked directly against real-world observations". According to Clarkson and Gilbert (1990, p. 199), "Transactional Analysis integrates intrapsychic dynamics with interpersonal behaviour".

TA considers that each human being has the potential to become autonomous, to understand his or her own behaviour and decide about a self-directed change process. According to Berne (1972, p. 31), the destiny of every human being is decided by what goes on inside his skull. Each person decides his own life. Freedom gives him the power to carry out his own designs, and power gives him the freedom to interfere with the designs of others.

TA introduces the idea of a contractual relationship between professionals and clients, based on mutual cooperation. Stewart (1992, p. 85) writes, "The principle of the contractual method remains a distinguishing feature of current practice in T.A."

In sum the values of autonomy, contracts and equality in relationships fit very well with the needs of the new millennium. The need to create a humanistic and cooperative culture in organisations is also supported by the TA concepts, that link the intra-psychic world, with behaviour and the possibilities for systemic change.

The *second contribution* is to provide alternatives to stimulate and sustain a friendly and healthy organizational climate that favours innovation, creativity, effectiveness and a social and ecological mindset. Such an approach requires continuous learning processes that facilitate the introduction of new values and behaviours and a sense of belonging.

Berne (1963, p. 150) mentions the importance of culture: "For a practical understanding of organizations and groups it is necessary to have a workable theory of group culture, since the culture influences almost everything that happens in a social aggregation".

The importance of culture is underlined by research. For instance, Krebs (2007, p. 8) indicates that lack of recognition, cooperation and compassion in organizations hinder the quality of relationships and influence not only the climate but also the products and services.

TA contributes to expand sensibility and self-knowledge, a process that supports and legitimates constructive values and corresponding behaviours that tend to promote growth and innovation. Change is a step-by-step process, sustained by recognition and respect as a continuous practice to be incorporated as part of organizational culture.

For instance, the positive impact of apparently prosaic behaviours such as a smile or a cordial hello are essential to creating belonging. Authentic positive strokes are a healthy, empowering and an effective antidote against psychological games played in corporations. Authentic positive strokes enhance self-esteem and invite individuals to recognize their qualities and learn, feel and behave in an OK/OK stance.

The focus on healthy boundaries and roles, the creation of cohesive teams and an emphasis on a culture that enhances autonomy are systemic interventions promoted by TA.

The *third contribution* is a powerful invitation to reflect on a renewed systemic and dynamic vision of human behaviour and how it impacts individual, team and organizational functioning.

As Berne wrote in *Transactional Analysis in Psychotherapy* (1961, p. xi), "This book outlines a unified system of individual and social psychiatry." The sub-title of his book, "A Systematic Individual and Social Psychiatry", underlines his intent to apply TA to the understanding of social aggregations.

Later, in the Preface of *The Structure and Dynamics of Organizations and Groups*, (1974a, p. vii) first published in 1963, Berne writes, "The object of the author in this book is to offer a systematic framework for the therapy of ailing groups and organizations".

The idea that all systems function simultaneously on three levels – structural, relational and psychodynamic – offers a powerful insight into the levels of intervention needed to create the organizations of the future.

Revisiting some key factors such as leadership, teamwork, organizational models and start-up phenomena using these concepts is helpful to better grasp the functional and dysfunctional aspects of organizations today.

The *fourth contribution* concerns the preventive character that stems from the knowledge and practice, theory and application of TA in organizations.

One example is the recognition of the negative consequences and different levels of harm caused by psychological games. Such dysfunctional interactions are sometimes absorbed and legitimized by certain organizational cultures and transformed in "official" organizational games, forwarding organizational and individual scripts (Krausz, 1993).

Permission-giving organizational cultures favour the emergence of OK-ness, cohesive teams, informal networks, participation and exchange of positive authentic strokes through healthy interactions.

The *fifth contribution* is the predictive potential of the theory and its application that may be used as strategic learning and development interventions.

The use of TA in the organizational context goes far beyond the limited theoretical information transmitted in conventional training events to "solve" the so commonly called problems of communication.

One example of the use of TA theory is the Existential Positions concept that provides a proficient predictive frame of reference. As Berne underlined (1966, p. 270), "Every game, script and destiny is based on one of these four basic positions". He also observes that an individual has "one basic position on which his life is staked, and from which he plays out his games and script" (Berne, 1972, p. 87), suggesting the predictive and observable potential of the concept.

McChristal et al. (2015, p. 84) reminds us that "prediction is not the only way to confront threats; developing resilience, learning to confront the unknown, is a much more effective way to respond to a complex environment" as, for instance, to enhance continuous learning, adaptability and autonomy.

When adequately applied, TA introduces new values, a renewed approach to sustain the emergent organizational models based on interdependent individuals working in teams.

A practical application: psychological safety in teams

As mentioned in at the start of this chapter, the relevance of teamwork is growing and being recognized as a potent alternative to enhance performance in organizations. Edmondson and Mogelof (2004, p. 109) recognize the importance of understanding "what factors enable people to experience a sense of psychological safety at work", considering that "the experience of psychological safety can allow team members to relax their guard and engage openly in the behaviours that underlie learning and innovation" (Edmonson and Mogelof, 2005, p. 110).

The Aristotle Project research (2017) aimed at discovering the secrets of effective teams at Google, also identified psychological safety as the most important element in effective teams. It was defined as "an individual perception of the consequences of taking an interpersonal risk or a belief that a team is safe for risk" (p. 11).

Looking through the lenses of TA, psychological safety in teams may be understood as a condition by which individuals function predominantly from an "I am OK/You are OK" position (+/+), contributing to a healthy and secure environment where they feel safe enough to:

- Recognise and learn from their errors
- Trust and respect team members
- Agree and disagree with comfort
- Give and incorporate authentic positive strokes
- Maintain self-awareness
- Voice opinions and concerns
- Ask for and offer assistance
- Exchange feedback

Ernst (1971, p. 33) on the basis of the Existential Position concept developed the classic OK Corral. He considers four outcomes of each encounter or interaction:

> "Brief or extended, at the conclusion of each encounter, no matter how many transactions between the parties, the outcome is resolved by one of the four categories of dynamic social operations":

GET-ON-WITH -	resulting in	I am OK and You are OK
GET-RID-OF -	resulting in	I am OK and You are not OK
GET-AWAY-FROM-	resulting in	I am not OK and You are OK
GET-NOWHERE WITH-	resulting in	I am not OK and You are not OK

He adds that an encounter "can bring about a chosen resolution for himself (the individual), his inside view, and his view of the particular companion in each encounter" (Ernst, 1971, p. 35). In other words, the GET-ON-WITH position, which results in I am OK and You are OK stance, generates constructive interactions that contribute to build and maintain a healthy and productive climate where psychological s tends to thrive.

The following table compares Ernst's four categories of dynamic social operation, Existential Positions and the resulting impact of each of those factors in the eight mentioned behaviours that may identify the existence, or not, of a psychological safety climate.

Table 12.1 Psychological safety, dynamic social operations and existential positions

Dynamic Social Operations	Get On With (1)	Get Rid Of (2)	Get Away From (3)	Get Nowhere With (4)
Predominant Existential Position	OK/OK +/+	OK/NOT OK +/−	NOT OK/OK −/+	NOT OK/ NOT OK −/−
Some Observable Behaviour Tendencies of Team Members	1. Recognizes and learns from errors 2. Trusts, respects team members 3. Agrees, disagrees 4. Gives positive authentic strokes 5. Self-awareness 6. Voices opinions, concerns 7. Asks for and offers assistance 8. Feedback exchange	1. Does not recognize errors 2. Does not respect nor trust team members 3. Imposes his or her ideas 4. Gives negative and false positive strokes 5. Self-awareness is contaminated by high self-esteem 6. Voices critical and prejudiced remarks 7. Seldom asks for assistance openly 8. Mostly evaluation	1. Recognizes errors but does not learn from them 2. Ingenious, naive, submissive 3. Seldom disagrees 4. Gives more positive than negative strokes 5. Self-awareness is contaminated by low self-esteem 6. Seldom voices critics and complaints 7. Asks for assistance/help and may offer help 8. Mostly positive	1. Does not recognize errors 2. Disrespect, isolation 3. Indifference, neither agrees nor disagrees 4. Negative strokes 5. Low/distorted self-awareness 6. Voices negative aspects 7. Refuses assistance and never offers it 8. No feedback
Probable Team Climate	Psychological Safety	Mistrust Competition Manipulation Games	Insecure Tense Dependent	Unsafe, no Trust Passivity Withdrawal
Drivers (Not OK Mini script)		Be perfect Be strong Please me Hurry up	Try hard Please others	Be strong Try hard

Besides the eight mentioned behaviors, we introduced one more set of observable ones, the Not OK Mini-Script drivers (Kahler & Capers, 1974, p. 28) defined as "a sequence of behaviour, occurring in a matter of minutes or even seconds that results in the reinforcement of patterns for life". This concept facilitates the identification of some not OK behaviors that tend to interfere with individual and team psychological safety.

This table may be used as a pre-diagnostic instrument to collect and organize observable information about individual and team interactional patterns.

The collected information may be cross-checked with other concepts, as for instance individual and team ego grams, games, discounting, organizational script and so forth.

Such a procedure will enhance the quality of a pre-diagnostic and contribute to the success of interventions to build/develop/maintain the much needed psychological safety in teams as well as in organizations.

Summing up

TA has the potential to develop and sustain Permanent or Lasting Competencies defined as

> an integrated combination of capabilities, experiences, talent and ways of being and interacting that provide the internal stability necessary to cope constructively with the external instability and transformation (Krausz, 2018, pp. 151–159). These Competencies are expressed through a coherent and integrated mind set, posture and consistency between discourse and action.

In the next years the workforce will probably be more and more challenged to update knowledge, exercise permanent competencies, learn and cultivate/enhance personal and interpersonal OK-ness, and TA facilitates this process.

Summing up, the emergent fluid organizational context may benefit from the resources offered by TA in the development of a predominant climate of OK-ness among individuals, teams and organization, stimulating/ intensifying conditions like sharing, participation, trust, "context leadership" (Cartolary, 2018, p. 2), optimized performance and well-being.

References

Berne, E. (1966). *Principles of Group Treatment*. New York: Grove Press.
Berne, E. (1974). *What do yoy say after you say hello?* New York: Grove Press.
Berne, E. (1974a). *The Structure and Dynamics of Organizations and Groups*. New York: Ballantine Books. First published in 1963.
Berne, E. (1975). *Transactional Analysis in Psychotherapy*. New York: Grove Press.
Cartolary, R. (2018). Soft Skills: Preparing the Leaders of Tomorrow. www.trainingzone.co.uk/leadculture/soft-skills-preparing-the-le. pp. 1–8.

Casciaro, T., Edmondson, A., & Jang, S. (2019). Cross-Silo Leadership. *Harvard Business Review*, May–June, pp. 130–139.

Clarkson, P., & Gilbert, M. (1990). Transactional Analysis. In W. Dryden (ed.), *Individual Therapy: A Handbook*. Buckingham: Open University Press.

Davenport, T., & Kirby, J. (2016). *Only Humans Need Apply: Winners and Losers in the Age of Smart Machines*. New York: Harper Books.

Edmondson, A. & Mogelof, J.P. (2005). Explaining Psychological Safety in Innovation Teams. In L. Thompson & H. Choi (eds) *Creativity and Innovation in Organizational Teams*. Lawrence Eribaum Associates, pp. 109–136.

Ernst, F. H. (1971). The OK Corral: The Grid for Get-On-With. *Transactional Analysis Journal*, October, 1(4), pp. 33–42.

Kahler, T., & Capers, H. (1974). The Miniscript. *Transactional Analysis Journal*, January, 4(1), 26–42.

Krausz, R. R. (1993). Organizational Scripts. *Transactional Analysis Journal*, 23(2), 77–86.

Krausz, R. R. (2018). *Análise Transacional Organizacional: Um Novo Olhar (Organizational T.A.: A New Outlook)*. S. Paulo: Ed. Scortecci.

Krebs, V. (2007). Managing in the 21st Century Organization. *IHRIM*, X(4).

McChristal, S., Collins, T., Silverman, D., & Fussell, C. (2015). *Team of Teams*. New York: Random House.

Passmore, W. et al. (2019). Reflections: Sociotechnical Systems Design and Organizational Change. *Journal of Change Management*, 19(2), 67–85.

Stewart, I. (1992). *Eric Berne*. London: Sage Publications.

The Project Aristotle (2017). https://rework.withgoogle.com/print/guides/5721312655835136/" ://rework.withgoogle.com/print/guides/5721312655835136/

Transactional Analysis Jornal. (2017). 47(4), p. 325.

Zuboff, S. (1988). *In the Age of the Smart Machine*. New York: Basic Books.

INDEX

Note: Page numbers in *italics* indicate a figure and page numbers in **bold** indicate a table on the corresponding page.

adapted power 16–17, 24; developing 26–27, *26*; elements relevant to 18
affiliate leaders 159
Agape 75
agility 105
agitation 93–94
Allende, Salvador 87
Alter, N. 28
Ambrogio, Italian Ugo De 4
amygdala hijack 127
anxiety *see* fear and anxiety, managing
Anxious Organization, The 128
Anzieu, Didier 54, 56
authoritarianism 159, 165
authority matrix *31*

balance, three drives in *72*
Balling, R. 45, 156–157, 163
Barnes, G. 81
Bateson, G. 124
Bazalgette, John 124
belonging 62
Berne, E. 2, 3, 8, 9, 13, 17, 24, 30, 33–37, 44, 53–54, 57–58, 62, 76–77, 81, 88, 91, 109–110, 119, 128, 131, 156, 174–188, 190–192
binding agent 73
Boon, A. 136
Bossche, Van Den 136
boundaries 2, 87–88, 175–177; Berne's classification of 109; complex system 90, *90*; dynamic diagram *183*; external 7, 88; immaterial 89; internal 7, 177; material 89; simple system 89, *89*; types of 88–90; visibility 89

boundary dynamics, managing 87–105; authority to intervene 98–99; clinical approach 100; consultant role 98; definitions 91; from diagnosis to problem resolution 101–104; diagram use 90; at the External Boundary 91–93, *92*, 95–96; facilitator's position 97–98; healthy system versus 95–97; internal boundary 93–95, *94*, 96, 97; intervention 97–100; levels of authority 98–99; visual representations use 90
boundary zones 64–66; Berne's representation of *65*; as a transitional space 67–68
brace 73
Burger, Yvonne 127

Cable, D. M. 116
Campos, L. P. 9
Canon 24
Capra, Fritjof 118, 119
C/D/E-model 32–34, *33*, 38–39; *see also* container
C-group boundaries 61–62
Change Competence Curve 139
change: management, transitional space importance in 68–70; of paradigm 118–119
character of a culture 13
circular techniques 83
circular transactions 83
circular working in a team, applying 82
Clarkson, P. 9, 190
clinical approach 100
clinical Force Field TA approach 52

197

INDEX

cognitive apprenticeship 133–136, *135*; *see also* workplace learning
cohesion in a group 11, *12*, 13
Cola, P. 165
collaborative reflection 141–142, *141*
combat groups *59*, 60
competence curve **140**, *146*
complexity: reducers 109; rise 78–79
complex system 90, *90*
composite groups 73
concept of boundaries 61
conflict 75
container 33–35
content 135
contracting, seven Ps of 137–139, **138**
contracts 44–46, 105; contracting practice 137–139; contractual Force Field TA approach 52; cooperation 45; expert exchange 44–46
Coyle, D. 113
Crespelle, Alain 21
cultural and historical power factors 24–25, *25*
culture: of challenge (spontaneous) 157, **162**, **167**; of cohesion (paternalistic) 157–172, **158**, **167**; culture of dialogue 46–47; of obedience (closed) 157, 163, **166**, **167**; of order (efficiency) 157, **160**, **167**; of rules and procedures (hyperbureaucratic) 157, **164**, **167**
curriculum development project 36–40
Cycles of Development 39

De Graaf, A. 45, 47
Dekker, Laura 125
democratic leader 159
Descartes, René 67
Désert, Alain 81
destruction 75
development groups 60
dialogue 46–47, 168
differences 33
double-digit growth 74
Drouin, Nicole Le 52
Dutton, Kevin 121
dynamics: at the external boundary 91–93, *92* 101–102; at the major internal boundary 93–94, 102–104

Edmondson, A. 192
effective leadership 8, 40
effectivity 3
emerging energy 178

emotions *see* feelings
energies: agitation/security 182; balance between 178–179, 182–184; emerging 178; imbalance, risks in the event of 179–180; planned 178–182; pressure/consistency 182; tension/regulation 182; three boundaries, three specific dynamics 182–184; types *179*
environment, working with 75
Eoyang, G. H. 32
Erasmus generation 65
Ernst, F. 193
Eros 75
Erskine, R. 172
etiquette 13
Euhemerus 8, 24
Ewenstein, B. 136
exchange 33
Existential Position concept 193
expert exchange 44–46
external boundary 7, 88, 177, *187*

Favez-Boutonnier, Juliette 100
fear and anxiety, managing 118–128; being focused 127; container of feelings 119–120; containment skills 126; on the edge of chaos 124; fearlessness, practicing 127; function of 121; individual psychology 123–124; linguistic interventions 126; organizational anxiety 123; real fear 122–123; script fear 122–123; smell of 121–122; stick to the contract 125–126; systemic fear and anxiety 125
feelings 119–120, 122
Force Field TA 51–85; balance, three drives in *72*; behavioural transactions 83; circular techniques 83; circular transactions 83; clinical approach 52; complex world 77–78; contractual approach 52; environment, working with 75; group imago, adjusting 81–82; systemic approach 52; "technical" society 77; *see also* boundary zones; groups; inescapable forces; tensional TA, facilitator's stance in
Fosset, Patrice 4
Foucault, Michel 67
Fox, E. M. 34, 101
Fradin, Jacques 63
Friesen, N. 137
functional feelings 122

INDEX

Games People Play 119
Gilbert, M. 190
global challenges outwards 108–109
Glouberman, S. 123
Goleman, D.159
Goodyear, P. 133
Gottman, John 122
Goulding, B. 120
Goulding, M. 120
Graaf, Anne de 4
Grand, S. 34
Grégoire, José 58, 81
group imago, adjusting 81–82
groups: boundaries 7, 58–59, *59*; combat groups *59*, 60; defining 7, 57–58; development 37, *37*, 60, 62–63; identifying criteria 57; large 54; as living organisms 52–53; misunderstandings about 56–57; organisation forms 60–61; process *59*, 60; rigid (closed) external boundary *62*; small 54; types of 58–60, *55*; work 58; *see also* C-group boundaries
Gurowitz, E. M. 9

Hackman, R. J. 31–32
Hay, J. 139
healthy system, versus boundary dynamics 95–97
hidden motive 181
hierarchical leadership 40
Hirsman, A. O. 163
Hug, T. 137
humanism 76
Hypnos 75

identity stretching 108
imposter syndrome 122
in-depth interview 168
individual psychology 123–124
individual stance 80
individual structure 11–13, *17*
inescapable forces 75
inner boundary 33
"Institutional Games" 3
internal boundary 7, 177; *see also* major internal boundary; minor internal boundary
internal tensions 73
intervention contract 99–100

Janet, Paul 67
Joseph, Isaac 58
justified power 24

Kerkhof 127
Kim, J. 136
Kohlrieser, G. 37
Kolb, B. 132
Krausz, R. R. 4, 8, 16, 156
Krebs, V. 191
Kübler-Ross, E. 139
Kühl, S. 41

Lacy, Mandy 4
large groups 54
Last of the Just, The 56
lateral leadership 40–44, *42*
Laugeri, M. 45
Laurier, Corinne 4
leader coach 159, 165
leadership 8; effective 40; of the individual structure (Level 2) 11–13, *17*; *Leadership: The Power of Emotional Intelligence* 159; levels of 9–14, 17, *17*; new challenges for 6–7; in the organizational structure (Level 1) 9–10, *17*; organizations and 7; power adapted to its purpose 16–28; in the psychodynamic structure (Level 3) 13–14, *17*; psychological 40; responsible 8, 39; styles 107, 159, 161; TA focus on 8–9; vectors, in a work group *110*; *see also* lateral leadership
leading 110: across 113–114; down 111–113; out 114–115; through people 107–116; up 110–111
learning practices at work 130–143; *see also* workplace learning
Lee, A. 35–36, 38–39
Levin, P. 39, 139
Levy, J. 45
Lewin, Kurt 54
life 52–53
linear causality 124
linguistic interventions 126
Little, R. 111
loads 73
love 75

major internal boundary 88; dynamic at 93–94, *94*; dynamic diagram *184*; security on *187*
management & organizational development (M&OD) 1
managers 168
matrix 73
Matthiesen, K. 41

Mazouz, Marleine 4
McKay, Sarah 120
Messmer, A. 37
method 135
micro-learning 137
Miller, J. A. 119, 123, 124, 128
minor internal boundary 88, 177; dynamic at 94–95, *95*; dynamic diagram *183*; pressures on *188*
Mintzberg, H. 125, 157
Minuchin, S. 35
Moiso, Carlo 119
Monod, Jacques 53
Moreau, Jacques 4, 34, 37
Morin, Edgar 79–80
movements 62
Mujica-Prodi, Lilianne 121

Napper, R. 132, 139
Newton, T. 132, 139
non-functional feelings 122

OK-ness *72*, 79–80
On the Edge 11
organisation 34
organisational complexity upwards 108
organisational power 18–20, *19*
organisational TA 132
organizational anxiety 123
organizational cultures 156–172; diagnostic questionnaire of **169**; elements of 13; pentagon of *170–171*; typology of 157–172
organizational script matrix *14*
organizational structure 9–10, *10*, *17*, 175–178, *175–176*
organizational theory, Berne's 174–188; boundaries 175–177, *177*; energy organization 178–179; psychological games 181–182; psychosocial risk situation 182; in psychosocial risks prevention 174–188; *see also* energies; organizational structure
organizations 7–8, 189–190; *see also* leadership
Oshry, B. 109
outer boundary 33

pedagogical team 46–47
Peeters, Flor 126
permeable boundaries, self-organising teams need 35–36

personal leader 8
personal power factors 21–23, *22*
Petriglieri, G. 3
Philia 75
Pinochet, Augusto 87
planned energy 178
Poelje, Sari van 3
power 41
power factors 18; *see also* cultural and historical power factors; organisational power; personal power factors
predecessors 24
preliminary meeting 168
primal leader 8, 24
private structure of organizations 8
process groups *59*, 60
psychiatric outpatient care 32–33
psychodynamic structure 13–14, *17*
psychological games 181–182
psychological leadership 8, 40
psychological safety, in teams 192–195, **194**
psychosocial risk prevention 184–186, **186**
public structure of organizations 8

rapid change 1–2
relational sequence 181
relationship-oriented leadership 8
responsible leadership 8, 39
Revived Humanism 79
rigid (closed) external boundary, Berne's representation *62*
Rock, D. 112
Rüegg-Stürm, J. 34
Rutz, Kathrin 4

Scharmer, O. 80
Schein, E. 156
Schiff, J. 126
Schmid, B. 37, 46
Schmid, G. 131
Schwartz-Bart, André 56
script fear 122–123
Seel, N. M. 135
self-organisation 36–40
self-organising teams 30–47; C/D/E-model 32–33, *33*; clear structure support 32–33; container 33; culture of dialogue 46–47; differences 33; exchange 33; leading 30–47; permeable boundaries need 35–36; psychiatric outpatient care 32–33; seeking autonomy 31–32; *see also* contracts; teams

200

INDEX

sequencing 135
Shah, J. A. 136
simple structure of organization 176
simple system 89, *89*
skeleton 73
Sloterdijk, Peter 71
small groups 54
social equilibria 71
sociological changes since Berne 76–77
sociology 135
Spector, J. M. 133
Steiner, C. 120
Stewart, I. 190–191
stick to the contract/task, mantra of 125–126
Storge 75
Structure and Dynamics of Organizations and Groups, The 8, 33, 175, 192
Summers, Graeme 4
systemic Force Field TA approach 52

teaching and supervising transactional analyst (TSTA) 131
teams 30–31; meetings 136–137; self-organisation 32; *see also* self-organising teams
techniques 13
tensional TA, facilitator's stance in 80–81
tensions 70–71
Thanatos 75
Tigchelaar, Mark 127
transactional analysis (TA) 1, 131, 189–195; call to action 189; contributions 190–192; as on the edge thinking 2; effectivity 3; focus on leadership 8–9; in friendly and healthy organizational climate 191; learning 132–133; organisational TA 132; in philosophical and humanistic nature 190; in predictive potential of the theory 192; in preventive care 192; rapid change 1–2; *Transactional Analysis in Psychotherapy* 191; *see also* tensional TA, facilitator's stance in
transformation heterotopias 67
transitional phenomena 67
transitional space, importance in change management 68–70, *69*
tread leader 159, 161
Treaty of Westphalia 62
trust 41
Tuckman, B. W. 39
Tutta la Vita Davanti 163
Tyrangiel, H. 133

van Beekum, Servaas 119
van Poelje, Sari 17, 23, 133
Virzi, Paolo 163
visionary leader 159, 161

Weber, Max 120
Web of Life, The 118
Whyte, J. 136
Winnicott, Donald W. 67–68
Wisdom of Psychopaths, The 121
Wood, J. D. 3
work group 58, *59, 110*
working relationships, managing vulnerability in 107–116
workplace learning 130–143; content 135; experience principle 133; method 135; micro-learning 137; pedagogy for 133–136; previous learning 139–141, **140, 148–155**; sequencing 135; seven Ps of contracting 137–139, **138**; sociology 135; team meetings 136–137; *see also* cognitive apprenticeship

Zimmerman, B. 123